C000259419

THE BATTLE
FOR BURMA

The Wild Green Earth

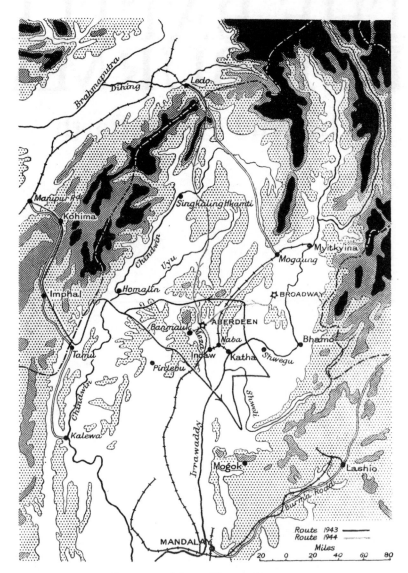

GENERAL MAP: UPPER BURMA.

over 6000 feet
   ,,   4000 feet
   ,,   2000 feet

THE BATTLE FOR BURMA

The Wild Green Earth

by
Bernard Fergusson

. . Still through chaos
Works on the ancient plan,
And two things have altered not
Since first the world began –
The beauty of the wild green earth
And the bravery of man.

T.P. CAMERON WILSON

Pen & Sword
MILITARY

Originall published by Collins Clear Type Press in 1946
Reprinted in Great Britain in 2015 by
Pen & Sword Military
an imprint of
Pen & Sword Books Ltd
47 Church Street
Barnsley
South Yorkshire
S70 2AS

Copyright © Bernard Fergusson 2015

ISBN 978 1 47382 715 8

The right of Bernard Fergusson to be identified as the Author of this
Work has been asserted by him in accordance with the Copyright,
Designs and Patents Act 1988.
A CIP catalogue record for this book is available from the
British Library

All rights reserved. No part of this book may be reproduced or
transmitted in any form or by any means, electronic or mechanical
including photocopying, recording or by any information storage and
retrieval system, without permission from the Publisher in writing.

Printed and bound in England
By CPI Group (UK) Lt, Croydon, CR0 4YY

Pen & Sword Books Ltd incorporates the imprints of Pen & Sword
Archaeology, Atlas, Aviation, Battleground, Discovery, Family
History, History, Maritime, Military, Naval, Politics, Railways, Select,
Transport, True Crime, and Fiction, Frontline Books, Leo Cooper,
Praetorian Press, Seaforth Publishing and Wharncliffe.

For a complete list of Pen & Sword titles please contact
PEN & SWORD BOOKS LIMITED
47 Church Street, Barnsley, South Yorkshire, S70 2AS, England
E-mail: enquiries@pen-and-sword.co.uk

Website: www.pen-and-sword.co.uk

To the Memory of All Ranks of

No. 5 COLUMN

AND OF

16TH INFANTRY BRIGADE

who were killed or died, as free men or prisoners, during the Expeditions into Burma of 1943 and 1944.

Truly if they had been mindful of that country from whence they came out, they might have had opportunity to have returned. Who through faith subdued kingdoms, wrought righteousness, obtained promises, stopped the mouth of lions, quenched the violence of fire, waxed valiant in fight, turned to flight the armies of the aliens; and others were tortured, not accepting deliverance; that they might obtain a better resurrection; and others had trials of cruel mockings, yea, moreover of bonds and imprisonment; they were stoned, they were sawn asunder, were tempted, were slain with the sword; they wandered about in sheepskins and goatskins; being destitute, afflicted, tormented; they wandered in deserts, and in mountains, and in dens and caves of the earth.

Hebrews xi

CONTENTS

MAPS

TOWARDS THE EAST

Remote from pilgrimage, a dusty hollow
   Lies in the Libyan plain:
And there my comrades sleep, who will not follow
   The pipes and drums again:
Who followed closely in that desperate sally
   The pipes that went before;
Who, heedless now of Muster or Reveille,
   Sleep sound for evermore.

In days of peace, when days of war were nearing,
   My comrades who are dead
Once in a while looked up the dark track, peering
   Where Fate and Glory led:
For these, the chosen of their generation,
   This was the path it took,
That ended in the sand and desolation
   Ten miles beyond Tobruk.

Their passing on that field and on that morning
   No second sight foresaw;
We spied no wraith, we had no seer's warning
   Like him of Inverawe,
Who heard, when yon dark memory was fading,
   Ticonderoga's name,
Grappled with Fate, and scaled the palisading,
   And died at grips with Fame.

Far off in Scotland at the hour of battle,
   As these her sons fell dead,
Above the herds of frosty-breathing cattle
   The winter sun rose red:
In every cothouse and in every city
   In those remembered shires,
The kettle sang its early morning ditty
   On newly kindled fires.

9

To those dear houses with their chimneys reeking
   In Angus or in Fife,
No spirit came, its words of omen speaking,
   To mother or to wife;
Yet in the homeless desert to the southward
   Before the sun was high,
The husbands whom they loved, the sons they mothered
   Stood up and went to die.

.   .   .   .

Once there were peaceful dawns in other places
   In days when war was not:
Friends sprawling with the firelight on their faces
   Around the cooking-pot:
Dawn on the Essex saltings, by whose marges
   The teal and widgeon hide,
Where up the brimming swatchways come the barges
   Creeping upon the tide;

Dawn on the Border, and the sound of shooting
   High up on Penchrist Pen,
The echoes rolling backward and saluting
   The firing-point again;
Dawn in the Castle, and the early scurry
   Of waking soldiers' feet,
And far below the grinding haste and hurry
   Of trams in Princes Street;

Dawn on the coast: the wind in bents and grasses
   Along the Buddon dunes,
Stumbling among the sandhills as it passes,
   Echoing ancient tunes;
Dawn in the ship, the sentry at the hatches
   Strange in his new abode,
The mugs for coffee passing aft in batches,
   The hammocks being stowed;

Dawn in Judæa, and the threat of pillage
    Upon the Holy Land,
The search at sunrise through a mountain village
    For a marauding band;
Dawn in Somaliland and dawn in Aden,
    Dawn on the hills of Crete,
Dawn on the cruiser's deck, with soldiers laden,
    And on the rescuing fleet.

.   .   .   .

For Time devoured our Day, and Night came creeping
    And Peace was lost in War,
And now upon my friends the sands are heaping
    (Who sleep for evermore);
And I, who shared their joys but not their dangers,
    Their pride but not their pain,
Mindful of them though in the midst of strangers,
    March to the field again.

I march at night; the stars come up to guide me
    Safe on the jungle track—
O for the friends that well might be beside me,
    The stout hearts at my back!
O for the piper, striding towards the morning,
    Half hidden in the gloom,
Playing my choice—"Steamboat," "The Gypsy's Warning,"
    "The Wee Man at the Loom!"

The jackals scream, the landmarks pass, the stages
    Are made and drop behind;
The stars that scan all warriors down the ages
    Look on me and are kind—
The soldier stars that pace the beats of heaven,
    To whom all things are known;
Who watch the fields where men of old have striven
    And who shall watch our own.

.   .   .   .

The night brails up her darkness like a curtain,
　　The morning star grows pale,
Till suddenly the hope is sure and certain
　　That death cannot prevail;
And in my need my comrades send assurance
　　That breaks on me with day
That from the grave that sealed their long endurance
　　The stone is rolled away.

The dawn is here: the sound of water flowing
　　Proclaims my bivouac;
Behind, the marching feet suspend their going
　　And leave the jungle track.
To-day, the little force that sleeps around me
　　Is marvellously increased:
To-night, with comrades who have claimed and found me,
　　I march towards the east.

　　　　　　　　　　　　Imphal, *January* 1943.

INTRODUCTION

I HAVE described elsewhere the adventures of No. 5 Column in General Wingate's first Expedition into Burma in 1943. Part I. of this book is an account of 16th Brigade in the second Expedition, the following year. 16th Brigade was the first formation to fight all our enemies in the late wars, Germans, Italians, Vichy French and Japanese. The other Chindit brigades went into Burma by air; we walked in from Ledo in Assam. Three hundred and sixty miles of the march was in single file, and it was very boring.

Part II. is a sort of Cottage Pie of learning derived from both Expeditions. It is an attempt to set down before they fade the lessons, military and otherwise, of two interesting years. We had to learn, by fumbling experience, knowledge which our primitive forebears knew by instinct, but which our advancing civilisation had discarded—how to live in forest. 1943 was a hard year, 1944 a disappointing one; but we learned a lot in both.

I must sketch lightly the situation in January 1944, the date at which the book opens. The Japanese possessed the whole of Burma, except for a few square miles of its uninhabited fringes; but at no point except in the extreme north-west were they actually locked with their opponents. In Arakan, on the Imphal front and in China they were in patrol contact, flaring up occasionally into a short-lived phase of minor fighting.

The exception was in the Hukawng Valley, where General Stilwell's Ledo Road, still under construction, was emerging from the mountains which, at that point narrower than elsewhere, divide Assam from Burma. Here Stilwell's Chinese were very slowly pushing forward, and had actually reached the young and narrow Chindwin. This river, whose name has been made familiar by the war, was the dividing line between Japs and Allies from the Hukawng Valley right down to the latitude of Tiddim, two hundred and fifty miles to the south-west. Across it, the patrols of both sides played Tom Tiddler's Ground; but although the Japs were present on the east bank in what, in that theatre, passed for strength, the British-Indian forces were mostly held back a little, in the tangled and forested mountains west of the river.

Wingate's original plan was to introduce his Special Force into the area of Indaw, the northernmost communications centre of any importance in Upper Burma. Part of the Force was to go in by air; my own Brigade by marching. The Force was then to seize and hold an enclave into which two ordinary divisions were to be flown, and towards which the Corps around Imphal was to advance. By this means, not only would the Japs opposing Stilwell in the north be cut off, but we should have delivered the British-Indian divisions from the defiles in which they had so long been confined, and put them in a bridgehead from which they could advance on a broad front.

Wherever in this book I refer to "Wingate's Plan," this is the plan in my mind. It was not until long afterwards—indeed, until after this book was completed—that I learned from General Sir William Slim, the commander of the Fourteenth Army, that the Plan was modified long before the fly-in of Calvert's and Lentaigne's Brigades and even before my own Brigade set off on foot. It seems that the Japanese advance across the Chindwin which materialised in March of 1944 was foreseen, and that General Wingate was warned that the "follow-up" could not take place.

This modification in the Plan was not made known to General Wingate's Brigade commanders. Perhaps he thought it would discourage us; perhaps he hoped to create such a favourable situation that the original Plan would be switched on again. After consideration, I have left the text untouched. To recapture the atmosphere of the campaign, I would have the reader know and think what we ourselves knew and thought. I have, however, incorporated here and there footnotes to refer the reader to this Introduction, where he might be misled by what is in the text.

Finally, I have plunged straight into the story, recapitulating as little as possible all the tedious processes of the planning. My Brigade alone was to march in, and it was finally decided that our route should be via Ledo. This part of the country was new to us all; but I had a small nucleus from the first Expedition who had experience of the district for which we were bound, and the conditions which obtained there. To that handful of stout-hearted companions who had shared the rigours of the first campaign, and who came again for the second, I am especially bound. But all who were Chindits, whether in the first campaign, or the second, or in both, belong to a family of comrades most closely knit in a common understanding.

PART ONE

I

LEDO

I THINK it was originally John Fraser's[1] idea that we should go in from Ledo. The easiest routes to the Chindwin were all closely watched by the Japanese, mindful of our exploits in 1943; and although we might have fought our way across, we could not have done so without giving ample notice of our coming. General Stilwell's so-called "Ledo Road" had crossed the Patkai Hills at their lowest pass, and had already reached the Chindwin in the Hukawng Valley. It might be possible to go so far over his road, and then to swing away on one flank or the other. By so doing, we should by-pass the battle which he was fighting, and, thus avoiding entanglement, be free to march southward the three or four hundred miles to our old stamping-ground near Indaw. Two other Brigades, under Mike Calvert and Joe Lentaigne, were to be flown into the same approximate area, and were scheduled to arrive there at much the same time as my own. Their detailed tasks were not yet settled, whereas mine was: to capture the two airfields of Indaw, and to hold them while one and possibly two ordinary (non-Chindit) divisions were flown in to exploit.

So Katie Cave of the Rifle Brigade, my splendid second-in-command, went off to Ledo to make contact with the Americans. Katie was a good deal older than I, but a friend of ten years' standing, who since 1937 had been my brother's commanding officer in the jungles of the southern Sudan. In order to come to grips with the war, he had, after much pleading, been allowed to relinquish his command of the Equatorial Corps, to step down in rank and to come to Burma. It was a good day for us when he did.

The Brigade was moving up by train. John Marriott, my Brigade Major, and I arrived by air on the 22nd of January, and

[1] Major J. C. Fraser, M.C., Burma Rifles ; 2nd in command No. 5 Column in 1943. Senior Officer Burma Rifles 16 Inf. Bde. in 1944.

19

met Colonel Cave at the Headquarters of General Boatner, General Stilwell's Chief of Staff. Colonel Cave had two patrols out looking for possible routes over the hills, and both of them had so far failed to find any. Stilwell's Hukawng Valley forces were heavily engaged in what constituted a defile, and it was clearly not practicable to cross in the same area and still avoid contact with the enemy. The Dalu Valley, the next along to the westward, had only one exit south of the Chindwin, which might be worth looking at, but which would probably be held. The weather was atrocious, the hills huge, the jungle hideous, topographical knowledge nil, maps bad, and outlook distinctly gloomy.

Stilwell was, as usual, forward with his troops, and I resolved to go and see him. His "Road" was a mass of mud and boulders, narrow and constantly blocked with land-slides. At best it took thirty-six hours to reach his advanced headquarters over the hills at Shingbwiyang (familiarly known as "Shing"). So I borrowed a couple of light aircraft off the genial Boatner, and set off with John Marriott in one and me in the other.

It was certainly big country, and my heart sank as I peered at it from the little aircraft. The map on my knees, at which little draughts of air kept twitching, boldly marked a track here, another there; but none were visible in the tangled jungle five hundred feet below us. I could not help feeling that the anonymous cartographer had assumed, with some excuse, that nobody would ever come here to check his work. Nobody with any sense ever would; and yet I was proposing to march a Brigade of close on four thousand men and six hundred animals over this hairy land.

Wreaths of cloud drifted round the mountain tops, while the aircraft dodged between. A few miles to the eastward I could see the brown scar of the Ledo Road, twisting and straggling through the forests and over the watersheds, scrambling painfully up to the crests, clinging there precariously for a few hundred yards, and slipping off again down to some preposterous mountain torrent, which it crossed gingerly on a fairy-tale bridge belonging rather to Willow-Pattern Land. Far beyond it were the huge hills towards Fort Hertz, across which the Chaukkan Pass was the only route. To the south was the thin ribbon of the Chindwin, bearing here some unfamiliar name; attenuated, but still a landmark and an obstacle. Across it at this very moment Stilwell's Chinese were forcing a hotly disputed passage, away in the eastern mists.

"Tagap . . . Nathkaw. . . ."

Through my headphones came from time to time the voice of the pilot, pointing out such landmarks as he knew. Away from the Road he was as lost as I. I kept him turning and weaving in accordance with my efforts to orientate myself, and to trace the alleged tracks in the forests below me. Sometimes I caught sight of a Naga village in its tiny clearing, and could see for a few hundred yards its domestic tracks, leading down to the water-point, or up to the patch of hill-cultivation. I could picture well the village life below me, remembering the loyal Kachin villages which had sheltered us from the hunting Japanese the previous year, on our original expedition. Although in the same moment my eyes could see both the Road and the village, one knew that the busy life on the one had not affected the primitive way of living of the other; that the village below had in all probability never seen a European, and was hardly aware of the alien races at war with each other ten minutes' air flight away.

But although I could see the domestic footpaths, and recognise them for what they were, I could see no sign of the "through" tracks of the optimistic cartographer. The jungle lay over all like a cauliflower. The high trees, the long feathery arms of the bamboos and plantains, the dark patches of monsoon jungle that lay in the bottoms and betrayed the hidden streams; the occasional escarpments many hundreds of feet high; now and again the lost village, with the upturned faces and the panicking pigs: there was nothing to be seen but these. And behind me, sixty miles to the north, at the ragged terminus of the long and laggard railway, would soon be piling up, night by night, the brigade which somehow I had to get over this nightmare country.

To land on the newly completed Dakota strip at Shing, we had to circle over the very Chindwin. When at last we were down, we were able to admire the strip and the amazing American genius for mechanical equipment which had made its construction possible. I once read in an old copy of the *Listener* a talk given by some American woman who had obviously a profound knowledge of our people as well as of hers. "I shall always think of England," she had said, "as a country where somebody is forever bringing you a cup of tea up six flights of stairs. The British cope; we fix." It is a sound observation; and I have never had brought to my mind so forcibly as on that first view of the jungle airfield at Shing the American determination never to use a man where you can more profitably use a machine. Their bull-dozers had torn up the jungle by its roots, dragged away the stumps, and smoothed out an airfield of fourteen hundred yards, ruthlessly stripping the skin from the earth, and laying bare what no man had ever before seen. But the earth is strong, and the jungle quick to reclaim its own; two or three years of neglect, and all will be green and impenetrable as before.

General Stilwell was away that day, and I did not meet him until a subsequent visit, when General Wingate was with me. Then the two of them talked in Stilwell's hut, while I gossiped with the American Colonel Willy a few yards up the hill. When at last I was summoned, I sat for ten minutes and discussed our plans with those two very forceful characters. Wingate, heavy-browed, broad and powerful; Stilwell, with his steel-rimmed spectacles, tallish, wiry and gaunt. Both had determined faces, with deep furrows about their mouths; both could display atrocious manners, and were not prepared to be thwarted by anybody. Both looked like prophets, and both had many of the characteristics of prophets: vision, intolerance, energy, ruthlessness, courage and powers of denunciation to scorch like a forest fire. I stifled a desire to hear them quarrel, and listened attentively to the terms of the bargain which they had struck.

General Stilwell had agreed to give me facilities up his Road as far as Tagap Ga: thereafter I was to strike into the hills to the westward, and to cross the Chindwin downstream of his battle at a point to be chosen by myself in the light of whatever knowledge came my way. In return, I was to seize on his behalf the town of Lonkin, a Shan city in the heart of the Kachin Hills. Lonkin lay twenty miles west of Kamaing, an important town on the main line of communication of the Japanese 18th Division, who were the backbone of the troops opposing Stilwell's advance.

Kamaing itself was only twenty miles from Mogaung on the railway, the advanced base from which the Japs were being supplied. If I could seize and hold Lonkin, Stilwell would try to relieve me there with some of his own Chinese while I pushed on towards my real task in the south. The loss of Lonkin would seriously threaten the Jap lines of communication, and loosen their hold on the passes south of the Chindwin.

I could sense that Stilwell was sizing me up: he looked horribly like Amos, Hosea or some other of the less matey figures of the Old Testament. I have the misfortune to wear an eyeglass, and its effect on Americans at first acquaintance is sometimes unhappy. At last he asked me how I felt about the plan. I replied that I liked it very much, and thought I should be able to do what he wanted.

"I like the sound of that," he said. "I'll give you a letter to Boatner."

A year later, I heard the contents of that letter. Apparently it read as follows:—

"Help this guy. He looks like a dude, but I think he's a soldier."

On the whole, I think I like it.

Wingate went back to the Headquarters which he had set up at Imphal in Manipur State, while I, in the Scots legal phrase, took avizandum as to the best route over the Patkais, down to the Chindwin, across it and south away beyond. Katie Cave, John Fraser and I raked Assam for people who knew or were alleged to know the country. Every now and then we would hear of some new potential source of advice, and one or other would make pilgrimage to see him, and to pick his brains. All these enquiries had to be carried out with the utmost discretion, for it was imperative that the enemy should not know of our presence in the area, nor of our intentions. It was now necessary also to learn something of Lonkin; and we actually found an Englishman who had been there at one time as a missionary. I asked him to come with us, and at first he agreed; but soon he began to make excuses, and it was evident that he had no stomach for the adventure, so I let him off.

Even after I had made up my mind roughly where I proposed to cross the Chindwin, we had made little progress towards finding a route to the crossing-place. We interviewed every sort and condition of man, in our quest for information: a Chinese general, who was supposed to have led his division out of Burma through Taro in 1942; two more missionaries; an Assistant District Commissioner, whom we submitted to cross-examination between two cross-examinations of his own, on the morning of his weekly assize; a police officer; two tea-planters who in 1942 had led parties of coolies into the hills to seek and succour refugees with food and elephants and litters; two young American officers, Quackenbush and Mac-Somebody, who had lately taken patrols into unknown country to investigate rumours of Jap penetration; Kachin refugees from the Hukawng Valley and beyond; opium-smugglers, big with trade secrets and coy beyond belief; Naga coolies, doing odd jobs on the Road in hopes of opium: the knowledge and ignorance of all were pressed into service.

While it was possible to disguise our real object from most of those whom we questioned, a few had to be taken into our confidence. And of all those to whom we put the straight question, "Is it possible to get a Brigade, complete with loaded mules, over that country?" only one, an American veterinary serjeant called Stahl, who had forsaken vetting for more exciting employment with a body of scouts, said "Yes." And even he added, "But it's gonna be goddam tough." Goddam tough was precisely what it proved to be.

Meanwhile, I was lent a medium bomber, a B25 (*anglicé*, a Mitchell), with which to reconnoitre. The Ledo strip was only capable of accepting light planes, and so I had to fly over to the big airfield at Dinjan, by the Brahmaputra, whenever I wanted to use the Mitchell. A month before, Phil Cochrane, the commander of No. 1 Air Commando, had flown Orde Wingate, myself and Brigadier Derek Tulloch (Orde's Chief of Staff) up and down the Chindwin between Homalin and Singkaling Hkamti, and eastward as far as the Indawgyi Lake. This time I took with me two of my commanding officers, John Metcalf and Dick Cumberlege, and determined to examine possible crossings of the Chindwin above Hkamti; the passes through the hills south of the River;

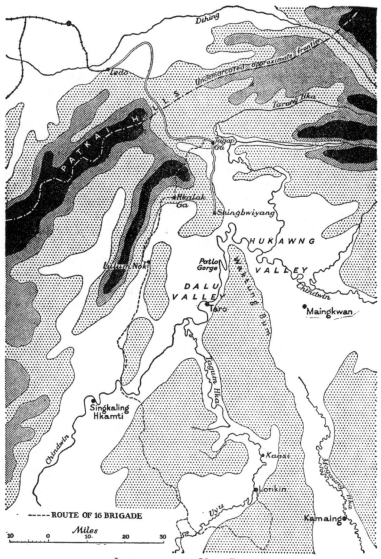

Dihing

Ledo

Undemarcated approximate frontier

Tarung Hka

PATKAI H.

Tagap Ga

Hkalak Ga

Shingbwiyang

HUKAWNG

Tulum Nok

Potlo Gorge

VALLEY

Chindwin

DALU VALLEY

Taro

Maingkwan

Singkaling Hkamti

Chindwin

Tagum Hka

Kansi

Lonkin

Mogaung Hka

Kamaing

Uyu

- - - - - **ROUTE OF 16 BRIGADE**

Miles

10   0   10.   20   30

LEDO TO THE UYU RIVER.

██████ ....over 6000 feet

▓▓▓▓▓▓ .... „   4000 feet

░░░░░░ .... „   2000 feet   25

and the approaches to Lonkin. I sat beside the pilot in the co-pilot's seat, Colonel John Metcalf stood behind me and looked over my shoulder, Colonel Dick Cumberlege was somewhere in the waist of the aircraft. Mitchells are far from ideal for reconnaissance, cruising as they do at two hundred miles an hour: but with their armament they give you a reasonable chance in the event of interception. I had intended to have a look at Indaw, which was frequently visited by allied marauding planes, and which could be visited once more without betraying our interest in the place; but this was forbidden by the over-cautious officer in command at Dinjan. I wanted to look at Lonkin too, in order to add a flesh-and-blood impression to what I had already gained from a study of maps and air photographs.

The north side of the mountains was shrouded in rain, as it often was; and I had difficulty in persuading the pilot, from my previous experience in twice visiting Shingbwiyang, that we should find sunshine beyond. We crossed the hills at fourteen thousand feet and burst through the cloud to see the whole land of Burma, as it seemed, spread out before us. I indicated to the pilot where I wanted to go by using the dual control whenever I wished to gain or lose height, or to change direction; and as we reached the Chindwin near Shingbwiyang, we turned down-stream towards Taro.

The Hukawng Valley and the Dalu Valley are both rather mis-leading names. The Hukawng proper (said to be derived from a Kachin word meaning "funeral pyre," and to record a great slaughter of Shans centuries ago) is taken to mean the flat lands on either side of the Chindwin through which runs the track from Ledo via Shingbwiyang, over the River, through Maingkwan and Kamaing to Mogaung. Stilwell had built his road along this track as far as Shing, and the Japs had built theirs from Mogaung to Maingkwan: there remained a short stretch in the middle which neither side had yet built. Over this track came many refugees in 1942, and on it many thousands died; it was the last remaining route out of Burma, save only the supposedly impassable Chaukkan (over which a few brave spirits, among them John Fraser, managed to struggle with infinite hardship).

West of the Hukawng, the Chindwin bursts through a deep

gorge, marked on the map as the Patlo Gorge, for some twenty-five miles, until it emerges in the Dalu or Taro Valley. The range which, on the south bank, separates the Hukawng from the Dalu Valley is known as the Waktung Bum. No track is marked on the map along this range, although a dotted one (signifying "impassable for animals") is marked across it; and it must have been traversed by somebody some time, because at one point beside a stream occurs the suggestive legend "Camp site."

I had some hopes that we might struggle along the watershed of the Waktung Bum, since game tracks are often found on crests such as these. I thought that if we could cross the Chindwin in the Patlo Gorge, and scramble up the backbone and along the crest, we might emerge in Kansi and Lonkin unbeknown to the Japs. (We knew there was a garrison in Taro.) Failing that we might somehow by-pass Taro, and either work along a track that was marked as climbing gradually on to the range farther south, or march up the bed of a small river called the Tagum Hka, which enters the Chindwin a few miles below Taro. The third and last possible course was to cross the Chindwin between the Japs in Taro and the Japs in Singkaling Hkamti. Between these two points the Chindwin again ran through a gorge, in which the ominous word "Rapids" occurred three times on the map.

The tracks leading southwards were therefore very few; and all ran through defiles where a Jap company might easily hold up a force many times its strength. This was an argument in favour of trying the Waktung watershed or the Tagum Hka river-bed. I resolved to look at both of these. Meanwhile, I was beginning to wonder just how good John Fraser's idea of coming via Ledo had been. As long as it looked a good idea, I was prepared to take the credit for it; but the more it looked like slumping, the more I was inclined to remind people that the idea had been John's in the first instance.

We flew low through the Patlo Gorge. The pilot wanted to shoot up a raft at its northern entrance, but I hastily stopped him: I knew that some of Stilwell's men were trying to force a passage through, and the raft was as likely to be Chinese as Jap. We circled Taro, but saw no signs of enemy; and then bore away southward between the Waktung Bum and the Tagum Hka, looking at both. The Tagum (*Hka* is merely Kachin for stream) started well, with a broad sandy bed; but it soon shrank into a nasty narrow overgrown affair, and then took to having waterfalls in a big way. The Waktung didn't even start well; and as we skimmed along, climbing gradually, fifty feet above the trees, I could feel my face growing longer and longer. The watershed was punctuated by high peaks and escarpments; and although one didn't expect to see signs of a game-track through the trees, one had no difficulty in deducing that it would be mighty funny game that tackled the Waktung Bum. It was no place to which to lead a Brigade that was in a hurry to keep an engagement near Indaw; I could not risk having to give the order "About turn."

We flew on south, gaining height so as not to tempt beyond endurance the Jap garrison in Lonkin. The country and the day were both beautiful, and it was tempting to forget what one had come there to do. Perhaps that is why I missed Lonkin. I saw a typical Kachin settlement on a hill, which I thought I could identify; but I looked in vain for the big village, standing in a paddy area several miles long, which I should recognise as Lonkin. I suddenly found that we were approaching a broad, shallow river that I knew must be the Uyu; and I swung the aircraft away, westward and downstream, until I recognised Haungpa, which I had seen from the air the previous month with Phil. South of it I saw my old friend, that fine hill Taungthonlon. Why one should get so fond of places which one can only associate with weariness, discomfort and a certain measure of fear, I cannot tell; but both Taungthonlon and the Uyu River, with its serpentine curves, have a strong hold on my affections.

At first I thought to go back and have another look for Lonkin, and actually turned the aircraft in that direction; and then I bethought me that, if we did, it would be obvious that we were on a reconnaissance, and the Japs would make deductions accordingly. So we turned north, and followed up the course of a stream to Singkaling Hkamti, keeping the hills on our starboard hand close aboard, and flying at a height of two or three hundred feet above the trees. The jungle was thick, but not comparably with what we had seen earlier; and the gradients were

reasonable. It was the best line of approach that I had so far
seen; and it looked as if the easiest way to tackle Lonkin would
be to come well to the westward of it, and then to assault up the
Uyu from Haungpa. Provided we could find a crossing place
near Singkaling Hkamti, and provided that we could find a way
from Tagap Ga, on the Road to Singkaling Hkamti, on the
River, we might manage yet.

We came out over the River near Hkamti, and noted several
places just below the exit from the gorge, where we might be
able to cross. The River broadened here, although it was still
twisting and turning as though not yet aware of its freedom
from the constraining mountains; which indeed still pressed
closely upon it on the northern side. At each corner, sandbanks
ran out from the inside bend, so that the actual expanse to be
crossed was little more than two to three hundred yards. I chose
first and second favourites, ten and fifteen miles respectively
above Singkaling Hkamti; and then the imp of mischief
whispered simultaneously in my ear and in that of the pilot.
Would it not be fun, it said, to sneak up on Hkamti from behind
the hills, catch the Japs unawares, and give them a bit of stick?
Both of us concluded without hesitation that it would. And so
we came near to our undoing.

We swung round once, roared up at tree-top height—and
missed the village by half a mile. The Japs must certainly have
divined our intention, and gone to ground; but we thought we
would have another try, and so circled again. This time we got
it right, and came out plumb at the monastery, standing in the
middle of an open space. We looked eagerly for Japs, and then
in an awful second my heart was in my mouth: for a great palm
tree, outsize among its neighbours like an animal out of
the wrong Noah's Ark, seemed to rise up out of the ground as
if to snatch at us. The pilot saw it in the same split instant of
time, and pulled back the stick so sharply that Colonel Metcalf,
craning his head over my shoulder in his search for Japs, went
backwards head over heels down into the well behind and below
us. There was a shock, and the aircraft shuddered; and then we
were rising above the River, gaining height and badly frightened.
Peering out at our port wing we saw four feet of fabric gashed
and tattered on the leading edge, and realised how lucky we had

been. We returned then to our proper task of reconnaissance, and flew at a respectful height through the gorge and back to Taro.

The River in the gorge was fast-flowing and narrow, and the rapids white and tumbling between sharp cliffs. The hills on the north bank (through which we must march if I stuck to my new plan of crossing near Hkamti and going for Haungpa) looked big and thickly forested but not so bad as the Waktung or the Tagum Hka. I did, in fact, stick to that plan, and this was the route we eventually followed.

I took over the controls on the way home, and soared with exhilaration over the Patkais. They still looked formidable, but this was now the sixth time I had flown over them, and I was rapidly becoming used to them.

Back at Dinjan, we looked at the damaged wing with awe, and felt rather foolish. The aircraft was out of commission for two or three days; but thereafter it took my remaining column commanders, in two trips, to look at the crossings between Taro and Singkaling Hkamti. There was a fair amount of air activity in the area anyhow, in connection with General Stilwell's operations, and I had no fears about divulging our purpose. I did not, however, allow further visits to Lonkin or the Uyu, which might have put ideas even into the thick heads of the Japanese. Meanwhile, I was busy at the bottom end of the Ledo Road with our final preparations.

Day by day the Brigade was arriving at the concentration area. To be more precise, it was arriving night by night, so that it should not be seen. The only troops at this end of Assam were Chinese and American, and British troops (my Brigade was all-British, except for the handful of Burma Rifles with each column) would have been highly conspicuous. The trains pulled on to a secret spur known as Jungle Siding; and the troops were brought in lorries under cover of darkness to a patch of jungle some hundreds of yards off the Road, by the side of the Dihing River. If by chance any train was so delayed that the troops must reach camp in daylight, it was stopped forty miles down the line, and brought on the next night. Katie met every train; I always took a full night in bed, feeling slightly guilty about it, but determined not to start the trek already weary. I had had a hard march the previous year, and was not feeling too robust in any case.

The lengths to which we went to conceal our presence were extreme and thorough. The only troops allowed to show themselves were military police at the two exits out of our forest camp on to the road, and the drivers of the few essential lorries. All these were dressed in American uniform and ordered to chew gum. The sentries in addition were made to sit, and forbidden to salute, except when spoken to, and then only gently. The result convinced me of what I had always suspected: that there is a definite American physiognomy; for even thus disguised, the Cockneys continued to look like Cockneys, the Cumbrians like Cumbrians, and the Jocks in the two gunner columns like Jocks. More surprising still were the negroes. There were hundreds of American negroes working on the Road as engineers and transport drivers; and I also had attached to me a section of Nigerians on loan from the 3rd West African Brigade, who had been carrying out a reconnaissance patrol on my behalf. These, too, had been thrust into American uniform; and yet they did not resemble in the slightest particular their American cousins. So little, in fact, that one American officer lounged up to Katie, and jerking his thumb at one of my West Africans in doughboy uniform just across the track, said: "I'll say *that* nigger never came from Georgia!"

Alas! for all our precautions. Even before we had completed our concentrations, the Jap-controlled Radio Saigon triumphantly broadcast a personal message to me, twice in one day, which ran:—

"O monocled Fergusson! We knew all about you and your Australians[1] at Ledo. You got out last time, but you won't get out this. We will bomb you day and night."

When I first heard of this, I thought it was a bad joke invented by some of the men; but an immediate investigation produced a number who had heard it, including N.C.O.s, and also one officer, whose account was identical. It was hardly surprising; Japanese information about Ledo was always good; and strenuous efforts

[1] This mistake presumably arose from our Australian-type bush-hat.

to discover the source of leakage had been unsuccessful. What
was more surprising was that no further broadcasts on this
subject were made. Possibly it was a bow at a venture, and the
Japs abandoned it when it apparently failed to draw blood. We
kept up our precautions, although strongly tempted to relax
them; and we know now that our eventual appearance in the Uyu
Valley took the enemy completely by surprise.

As soon as I got back from the reconnaissance over the
Chindwin which I have described, I stopped swithering about the
plan, and decided, for better or worse, on the following. General
Stilwell had promised to help me with my transport as far as
Tagap Ga, which was about seventy miles up his Road, and some
little way beyond its highest point. Thence a track ran up into
the hills which Serjeant Stahl, the American vet., had been over
a year before. This track, known to the Americans as the "Salt
Spring Trail" (shades of the Wild West: the Americans called
all tracks "trails") was alleged to go to Hkalak Ga, where the
Chinese had an outpost watching for Jap movement from the
direction of the Dalu Valley and Taro. This post was kept
supplied by air and was normally reached by a bad track from
Shingbwiyang. For us to go by Shing would be a long way
round; and the logistics of the Road in relation to my Brigade
would not allow us to be carried farther than Tagap. Shocking
as the Road was to that point, it was said to be even worse thereafter. Almost every yard of it was being worked on; the lorry
capacity was entirely taken up with sapper materials, and the
supplies necessary to support the labour working on the road;
Shing and everything beyond it was being supplied by Dakotas
on to the Shing strip, and thence forward by Jeep. So I decided
that the first leg of our march should be to Hkalak Ga.

Beyond Hkalak was Lulum Nok. One of Katie Cave's reconnaissance patrols had been somewhere near Lulum, which was
said to be held by another Chinese outpost; but this patrol,
operating south-east of that area, had bumped trouble in two
places, once in a village, and once on a track. It was extremely
hard at Ledo to find out the detailed Chinese dispositions, which
included many scattered outposts in places which were either not
shown on the map, or, if shown, were often ten miles out.

However, the existence and whereabouts of Hkalak were

certain and so was its garrison; the existence of Lulum was
pretty certain, though there were doubts about its garrison;
beyond Lulum all was doubt. The map showed large blobs of
country pure white, with "unsurveyed" printed brazenly and
unashamedly across them; and other areas were studded ingenu-
ously with question marks printed in a neat and symmetrical
pattern. It wouldn't have been a bad thing if there had been
question marks all over it.

From Tagap to Hkalak, then, by the Salt Spring Trail (hoping
that Serjeant Stahl was right); Hkalak to Lulum: so much was
clear. After that, we must see what offered. Meanwhile, as soon
as I had a few troops under my hand, I put together a party of a
hundred and fifty sappers and fifty infanteers, with a few Kachin
Burma Riflemen to act as interpreters, and sent them on ahead
under Robinson, my sapper Major, to find the Salt Spring Trail
and to clear it ahead of us. It was as well that I did so. If it had
not been for Robbie's pioneering, the march to the Chindwin
would have taken us twice the time.

Robbie Robinson and I were old allies. At the beginning of
the war, he was second in command of the field company attached
to the Brigade in which I was Brigade Major. He was a proper
soldier. He got his commission on the outbreak of war, after
some eighteen years' service; and he was already two years over
the maximum age laid down for being a Chindit, when his field
company was selected for Chindit service. But would he accept
that ruling? He made the life of every doctor in the neighbourhood into sheer hell until, with their heads bloody and bowed,
they passed him fit. During the march to the Chindwin, enough
blessings rained on his head to ensure him a tangible, eighteen-
carat halo. Of this, the ribbon of the M.B.E., which he wears
to-day, must be taken as the outward and visible sign.

Robbie left on his mission before any mules had arrived at
Tagap, for the animals were marching up the Road: there were
not enough lorries to carry them as well as the men. In consequence, I had to send him off without any wireless, and his only
means of communication with me was by runner to Tagap, and
thence back down the Road. I had to fly to Imphal for a final
conference, and owing to bad weather did not get back for three
days. When at last I arrived, I found that first reports from

Robbie were bad. Even so, I could not leave for roadhead: for Tagap was twelve hours' drive from my camp by the Dihing, and I had still much to do there. Every night one column (two columns equalled one battalion in our organisation) left camp at dusk for roadhead, where we had established a ration dump, and where some of my staff were running a forward concentration area.

On the 1st of February, General Sir George Giffard, the Commander in Chief of 11th Army Group (afterwards known as Allied Land Forces, South East Asia) came to say good-bye. Most unfortunately, his old regiment, the Queen's, had already left for roadhead, and he did not see them. He was an old hand at jungle, having spent much of the last war chasing Von Lettow-Vorbeck round German East Africa, and having since been Inspector-General African Forces. I think he enjoyed his night with us, even though we had nothing whatever to offer him; I opened my heart to him about my many preoccupations. When at last it was time for bed, he rolled himself up in a blanket and slept on the ground as if he had still been on column in German East. It was fun having him, the only senior officer in either the British or Indian Armies, so far as I know, who as a junior had had long experience of jungle in war conditions.

Then, a day or two later, came General Wingate. I bade farewell to our wet and clammy camp by the Dihing River, and set off with him, and George Borrow, his A.D.C., up to roadhead in a Jeep borrowed from General Boatner. Before leaving, we had a meal in a Chinese eating-house by the side of the Road, feasting greasily on sweet and sour pork, Eggs Fu-Yong, chicken noodle soup, and a delicacy which the proprietor called "Flied Lice," but which I was relieved to recognise, when it came, as nothing more exotic than "Fried Rice." Then, after dark, when the ordinary Road traffic had ground itself to silence for the night, we set off up the long climb to the 70th milestone and Tagap.

I have not yet mentioned the rain. This corner of the world, where Assam, Burma, Tibet and China all nearly meet, has the heaviest rainfall known. At that season it is almost incessant. North of the hills it is often fine and clear; but once within them it is raining far more often than not. Our camp by the Dihing was just on the fringe of the grey curtain; once we moved southward, the curtain closed on us for good and all, and was not to lift again for several weeks. From the moment we started up the Road until we came into the Chindwin Valley, not a day passed without rain: steady, solid, cold and merciless. In every sentence as you read it, you must strive to hear the swish and feel the chill of grey, implacable rain.

Our driver, a cheerful gum-chewer from Michigan, cursed it as he drove. I had thought to find the Road something like the Manipur Road up which we had marched into Burma on the first Expedition just a year before, which boasted tarmac for much of its length, and whose surface at least was reasonable: but the Ledo Road was immeasurably worse. It was everywhere a foot deep in mud and shingle, and every vehicle (driven either by negroes or Chinese) had to have chains permanently on the wheels. Even with no traffic moving, it took us all our time to average ten miles an hour; and it was one of the most fatiguing drives I ever suffered, since one had to exert muscular effort all the time to remain in the Jeep. Time and again we had to lift it out of ruts a couple of feet deep, and to set it carefully on its wheels again so that the ruts were straddled.

It was about two in the morning when I suggested to Wingate that we might arrive at our destination before dawn, and pass it by mistake in the darkness. We were all exhausted, and decided to sleep for a couple of hours by the side of the Road. The rain slackened to a Scotch mist, and we didn't fare badly. When dawn came up, we eased our stiff limbs, motored a couple of miles farther on, past labour gangs just waking up to work, and found the Brigade sign by the roadside.

My advanced party had done its work well, and all columns had settled into a bivouac area by the side of a broad stream half a mile below the turmoil of the graders and the bulldozers. Breakfast was brewing up, and every man sat with his mess-tin on the fire before him. I had given permission to let beards grow a few days before, and people were looking rather ruffianly. But they were well and cheerful, and the word spread rapidly that Wingate had arrived. Few of the men had seen him before, as he had had typhoid during most of the training period. Barely six weeks ago, he had been on the Dangerously Ill list; now he was in his usual compelling form, making light of all difficulties and dispersing all doubts. He had just sent reconnaissance patrols across the Chindwin a couple of hundred miles farther south, with the characteristic order: "No patrol will report any country impenetrable until it has penetrated it."

There were difficulties and doubts enough. Robbie had sent back a runner with word that the going was worse than we had feared in our most downcast moments. He feared that we would never get loaded mules over, and asked if it were not possible to take them light, and to have their loads dropped beyond the mountains. This, I knew, was out of the question.

In giving Robbie Robinson his orders, I had told him to work his way the thirty-five miles to Hkalak, carrying a week's rations. This I hoped would last him until he got there; and knowing that the Chinese outpost at that point had cleared a dropping area, I proposed to drop him his next supply when he got there. But Wilkinson, my senior commanding officer (of the Leicesters) who had been in charge at roadhead pending my arrival, had already had an SOS from Robbie to say that progress was desperately slow; he was fast running out of food, with no sort of prospect of reaching Hkalak within ten, let alone seven days. Colonel Wilkinson had therefore organised a carrying party from his own unit, to carry food for Robbie's men as far out along the track as could be managed in a day; and had gone ahead of it himself, so as to see the conditions with his own eyes. No mules had yet reached roadhead, and the stuff had to be carried by man load. Wilkinson had already started when Wingate and I arrived, and the carrying party was in process of breakfasting before loading up.

We, too, had a hurried breakfast, and set off in pursuit of Wilkie Wilkinson—Wingate, myself and my two Intelligence Officers. We walked a mile down the Road, to where a rough wooden bridge spanned the stream by which the Brigade was camped, and crossed it. Chinese were working on it, and Wingate greeted them in what he confessed was his only word of their language. It sounded like "How!" and he described the *succés fou* he had enjoyed when he tried it on Chiang Kai Shek. Immediately across the bridge, the Road bore away downstream, and we began to clamber up a brown, muddy butter-slide which was the first stretch of the Salt Spring Trail.

To get up that first hill, less than a mile in length, un-impeded by packs or weapons, took us a full hour. Two or three hundred of my men were working on it, building steps and traverses with bamboo and other wood, felled by its side. I wanted to concentrate on traverses, like those which on a larger scale General Wade built up Corryarrack two hundred years ago; I thought they would stand up better to the enormous strain soon to be put on them. General Wingate ordered steps, and I was not sure enough of my ground to stand out against him; but it proved an exception among the many arguments which I had with him: on this occasion I would have done better to have stuck to my guns. When, two or three days later, the mules began to tackle the hill, they knocked the steps sideways in the violence of their struggles, so that they had to be rebuilt after every two or three animals had passed; and I got a message sent forward to the workers, far ahead along the track among the pioneers, that all steps were to be replaced by traverses wherever it was possible.

We struggled on up the hill. Far below us in the valley, the roar of the traffic on the Road continued, and the bulldozers pushed and pulled at the reluctant mountain; deep blue smoke rose from the wet fires of the Chinese labour camps. Sometimes for a few moments the rain lifted, and one saw out across the valley to the towering mountain on the other side.

At the summit, we passed into the green tunnel which, with only two glimpses of the outer world, had its other mouth at Hkalak. The trees closed over our heads: we were already beyond the range where the labour parties sought for timber for the Road or firewood for the camps. The track was an old one; not having been travelled since last monsoon, it had almost grown over. Every yard, however, bore witness to Major Robinson's pioneering: bamboos and vines cut back; steps and traverses built; new paths cut round fallen trees; stumps with raw white gashes sticking reproachfully out of the ground or out of the bushes; light brown earth, lately turned for the first time, standing out against the dank and sodden leaves. Level going there was none; but the gradients were not bad, once the path had reached its destined crest. In some places, it was thrust off the watershed by some especially big trees, and here the new trace would be cut out of the side of the hill. After a couple of miles it took a definite downward trend, following first a spur and then a stream-bed, until it achieved a gradient of one in one. Here too, Robinson had been at work; but even so it was all one could do to keep one's footing; and indeed all of us slithered some of the way.

At moments during the descent, a vista opened to show the opposite side of the glen into which we were descending; it seemed bare of jungle on its lower slopes. At last we came out into a clearing, through which were leaping the swollen waters of a mountain stream. Across it, our pioneers had built a causeway of boulders, level enough for the passage of mules, where the water was no more than knee-deep. This was Salt Spring; and I noted with satisfaction that on the far side there were small terraces a few yards square, on each of which it would be possible to camp a section of men, or two or three mules. With a little reconnaissance it should be possible to make some staging post of a kind at this point.

On the far side of Salt Spring, the path immediately began to climb once more, at a fantastic gradient: for a thousand feet which we had lost in the descent had now to be won back. We struggled up to the lip of the glen, and for about a mile beyond; and then we turned back, for Wingate had seen all he wanted to see. He refused to be daunted by the obvious difficulties which lay ahead.

"That's all right," he kept saying: "that's not too bad. You'll manage that all right."

I am glad he said so; for his certainty that we should get through buoyed me up, so that we never really thought of failure. Weeks later, at the Chindwin, he confessed that he had in fact thought otherwise, and had been expecting every day what he described as a *non possumus*. It was one of his rare pats on the back, and more precious than a peerage.

On the way back, we met Colonel Wilkinson's carrying party under Major Dalgliesh. They were carrying immensely heavy loads of rations, which they succeeded in getting beyond Salt Spring before having to dump them. We also passed Bill Smythies, one of the two Burma Forest Officers attached to my headquarters, whom I had ordered forward to help Robbie with professional advice. He was groaning under eight days' rations; the sweat was pouring from him, and he must have been bitterly lamenting the days of old civilian Burma; when (so I gather) one walked light, and put the peace-time equivalent of one's pack on an elephant.

I could not imagine, that evening, why I felt so exhausted, and so unaccountably seedy. The answer came when I woke in the middle of the night, shivering and hot by turns, and knew I was in for a dose of fever. I was glad to accept the farewells of Orde Wingate and George Borrow, to see them depart in their Jeep a little before noon, and to stagger down the hill to my bivouac; to tell John Marriott to carry on, and to roll myself up in my blankets and wish I was dead. I still retained the power to marvel when Jimmie Donaldson the doctor produced from his "Medical Comforts" no less a wonder than a hot-water bottle; and I dozed fitfully, working out wild logistic calculations, based on the problem of getting us to Hkalak. The alternatives appeared to be either cannibalism or carrying parties under Duggie Dalgliesh.

II

THE MULES began to arrive; their natural frivolity abated by the rigours of the Road, and their muleteers blasphemous and jealous of their comrades' having ridden up it in trucks. There arrived, too, the teams of men out of each column who had been collecting and training with our latest weapons, the Lifebuoys. Wingate had seen and ordered these during his trip to the United Kingdom; they were the latest thing out. For the first time in the history of the war, thanks to his persistence, troops in this theatre had been given priority in a new weapon. The Lifebuoy was a flame-thrower, and received its name for security reasons; its circular fuel-container did in fact resemble the type of lifebuoy usually hung along the side of a ship. On this occasion, as on so many others, security had led to confusion. The first consignment had never arrived; many months later they were found in a naval store at Bombay, which had seemed to somebody in the course of their journey a more natural destination for an article called a lifebuoy than a Force planned to operate hundreds of miles from the sea.

We tried them out by the river-bank, in a demonstration attended by all officers. I remember it well; I remember also shivering from my ague despite the British Warm which I had managed to bring thus far. Beyond the river, the huge trees dripped sullenly. A subaltern, fresh from his course, described the weapon's virtues and limitations; and then an operator played it on the beach, on the undergrowth beyond the river, and on the river itself. The flames leapt up from the fuel as it pitched; great pools of it went floating and burning smokily down the river like fireships. It was a formidable weapon, but an abominable mule-load: not from its weight, a mere seventy pounds, but from its awkward and intractable shape. Try as we would, we could only carry it as a top-load, which raised the minimum mule-height, for which the tunnels through the jungle must be cut, by fully six inches.

The first columns to start were those of the Queen's. The order of march, and indeed the order of battle at Indaw two months later, were dictated not by choice, but by the order of battle on our final training exercise early in January. We had entrained for Ledo directly it ended, according to the order in which the columns reached the railway station from the mock battlefield; and since then we had been racing against time. The Queen's reached Ledo first, and thus were ready to start first up the Road; they were the first to complete concentration of mules and men to Tagap, and thus the first to tackle the track to Hkalak. I allowed their mules two days to recover from the hardships of the Road; and then they started off.

I knew that the first hill would prove a serious obstacle, but I still hoped that they would get beyond Salt Spring on the first day. Vain hope! The rain had intensified, and the first mules to leave the Road above the wooden bridge sufficed to kick away the steps and traverses so painfully built. The water had under-mined the logs which shored them up, and none survived the passage of so many as four mules without having to be repaired. By the end of the first day, of the two columns, something over half the mules had reached the top of the first hill, barely a mile from the Road; most of their loads were still at the bottom of the hill, or at various points on the way up. All except the first few loads had had to be man-handled; the elaborate steps and traverses were in ruins; and the whole hill was one unsavoury chute.

From bitter experience with these first columns, I had to revise my whole programme. It was only four miles from the point where the track left the Road to the top of the hill beyond Salt Spring; but it took three days for any one column to get there. One whole day was needed to reach the top of the first hill; another to the bottom of the Salt Spring Hill; the third to climb out of the Salt Spring ravine. And the area in which I was required to fight, in six weeks' time, lay 350 miles away, across country little of which was known, but which looked from the map and from the air to be of the same quality as that in which we were. Our only hope lay in the prospects of better weather once we were over the watershed, and dropping down to the Chindwin River.

I had settled my order of march at five columns ahead of my headquarters and three thereafter. The Queen's led, followed by those of the Leicesters. Then came the first of the two columns formed from the 51st Field Regiment, Royal Artillery (recently converted to infantry); then Brigade Headquarters, a huge cumbersome unit of nearly two hundred men and over sixty animals; then the second Gunner column; and finally the two columns of the 45th Reconnaissance Regiment, who had also just become foot-soldiers. To be tail column of a long line of columns is misery; and to be in that position for a period of two months an abominable cruelty which I should have avoided inflicting could I possibly have done so. But to pass columns ahead of each other was impossible without loss of time; and time was all-important.

I resolved to push ahead of Brigade Headquarters so as to watch the progress of my earlier columns. I could keep in touch with Brigade and General Wingate's Headquarters by exploiting the hospitality of wireless sets other than my own. Back at Imphal, my rear Brigade Headquarters, located two miles from Wingate's, and linked with his by telephone, accepted my news and passed me his orders. There sat Katie Cave, chafing at his distance from the field, but glorifying in every little thing that he could do to help us; and with him a little group of signals, ciphers and watch-keeping officers, whom former wounds or sickness had rendered less fit than we for the heavy marching under heavy packs. We had another group working for us as well: the party under Major John Stobbs at Air Base Headquarters, at Sylhet in Assam; whose job was to note our requirements and to load up the supply-dropping aircraft accordingly. We were always conscious of these friends and comrades away behind us, who in their warm and wakeful interest for us seemed indeed very close.

Better of my fever, though feeling rather limp, I set off from Tagap with Captain Noel Catterall, the junior of my two Intelligence officers. I forget which column was on the hill that day; but I do not forget the sight of the struggling, plunging mules with heaving quarters and steaming flanks. We reached Salt

Spring at dusk. The spring actually existed, in a little grotto just above where the track crossed the stream, from which it mingled its salt waters with the main torrent. It may at some time have been inhabited, although it was an unlikely place to be chosen by the stronghold-loving Nagas; more likely it was an old staging camp for Naga parties on the march: I cannot otherwise account for its being cleared of trees. It was a pretty little spot, to my way of thinking: I had long since despaired of persuading John Fraser to agree, since he was no longer interested in any views save those around Edinburgh, which he had not seen for nine years. But the deep ravine, with its matted jungle, was lovely to those whose eyes had not been unduly filmed by prolonged exile; and although the hut which Noel and I built that night with groundsheets and plantain leaves was not entirely water-tight, we supped and slept there well enough.

Next morning, I passed the column which had finished climbing out of the ravine the previous afternoon. Soon I came to the spot where Wingate and I had turned back a few days previously; this time I pressed on into country still unknown to me. The going here was not bad, though steep and weary; and soon I met a man coming back from Major Robinson. The letter which he bore, and the story which he had to tell, were both depressing: he had left Robbie only the day before, and had covered in a few hours the distance which had taken them a week to traverse southward-bound and pioneering. Robbie was still short of Hkalak and out of food; he had taken the decision to press on into Hkalak with his men, clearing the track only to the extent necessary for his own passage. Once there, he intended to get food, and then to set most of his men working back while he himself pushed on with a small party to Lulum. The runner said that the worst of all the hills was barely a mile ahead, and that a column was spreadeagled on it at that moment.

There were still three columns ahead of me; so presumably the first two had got up all right, and my spirits did not therefore decline unduly. A few hundred yards on, I came to a group of three Naga huts, temporary shelters obviously intended for the use of travellers, with a ravishing view across a valley fifteen hundred to two thousand feet deep, so far as I could guess: the bottom was invisible below my feet. Here there was a small trickle of water running through an improvised bamboo pipe, and unmistakable signs of a column having bivouacked the night before. Here also, to my disgust, the curtain of the jungle being slightly lifted, I found I could still hear the noise of the traffic on the Road, and realised that, after all our struggles, we were still in earshot.

Soon I came to a small opening in the jungle beside the track, where mules were cropping the bamboo leaves, with their loads lying on the ground beside them. The muleteers were making tea, despite the pouring rain. Already they had learned the trick of making fires in sopping jungle: how to cut dead branches from the trees instead of taking those more temptingly lying on the ground; how to strip off the bark and outer shavings, so as to win through to the dry wood inside. Now, leech-hunting below their rolled-up trouser-legs, they were awaiting with patience the fruits of their firebuilding.

Colonel Wilkinson, they told me, was somewhere on the hill; and there eventually I found him. It was a brute of a hill, indeed. It climbed eighteen hundred feet with an average gradient of one in two, and frequent relapses to one in one. Sometimes the ladder (for that is practically what it was) climbed the back of a ridge, sometimes the bed of a stream; sometimes it lay in a hollow where the succession of mules had kicked away the earth and exposed the slippery rock. Again Robbie's hand was visible in the cut-back branches and frequent traverses; but at times there was no scope or option for a traverse and one had to follow straight up the incline.

The first two columns had again resorted to sending the mules up light, and man-handling the loads. The third, whose progress I was now watching, had evolved a new technique, so successful that I made it the standard practice in the Brigade. Men were stationed at intervals on the hill at points where there was a little flat: their job was to catch and rest the mules, who were allowed to come up free, loads and all. Wherever there is a steep hill, the mule likes to subscribe to the old Scots saying: "A stout hert to a stey brae"; he likes to take it at the double. Woe betide the muleteer who gets in the way; unless he can keep a firm hold on his beast he is flung down and trampled. And when, as was the case with us, a man carries seventy pounds on his back (far more, in proportion to his weight, than a mule has to carry) he cannot hope to double up the Naga hills, be his heart ever so stout.

So here they came, these gallant mules: trotting or galloping up the hill, with nostrils dilated and an uncommonly wild look in their eye; completely masterless, and deeply resentful of being halted for a compulsory breather. Many a man whose duty it was to stop them went flying when he tried it, howling horrible blasphemies as he hurtled into the wet jungle. A few loads slipped; more often a portion of the track collapsed, and the mule rolled over and over down the hillside until he lay, breathing great gollops of air, helpless until his load was taken off him. Even this wasn't an easy job: first the surcingle had to come off, then the load, then the girth; and before you were ready for him, there would be a heave and a plunge, and the beast was on his feet—and, like as not, on yours.

That was the way of it, however; and once we discovered it there was little more man-handling of loads. It was so successful that some columns carried it too far, and even on comparatively level going would allow the mules to trot along in their own time, until held up and rested by squads of men posted for the purpose. I put a stop to this, however, except upon hills where it was essential; because I feared that the mules might come to look on it as their normal mode of progression, and refuse all others. This would hardly do when it came to coping with Japs as well as with mountains.

There was one mule in 69 Column (a Gunner one) which went completely screwy. Having had a taste of individual progression it refused to revert to normal; and when normal methods were attempted, it would toss its muleteer like a Highland smith the caber. It became widely known as the "Mad Mule"; and one would hear from far behind in the column cries of "Make way for the Mad Mule!" Everybody would clear the track, and the beast would come by at a fast trot, its load swaying, its reins trailing, and a look in its eye as of one with a train to catch. Eventually one would catch it up again and pass it, having a snack of bamboo, and waiting for its muleteer to come up. The men would greet it with facetious cries, to which it paid no heed; until its own boss would arrive, take hold of the rein and try to resume control: upon which it would shake him free, and trot doggedly on until again it judged a meal was due.

This long hill, which became known as "Robbie's Steps," was in some ways the worst of all. Columns averaged nine hours to get up; and although there was water at the bottom, where the Naga huts were, there was none at the top, nor for a long distance beyond it. Paradoxically, water was our acutest problem, despite the rain; for Nature in her wisdom has decreed that water shall not flow along watersheds, although she has ruled that watersheds are the best alignment for tracks. Hundreds or thousands of feet below us there was water in plenty; rain beat on us without pity day and night; yet water-points were few and far between. Columns found different ways of getting over the difficulty. One had water dropped on it from the air, at one of the rare openings in the jungle; some cut precipitous descents, involving an extra hour's work on top of the day's toil; some found enough in bamboos to supply animals and men alike, tipping their contents into inflatable rubber-boats which we carried as part of our equipment; some inflated their boats and left them out to fill with rain.

The same process that we had first experienced on the hill above the Road, whereby the rain washed away our carefully constructed steps, still continued. Until we eventually reached Hkalak, I do not recollect one single stretch of level track so much as a hundred yards in length. The falling gradients were not so bad: the mules slithered down them, keeping their balance with remarkable skill; but the up gradients had not only to be built, but to be rebuilt half a dozen times during the passage of a single column. Everybody shared in the work; none was exempt; and hewing, digging, hauling, carrying went on continuously. Sometimes the track led through a thick bamboo clump in which a tunnel had been cut and carefully propped up; a mule, frightened or awkward, would swing a little bit off the track, and catch its load or its feet in one of the carefully placed props, so that the whole edifice would fall. Sometimes an exhausted mule would subside in the mud, right in the fairway; and the whole procession would be held up while its load was removed, carried up by manhandling, and the track cleared. On the whole, however, the beasts were sure-footed even beyond their reputation; and nobody in the Brigade was ever heard to "lightly" them after the journey through the Patkai hills.

I went back that night to Salt Spring, and found the column with whom I had shared the western side of the stream the previous night safely up the hill. The advanced party of my own Headquarters was just beginning to come in; and as I watched my servant, M'Clung,[1] brewing me up some tea, I could see the leading mules slipping and sliding down the opposite hill through the little gaps in the jungle. An hour's respite from rain, with a warm sun to dry our clothes in, had just ended; and Noel, stripped to the waist to keep his spare shirt dry, was showing the newcomers where to bivouac. When I had finished my tea, there was still an hour before darkness; and I set out along the track towards the Road to see how well the tail was coming in. I met odd parties coming along, chiefly those who had tackled the first hill in the morning; and before long I met John Marriott, my Brigade Major, fifty feet down the hillside, grappling with a signal mule below whom the track had slipped away. I helped him unload the frightened beast, and to haul first it and then its precious wireless load back up the hill to safety: by then it had gone full dark, and no moon could shine through those thick clouds. By no means all of Brigade Headquarters was in that night; and the bulk of it had to bivouac half-way between the Road and Salt Spring.

So it went on, day after day. It was no unusual thing for a column to sleep in two halves, with one of those major hills dividing the two; and supper was often a dry meal, with no water within reach, save that which we caught in our mugs or groundsheets from the rain. A dry bivouac was unknown; and all bivouacs over five thousand feet were bitterly cold. There was an unpleasant plague also in the shape of the *polaung* fly: a tiny creature, no bigger than a sandfly, with a particularly vicious bite which drew blood and hardened, with those most allergic to it, into a septic spot as tough as a wart. This gentleman pitched into us at all camps over four thousand feet up. Working hours were from dawn to dusk; we had meals in relays,

[1] Pte. R. M'Clung, The Black Watch, an ex-ploughman from Kilkerran, my home in Ayrshire.

but the work was continuous, and would have gone on through the night but for the inky clouds that hid the moon.

It soon became apparent that the seven days' rations we had carried from roadhead would not last till Hkalak Ga. From the leading column, to which had been deputed the duty of organising the supply drop at Hkalak, came a report that they were down to their last day's food, with half the distance still to run. I had already warned our Air Base by wireless that we should almost certainly need a supplementary drop to carry us on to Hkalak; and told John Metcalf, the colonel of the leading column, to keep an eye lifted for a suitable place to have it. He got his drop, and taking a few platoons pushed on ahead to Hkalak, leaving all his mules and the rest of his men to come on with his second column under its commander. Each night he reported progress, until at last he sent the glad tidings that he had reached the village. Most welcome item of his message was the list of water-points which he included in his report; and most depressing the news that he had had to go right over the crest of Saya Bum, a high mountain which the track, had it abided by the map, should have skirted: his nessage said plaintively, "no choice."

To labour the difficulties of that march would be tedious as well as unbecoming; and it will perhaps be forgiven me if I sum it up in an extract from my official report written just after we got out:—

"This march was the heaviest imaginable. The rain was torrential and almost continuous; the gradients were often one in two; no single stretch of level going a hundred yards in length existed between TAGAP and HKALAK, and few thereafter. Many mule loads had to be carried by hand up steep slopes, and the path had to be remade, or the traverses rebuilt, two to three times during the passage of a column. The cold was intense, particularly at bivouacs over five thousand feet. The 70 lbs. which men were carrying were greatly increased in weight due to saturation with water. A dry bivouac was practically unknown. Leeches, which were innumerable, were the least trying of the conditions. . . . Wireless communication was difficult, and the supply dropping on the whole atrocious, up to forty and fifty per cent. of the supplies dropped falling hundreds or thousands of feet down the cliffs and becoming a dead loss. Columns averaged nine days to cover the thirty-five miles from roadhead to HKALAK."

We of Brigade Headquarters had our first supply drop of the campaign on a small natural clearing rather over five thousand feet above sea-level. It was far from ideal, in that the clearing owed its existence to a marsh, with which its dimensions precisely coincided; but it was by far the best site anywhere between Tagap and Hkalak. The leading gunner column, No. 69, which was immediately ahead of Brigade, had had its drop a day earlier and at a far worse place; where any "overs" which missed the dropping zone floated mockingly a couple of thousand feet below, to places where it would have taken a week's work to reach them, even if they could have been located. It was the first drop we had had from American aircraft, and they did not appreciate at that early stage of the campaign the vital importance of accurate dropping. We longed for our old allies of Burbury's 31 Squadron who had done all the air supply for us the previous year.

But our marsh worked well, and this time the drop was excellent. Every parachute but one fell plumb in the dropping zone, small as it was; and the one miscreant missed it by not more than ten yards. This was the first drop carried out on my Brigade by 117th Squadron R.A.F., who had been especially imported from the Middle East at Wingate's request, and whose high standard was never to vary throughout the whole campaign. Long after 16 Brigade had come out, right through the miseries of the monsoon, 117 went on dropping beautifully to our comrades in the other brigades, and earned a platinum coconut every time.

On the eighth day after leaving Tagap I again pushed ahead, taking John Marriott the Brigade Major with me, so as to reach Hkalak and see my forward troops. Over Saya Bum we went, and down the other side; and then on a sudden we emerged from the green tunnel which had so long walled us in, and there burst on us the most glorious view. The rain had stopped; and we saw before us many miles of leaping crests, flanked to the westward by hills running up to nine thousand feet, but, to our front, definitely lower than what we had come over. In the sunshine of that morning they showed a soft green olive colour, instead of

W.G.E. D

the harsh vegetable shades of the past weeks. In that time we had sweated by day and shivered by night, and been wet and stiff all the time: yet I swear that in that moment when the view burst upon us, the memory dropped from us like Christian's burden.

Below, on a crest no more than a mile away, lay the stockaded post of Hkalak. Smoke rose from it, a heartening thing to see. The crest was clear of jungle, and neat houses circled it. Here was no straggling Naga village; it was a secure fort. A watch-tower thirty feet high, built of logs and roofed with brown plantain leaves, dominated the countryside. The whole was spread below us, as one of the men said, "in glorious techni-colour." We halted for a smoke and to admire the scene; and it was my fancy to lie hidden where the column, pressing along a few hundred yards behind us, would emerge in its turn, so that I could hear the comments of the men. I was not disappointed; for each bearded, ragged, soaking soldier could contain himself no more than I had, and burst out in rapture as he saw it.

Already, in and around Hkalak, Queen's and Leicesters were disposed. Supply drops had been taking place daily, and the men had had their first mail for a month. Spirits were correspondingly high, and Colonel John Metcalf, who had already been there four or five days, told us all about the place. There was a company of Chinese, under a Captain; there were three American officers: one a doctor, with an excellent little hospital; one a liaison officer with the Chinese; the third was the owner of the watch-tower, whose duty it was to report any aircraft seen. John Metcalf had already had trouble with the Chinese, who were busy at each supply drop looting any statichutes which fell out-side the dropping zone; he had got no change out of the Chinese Captain; but the position had improved since he had caught twelve of the thieves red-handed and given them a beating. (The American liaison officer, deeply shocked, had all the same greatly enjoyed witnessing a performance which was strictly forbidden to himself, but which he had been longing to stage for a year.) John had served in China with Boatner, and knew the form.

Reports of the onward track to Lulum were good. Robbie had gone on before John Metcalf's arrival; but a runner was already back who, travelling light, had taken less than three days to do the return journey. There had been a Chinese post in Lulum, but it had now withdrawn. There was no definite news of the Japs, although rumour put them in Gum Ga, Tekti and various other villages beyond. My orders to Robbie had been not to press on beyond Lulum, partly to keep him out of trouble, and partly to give no hint to the Japs on the Chindwin that I was going so far.

We spent a couple of days at Hkalak, and pleasant days they were. The doctor at the hospital was a grand fellow, who accepted various sick men from us whom our own doctors thought unfit to continue, and also various men who had the ill luck to be wounded on Chinese booby-traps, which infested the area. His hospital, remote though it was, enjoyed the advantage of equipment the like of which my medical officers had never seen since they joined the Army. Doctor Farr himself was a neat, bearded man with a peace-time practice in Newark, New Jersey, which I had visited many years before: I hope it was not too apparent to him that I could recall nothing whatever of his beloved city. With the two younger officers I dined one night, and altogether it was a pleasing interlude. All three were surprised to see us. They barely knew that the Salt Spring trail existed, having themselves come up from Shingbwiyang, and having received all stores and material by supply drop. They had had a wireless message telling them to expect a " patrol "; but they had hardly expected it to amount to four thousand men, until Robbie Robinson arrived and warned them.

The local Nagas had been equally surprised, but they had had some measure of warning: unknown to us, the bush telegraph had been in operation, even though the only Nagas we had seen had been a party of three on their way to the Road. The chief item of interest to the Nagas were our mules and ponies, the first they had seen.

I held at Hkalak the last conference of all my column commanders which I was able to hold through the whole campaign. It meant bringing Colonel Dick Cumberlege and Major Bill Varcoe sweating up from the tail of the procession (which required three days' notice) and keeping back Wilkie Wilkinson (now to lead vice John Metcalf) a day or so behind his troops.

The Queen's had had a hard time of it as the spearhead, and it was now the Leicesters' turn to be pioneers.

Hkalak to Lulum finally took four days, and except for two steep pulls the going was not too bad. There were no more *polaungs* at this height, but the leeches increased both in number and appetite. Out of one bivouac, beside a chilly stream, we were driven by fair weight of numbers to seek immunity on higher ground. We passed through several Naga villages, and learned from them that we were not, as we had idly hoped, the first Europeans to come there: a party of five had visited them seven years before. That would be in 1937, we reflected: what eccentrics had they been? Surveyors, prospectors, forestry people, police? I still do not know: but if they were surveyors, I would dearly like to meet them, to tell them what I think of their surveying.

We were now on the fringe of white spaces on the map boldly marked "Unsurveyed" and surrounded with question-marks. It was of this period that we were afterwards alleged to have sent our evening location over the wireless as "Estimated position two miles south of the 'Y' in 'Unsurveyed.'" If we did so, and I have no clear recollection of doing it, we were either:—

(*a*) a different number of miles in a different direction; or
(*b*) lying.

Even where we were, where the maps claimed to know all about it, they bore little relation to actuality. Immediately west of us, towards the white patches, they had the grace to strew question-marks every half-inch; but east of us they surprisingly became more positive for no good reason. Their rashness in so doing may be fitly illustrated by the information which they gave concerning a stream called the Puk Yu, which was shown as rising some eight miles south-east of Hkalak. Apparently it started high up on a range; gathered impetus, thickness and enthusiasm as it flowed south; and then climbed painstakingly up another range, growing ever thinner until it culminated in a second source due east of Lulum. Odd as the country was, it was hard to believe it as odd as all that.

I liked what little we saw of the Nagas. They were much more jungly and primitive than those other Nagas who live near the Manipur Road, a couple of hundred miles away to the south-west: although they looked much the same. They had frizzy hair not unlike Polynesians, and I swear you could smell them before they came round the corner. They would do nothing for money: opium was their only currency, and General Wingate's scruples would not allow him to let us trade opium. This was infuriating, and to my mind wrong. The country was unadministered; opium was the currency not only *de facto*, but, so far as there was any *jus*, *de jure* as well. To refuse to recognise it was as insular and unpractical an attitude as to refuse to recognise French francs in Paris. I managed to get a small quantity of opium by stealth, but it was nothing like enough for my needs, and without it the Nagas would neither work nor give us information. It may be thought that I did wrongly deliberately to flout the General's wishes in this matter. I am quite unrepentant, and would do the same again. I hold that this was an occasion when his principles led him militarily astray.

The Nagas were the most parochial folk I have ever met with. In most of their villages there was someone who could speak Chingpaw, the tongue of the Kachins, and old Agu Di or one of my other Kachin soldiers (I had about thirty with the two gunner columns) could usually get some gossip out of them. But the villagers had not much information to give us, since between the areas where the Japs had been, and those where they had not, there was no coming or going. Furthermore, the relations between the villages were strained; this and that village were allies against the other and the next; they would not band as a nation against us or against the Japs. We had amusing confirmation of this some weeks later, when we intercepted a runner carrying mail for the Japs south of the Chindwin. Among his despatches was one from a junior Jap officer to a senior, complaining (for what appeared from the tone of the letter to be for the umpteenth time) that the Nagas wouldn't help the Japs against us, but were continually asking the Japs for help against each other.

I have heard, with what truth I don't know, that Naga religion tells them they have two lives to live: this one on earth, and one more, of the same length, in the Village of the Dead. The number of slaves that they will have in that second life amounts to exactly the number of heads which they succeed in bagging in this present one. Hence the jolly, old-world pastime of head-hunting, which they still pursue with all the keenness of Rugger players. I learned a few words of Naga from some grinning children one day, when Private Stephens and I were forging ahead of Brigade Headquarters; but not enough to discuss higher metaphysics such as these. And alas, I have long since forgotten even those few words.

Lulum was a deserted Hkalak, though obviously never so large or elaborate. Here we had a great reunion with Robbie Robinson, who, since we had last seen him, had sprouted a bushy and grizzled beard. The Chinese were long since gone, and the Nagas had regained possession; but the open space which had been cleared for supply-dropping was still free of jungle, and we had some moderately good dropping of our own. We had at last managed to establish wireless contact with our light aircraft,[1] who came and dropped messages on us, and grabbed messages from us, from a wire strung between two poles. Andy Rebori, their amusing and witty commander, dropped me a long typewritten letter, headed:—

REBORI FIELD, TARO.
The only United Nations Airfield beyond the Chindwin.

This proud claim was, in fact, correct; for since we left Tagap, General Stilwell's Chinese had managed to complete their single-file through the Patlo Gorge, and to emerge in the Dalu Valley south of the Chindwin. Andy was quick to profit by this, and to establish his light planes in a paddy near Taro village, thus avoiding both the rain north of the river and the danger of being annexed by General Stilwell, under whose constant eye he would be if he remained at Shingbwiyang.

From Lulum onwards we were in new country, of which we had no information. Rumours of Japs were numerous, but we never caught up with them; although at one village we arrived the day after a small party of Japs had paid it a visit. They had come to seek food, from somewhere over to the westward, where they had for some time had an outpost. They had heard whispers of our coming, and questioned the headman with beatings.

[1] These belonged to the American "Light Plane Force," of which more—much more—hereafter.

Although he himself had heard only the vaguest rumours, he had confirmed that we were in great strength and advised them to begone—which advice they had taken, without waiting for the food which they had come to demand. The headman, who was obviously making the best of his tale, and trying hard to impress us with his heroism, said that his visitors had been in poor shape and very frightened, whereas he hadn't, of course, been frightened a bit. He had never seen British before, but he had always heard they were the most delightful people, and he'd brought us a chicken.

The going had gone slow again, although we were now on paths which Japanese patrols had occasionally used; and at one point we even found some foxholes at the side of the track. Occasional heavy rainfalls held us up, as for much of the way the track coincided with the bed of the various streams. The legend on the map, "Path follows bed," is common enough throughout Upper Burma, and to the initiated it means weary, heavy wading in depths varying from ankle-deep to waist-deep. The risks of foot-rot are very real unless discipline is strict; by which I mean the drying of socks and the compulsory massaging of feet in the evening, or whenever chance offers. Whether or not "path follows bed," you must resign yourself to the knowledge that your feet will always be wet: if you are not travelling along a stream, you will be crossing them frequently. The wetting of your feet is the least part of it: it is the introduction of innumerable grains of sand between socks and feet, and between socks and boots, which makes life hell.

At one stage between Lulum and the Chindwin there was an apt misprint on the map which caused its share of hollow laughter. The printer had substituted a "B" for a "P" so that the usual legend read "Bath follows bed." It was a poor joke, but life was dreary; and it gave us pleasure at the time.

As progress got slow, so information got bewildering. The track never went where either the map or the natives said it should; and information coming in from India only fogged the issue. My old acquaintance Major Dick Wood of the Burma Rifles had been wandering for some months with a wireless set in the wilderness between Kohima and the Chindwin; and I had asked him to send me whatever "dope" he could get on the crossing area on which I had set my heart. What he sent me was evil. He was being chased by inquisitive Japs; the headman of such and such a village was the centre of a network of information; such and such a track was overgrown; most of the area was dead bamboo. (Dead bamboo is almost the worst jungle you can get.)

All that we knew or learned about the route proved false. There was never any choice of paths, but there was always one path leading vaguely nearer the Chindwin, and I let ourselves be sucked along it. Only once, near Lapyep Ga, did I make a strenuous effort to assert myself, and to stick to yesterday's plan; I sent Robbie Robinson and Oscar Palmer (Recce Platoon commander in 22 Column of the Queen's) to find a way along an alternative track shown on the map. They got a little way, and then signalled me by wireless such a piteous report about their miseries, that I bade them rejoin the main body.

Every day I made concessions to that day's discoveries, and modified my plan accordingly. Every day I had to abandon yesterday's purpose and go on wherever the path wanted to take me. John Fraser I made commander of a special flank guard known as Fraser's Force, consisting of three platoons levied on various columns; his rôle was to guard our flank from the westward, whence Dick Wood, literally a voice crying in the wilderness, was sending me ominous warnings on his wireless. But John Fraser was also track-bound; he couldn't get off it, and eventually he acted as a sort of spare advanced guard across the Chindwin when we got there.

For get there at last we did. During the last few miles of our march, characteristically, path followed bed. I knew the Leicesters had made it, for they signalled back to tell me so; and, leaving Brigade Headquarters bivouacked at the little village of Kawala—the first Shan village, some four miles short of where we hoped to hit the River—I splashed with a companion whose identity I forget, onwards down the stream. It was a brute, of the knee-deep variety; it was hemmed in by high forested banks; round every corner I hoped to see my old friend the Chindwin, yet every corner showed another five hundred yards of gorge without promise.

At length, after a right-angled turning, I became aware of a long green bank on my left, like the bank of a railway cutting;

beyond it I could see only sky, and no more high ground covered with trees. Now I knew we were getting warm; and soon I saw close beneath the bank a group of soldiers and a mule or two: I recognised Ralph Leyland, the Animal Transport Officer of one of the Leicester columns. He told me of how a wireless signal had just come in from Wingate. It read:

"Well done, Leicesters. Hannibal eclipsed."

III

OUR CROSSING of the Chindwin in 1944, with what one of my officers called "every mod. con.", still strikes me as an extraordinary affair. It was a Twentieth Century performance, compared with which our crossings of major rivers in 1943 were Early Victorian. We had become so accustomed to relying entirely upon our own ingenuity that the use of motor boats, brought in by air to these back-blocks of the world, seemed as out of place as the Yankee at the Court of King Arthur. Chindit warfare had hitherto been primitive; suddenly we found ourselves so up-to-date that we were leading the field.

On the first Expedition, the crossing of wide rivers had been one of our principal problems, the subject of much study and practice. Within limits, we had solved them. The principles which we had learnt, and the training which every man—and animal—had received, stood us in good stead when we suddenly became modernised. I do not regret having allotted a high proportion of our short training period to river-crossing; another formation, which had to cross the Irrawaddy in the course of the campaign, suffered severely from having allotted too little.

Until the majority of the Chindits became airborne, the Chindwin River, alias the "Jordan," had to be crossed before the campaign proper could begin—an operation which corresponded to the throwing of the double-six at dominoes. All seven of the 1943 columns got across the Chindwin without mishap; five of them subsequently crossed the Irrawaddy; and innumerable small parties crossed both on the way home. We thus had plenty of experience on which to base our principles.

River-crossing, under Chindit conditions, cannot be learnt in theory: it needs packets of practice. That practice must be carried out on a river with a current: to think that it can be done on a lake or a reservoir is a grievous fallacy, and will only lead, as one's Nanny used to say, to tears in the end. I have had anxious moments during such training, such as when Alan Sheppard, with a dozen other officers, disappeared round a corner of the fast-flowing Bhadra River in Mysore on a rapidly disintegrating raft; or when two officers, trying to wade the Tista near Darjeeling in full kit, lost their footing and went sixty yards downstream with their rifles and packs round their necks. But it is far better to train in such places as these than on the smooth, safe waters of a reservoir: for the Chindwin and the Irrawaddy are both fast-flowing, and, for tactical reasons, were highly unsuitable as the first stretches of water on which to encounter a current.

The principles never changed, whether your means of crossing were modern or medieval. The first was never to attempt an opposed crossing. In 1943, three crossings were interrupted, and of these two had to be called off. The third was Mike Calvert's first crossing of the Irrawaddy, somewhere near Tagaung, when he was interrupted from the near bank when most of his force was over. He engaged the enemy with mortars and machine-guns from a sandbank half-way across, and got away with it, except that he lost more than half his animals (including an elephant which he had co-opted some weeks before, and to which he had become deeply attached). He carried on with thirty mules instead of the statutory sixty, and at the end of the campaign wrote a characteristic report claiming thirty as the ideal number.

With air support, such as we enjoyed in 1944, the chances of an opposed crossing being successful slightly improved, except that, on a really wide river, observation, from which to direct the air support, would be hard to achieve, particularly in the case of the Irrawaddy. That beastly river is a mile wide at most places below the defiles; and even though much of that mile is taken up with sandbanks it remains a nasty obstacle. Usually it was possible to bluff your way out of having to force an opposed crossing; it was certainly advisable.

A crossing-place had to be chosen in the first instance either off the map or as a result of aerial reconnaissance, having regard to the enemy's dispositions and the possibilities of a good deception plan. You could not approach the river with your column, and wander along looking for a suitable place at which to cross. Having made your choice off the map, you had to delegate the decision as to whether or not it would serve to a trusted officer, who, in a column, was normally the commander of the Reconnaissance Platoon.

Of all the jobs in the column which a junior officer could hope to fill, the Recce Platoon was the plum. It was commanded by an officer of the Burma Rifles, with a second-in-command from the column which it served. It consisted of one section of Burma Rifles and three of British troops, and operated—at least in theory—a couple of days ahead of its column. When reconnoitring for a river-crossing, it would set up a bivouac within reach of the river, in hiding, while the reconnaissance was carried out, and wireless back its report to the column commander behind.

Several factors could spoil a potential crossing-place. Japs; the presence of villages, with their inevitable informers; lack of cover on either side of the river; high banks; muddy banks; submerged snags; and impossibly strong currents. An ideal crossing-place is rarely found; one or another of these drawbacks is bound to be present to a greater or lesser degree. But as soon as the column commander gets his report, he must make up his mind; the Recce Platoon cannot go for ever undetected; and once committed to the crossing, the best security lies in speed.

So, when I looked across the Chindwin on the morning of the 29th of February, 1944, I had a number of things on my mind. The Japs were reputed to have a garrison of a hundred and fifty at Singkaling Hkamti. They were not strong enough to prevent our crossing, but they were strong enough to make it more difficult. We had actually emerged from the hills five miles downstream, five miles nearer the garrison than the crossing-place which I had chosen from the air. We had no choice. If we had left the track for the tangle of dead bamboo between us and our chosen place at Ninghkau Ga, we should have added at least two days to our journey, and increased the risk of the Japs getting warning of our approach.

The garrison of Singkaling Hkamti was maintained from the Uyu Valley, some five or six days' march away. Only one track linked the two, and this route had been traversed by one of our escaping parties the previous year. From Hkamti to

Ninghkau Ga it ran south of, and parallel to, the river a little way inland, behind the cliffs. If the Hkamti garrison knew of our approach, it would be an easy matter for them to take up positions opposite us to harass our crossing. We should then have to cut our way painfully along our own bank until we found another point; for it would be impossible to land the gliders with our equipment, as we had planned to do, on one of the sandbanks if the enemy had it under fire.

We had therefore devised two plans to deal with the garrison at Hkamti, both of which involved the use of Andy Rebori's light planes from Taro. A patrol from my own regiment, The Black Watch, serving in another Brigade, was flown on to a sandbank some ten miles below Hhamti, in the hope (which was justified) that the garrison would sally out downstream to see what was (in the elegant American phrase) cooking. Secondly, Jim Harman[1] with a small party was to be landed on one of the sandbanks immediately opposite where I was now standing, to climb the cliff, make towards Hkamti, and block the only track with copious booby-traps. He had for company Captain Peter Bennett, a survivor of the first campaign who had been one of the party which used this very track on its way out. Bennett was now serving at Karachi, and I had borrowed his services to advise me about the route to the Uyu; at his earnest request, in payment for them, I allowed him to accompany Jim.

Both Jim's and The Black Watch party had been flown in the day before, and I now had the satisfaction of knowing that the only route between me and Hkamti had a block on it. Colonel Wilkinson already had a couple of platoons under Major Duggie Dalgliesh across as a bridgehead, and "Fraser's Force" came past me as I watched, and began crossing as well. I told John Fraser to try and make contact with Jim Harman westward towards Hkamti, and also to push eastward along the track to Ninghkau Ga, so that we should have ample warning of any enemy approaching from that direction.

Wilkinson's leading elements had reached the River the night before, in time to push across in the dark in inflatable boats. Half-way over, they had become aware of a sound a little way

[1] Captain J. B. Harman, Gloster Regiment, O.C. Commando Platoon, No. 5 Column, 1943.

upstream of them, and had rested on their paddles. The sound came nearer, and then, in the moonless dark, they had seen glide slowly past them on the current a long canoe full of men. Whether they were Japs or Shans we did not know, nor whether they had seen the motionless British; they had gone on down-stream without showing any sign of interest, and our specula-tions added to the piquancy of the next day or two.

That was all we knew about the enemy. Of villages, there was one half a mile upstream of us, on our own bank, not shown on the map; and we had not spotted it, hidden as it was in the trees, on our air reconnaissance. Nor, more curiously, had it been seen on the air photographs, even by the experts. It was no more than a collection of huts where local cultivators occasion-ally spent the night. Two or three of them came to see us, and produced some scanty information. They confirmed the number of Japs in Hkamti; they told us that the few villages between the Chindwin and the Uyu had been evacuated by order of the Japs (in any case, only two were shown on the map). They them-selves had been left in peace because they were growing opium. I fancy they were Shans, of a sort: they were very primitive, and had not previously seen Europeans; they were simple, and wholly devoid of shyness.

As a crossing-place, the spot where we were seemed nearly perfect. There was ample cover on both sides of the River. The bank on which we were was high, but there were plenty of places where mules could get down. At the foot of the bank was a broad beach, and on the opposite side, shingle jutted out at least six hundred yards. The actual width to be crossed cannot have exceeded three hundred: and the current was no more than a knot—far less than at my crossing-places of the previous year, a hundred miles to the south. The forests across the river were silent and mysterious; we were looking into the sun, and the shadows lay thick on the farther cliffs.

I had sent warning orders some days before that the gliders were to be loaded ready at Air Base, so that they could fly in with the river-crossing equipment on the receipt of the single code word "Trip." The code word had been sent, but the gliders had not come. I forget now the reason for the delay; but I spent that day champing with a feverish impatience, and straining my ears for the familiar drone of the dignified Dakotas. Both Leicester columns and the leading column of the Queen's were already either arrived, or bivouacked within a mile or two of the River. The sooner I could get across and be on the move southward, the better I should be pleased. Meanwhile, I was heartened by the news that, two days before, a long-planned air raid against the site of the Japanese wireless station a mile outside Hkamti had duly taken place, and was thought to have destroyed the station: it had at least revealed and destroyed two huts in its supposed location.

While I was fuming at the delay, the men were revelling in it. For the first time for many weeks they were no longer being urged to keep moving. Both in the *chaung* leading to the River and in the River itself, the men were bathing, washing their sweat-stiff shirts and trousers, and scrubbing their now well-grown beards. I passed the time of day with many of them and with their officers, and heard their pungent comments on the trip so far, and the gradients obtaining in the Patkais. One remark reported to me was: "When I retire, I'm goin' to buy myself a bloody bungalow, and it won't even 'ave a ———— doorstep."

In the afternoon the Leicesters began to cross under their own steam, using their inflatable boats and rubber dinghies. John Fraser had already got his force across (he had no mules to cumber him) on groundsheet "sausages." This was a system, by no means peculiar to Chindits, of putting the weapons, boots and clothing of two men into their two groundsheets, and tying them up tight with thin cord; the resulting bundle is wholly watertight, and supports the weight of a non-swimmer. Here, again, one of my invariable rules in river-crossing is that a man must not cross with nothing on his feet: he can go across naked if he likes, provided always that he is able to walk about freely on the other side.

At last, at six in the evening, an hour or so before dusk, we heard the veritable sound of Dakotas; and the busy men, working on both beaches now, stopped to listen and to look. I saw the men on the far side pointing and waving; we on our side could not yet see the aircraft, which were coming from behind our right shoulders, and were still defiladed from our view. Their drone got nearer and nearer; and at last with a *crescendo* they burst out over our heads. The first came at about a thousand feet, flying very slowly, towing its glider behind it like a reluctant child. It flew on upstream, and its neighbour followed it into view, flying in the same track. They circled away behind us, and then the first came round again, this time much lower, and released its glider opposite where I was standing. The glider circled once, in the same orbit, and then appeared again at the bend in the river, broad-winged and silent as a hovering albatross. Lower it came till, with what seemed like a sudden acceleration, it was skimming the shingle bank opposite; and then it touched with a flurry of dust, and came to a stand-still. Some of Duggie Dalgliesh's men, warned for the job, dashed out from close under the cliff, and dragged it out of the way. Soon its neighbour was also down, and both were being unloaded.

The noses of the gliders were pulled up, and out from the box-like body were dragged the assault boats, with their out-board motors. I had left some of my sappers in India (wise provision of the sage Robbie) to tend these motors, so as to be sure that they would work immediately on arrival. Within five minutes the first craft was in the water, and chugging across to where I, entranced, awaited it. And from then, all night long, across the "Jordan," the assault boats sped to and fro. The Leicesters were crossing.

It had been intended that the gliders should be snatched off that night, and towed back to their base. Both were set ready, their tow ropes extended between two poles so that the Dakotas' grapnels should duly catch them. The two glider pilots were sitting in their seats waiting for the snatch; they could see the Dakotas wheeling in the air; and then they heard them coming up fast from behind, and braced themselves for the pull. Instead of the expected jerk, they heard the sound of heavy weights falling all about them: they were in the middle of a supply drop which had been arranged for us from a different base. The two original Dakotas—those which had towed in the gliders—had been feeling lonely, high in the air, awaiting the completion of their task. Theirs had been the loneliness which engenders nervousness; and when they suddenly saw two unexpected aircraft approaching, the thought that shot through their joint mind was—"Japs." They beat it for home; and the two new-comers, knowing nothing of the panic which they had started, calmly proceeded with dropping us supplies. Heavy loads of boots, clothing and rope coming down without parachutes, thundered on the shingle about the ears of the shrinking glider pilots. It was not until the next day that they were finally and successfully snatched off and towed back to India. Even then, they returned five days later to retrieve the motor-boats when we had finished with them.

I lay that night listening to the welcome and efficient sound of the boats chugging to and fro across the River. Inevitably I thought of our other crossings of the Chindwin. I recognised, in the exhilaration which I now felt at having reached it across those appalling mountains, the same sense of "Now the show is on!" as I had felt the previous year. The Chindwin was our threshold, and we stood on it once again. Last year, when we crossed it, we were only a day from roadhead, and far nearer our objective; this year we had started from roadhead a fortnight earlier, and reached the River a fortnight later. My original orders from Wingate had been to arrive in the Banmauk-Indaw area about the 5th of March; in a few hours it would be the 1st of March, and I had well over two hundred miles to go, through country which I did not know, past garrisons of which we did not know the strength, among people of whom we did not know the temper. However, I felt clear in my conscience that we had nothing with which to reproach ourselves in being thus behind schedule; the miracle was that we had got here at all. I thought then, and I think still, that the country behind us was the worst that animals could possibly go over; and had it been just a little bit worse, or had any one of several defiles been a trifle stickier, we might not have made it for several weeks more. Luck had so far been with us.

With dawn the tempo of the crossing increased, particularly so far as the animals were concerned. They do not greatly care for river-crossing at the best of times; in the dark they look on it as President Coolidge's preacher looked on sin: they are against it. With daylight they can see what they are in for, and some of them are prepared to have a shot at it.

I am not fond of horses. My regard for them has slightly

increased (I enjoy saying this) ever since I ate my charger in 1943, when I was hungry. But my attitude towards horseflesh, whether alive or as foodstuff, whether quick or dead, is lukewarm. My love for mules, on the other hand, is unabated. I like their appearance, their stout hearts, their loyalty in evil moments, their very obstinacy and their sense of humour, misplaced though it so often is. Do I not recall my efforts once on training, to cross the River Betwa in the Central Provinces of India? How one of my mules (was it the homely Betsy, or the more patrician Star of Baroda?) resisted the efforts of ten men for twice that number of minutes? I called a halt at last, exhausted, for a cigarette and a review of the situation. And as we lay on the bank, naked, out of breath and aching in every limb, one of the men gave a loud cry: Betsy (or Star of Baroda) had plunged into the river, and swum over of her own accord.

Bill Smyly[1], my youthful Irish Animal Transport Officer of 1943, was still at this moment intriguing to join me for 1944. (So far his obstinate commanding officer was refusing to make him available, though in the end the united efforts of Bill and myself triumphed, and he flew in to me at a village near Indaw.) Bill had compiled for me some notes on his ideas of animal management, and they were full of wisdom. Spelling was as much his weak point as animal management was his *forte*; but that need not deter me from quoting him on the three schools of thought among mules in the matter of crossing rivers. Nothing wiser on the subject has ever been said.

"With regard to river-crossing," wrote Bill, "there are three tipes of mules. The first tipe will go quitely, if they have good mulatiers. The second tipe have to be ceduced. For the third tipe, there is nothing for it but WRAPE."

All day the work went on. I made sure that all my fads were being attended to: that no boat was being delayed for so much as a split second; that there was an officer in charge of either bank; that platoons had been posted up and down the river on either side; that the banks were being kept clear of kit and stores; that machine-guns and mortars were sited in case of interruption; that signal lamps were in communication across the river. The crossing was going well. The mules were unloaded in turn, and

[1] Lieut. W. Smyly, 2nd Gurkhas, A.T.O., No. 5 Column, 1943.

their loads put in the boats. The muleteers took the saddlery off
their animals, and got into the boats with them; the reins of the
mules were put into their hands; the boats pushed off, with the
mules towing astern. Some of the more ambitious and expert
columns were swimming their mules free, and one lot of thirty
went over by themselves, swimming grandly and superbly across,
their tails streaming astern. The usual recalcitrant beasts were
playing up, and the usual indefatigable men were dealing with
them. The whole river was alive with activity, and it was a fine
sight.

I went across myself soon after midday with the leading
elements of my headquarters, and saw the Leicesters off on their
way. General Wingate was coming in that afternoon, and I had
asked him to bring with him Katie Cave and Douglas Kesting,
my base signals officer. Wingate arrived about half-past four,
in a C 64 (or Nordin Norseman) piloted by Clinton B. Gaty,
Colonel in the United States Army Air Force, and one of Phil
Cochran's right-hand men. I met him then for the first time,
but he became a close friend; we had many ploys together thereafter, including a wholly private and unlicensed raid on Akyab.
His death in the last few weeks of the Burma campaign of 1945
was a sad blow.

I looked in vain for Katie and Douglas behind Wingate's
shoulder, as he emerged from the aircraft. Phil Cochran and
George Borrow got out, and them I was always glad to see; and
four complete strangers, who turned out to be War Correspondents.
I stood, black with fury, while Wingate explained blandly how
he thought it even more desirable for our march and crossing to
receive proper attention in the Press than for me to see my second-
in-command and signals officer. I yield to nobody in my willing-
ness to help the Press, but on that occasion I could cheerfully
have murdered these unfortunate journalists. When at last
Wingate forced me to see them, I am afraid that I gave them an
inhospitable reception.

That was the first occasion on which Clint Gaty put me under
an obligation to him; for he offered to take off at dawn, go back
to Imphal and fetch Katie and Douglas. He endeared himself
further by saying "Would any of your boys care to come for the
trip?" I thought at once of my muleteers; the trip over the

mountains had fallen on them with a heavier hand than on any one else, and I told my Brigade Animal Transport Officer to pick out a deserving man for the treat. He selected a little North-countryman whom I had noted for being indomitably good to his animal even under the worst conditions; and so it came that Private M'Glinch got his first trip in an aeroplane, and his first lesson (from Clint) in how to fly one. His broad face remained cloven in a lasting smile for a full month thereafter.

My temper restored by Clint's offer, I took Wingate, Phil Cochran, George Borrow and Clint himself along to my Head-quarters, newly established on the south bank, for a cup of tea: so much tea, indeed, that my batman's face grew rueful at the inroads we were making on our meagre ration and I had to ask Clint to bring some more back with him from Imphal next morning. Then I offered Wingate a bathe, for bathing was his delight; and we both went and had a swim in the busy river. "Last time I swam in the Chindwin," he said, "was on the way out, last year, when John Jeffries nearly drowned."

Then, by bad luck, we met one of the opium-growers on the beach selling turtle's eggs. Wingate bought the lot, amounting to twenty or thirty; and distributed them to men whom he met on the beach, standing over them while he made them eat the horrible, jelly-like substance raw, declaiming that it was good for one. An obsequious N.C.O., thinking to please, ate four or five in a row; qualifying for commendation from Wingate, and retribution (so he later confessed) from his tummy.

That night, as we sat round the fire, we heard once again the drone of approaching aircraft. We dowsed all lights, in case it should be an enemy; but flying low up the river he flashed a recognition signal, and immediately a row of fires sprang up in the sand, from petrol poured out for the purpose. It was another supply drop. Every evening, as a new column reached the Chindwin, supplies were dropped for it on the same shingle beach as had been used by Jim Harman, the gliders and Clint Gaty's aircraft.

Wingate was frankly pleased with our march, and said so warmly. (Phil Cochran said, "That was certainly bad country. You guys will have one leg shorter than the other for life.") But Wingate was worried about our being so much behind schedule. Brigadier

Mike Calvert was due to fly in within the week, when the moon served as it would not serve again for another month; and Joe Lentaigne was to follow as soon as Mike was fully in. The plan had matured a great deal since last I had seen him, a month or so before. I told Orde that, with the best will in the world, and with what would almost amount to co-operation on the part of the Japs, I didn't reckon I could reach the Banmauk-Indaw area before the 20th of March. He agreed, but only stipulated that I should not lose a moment that I could avoid. He also gave me, and commended to my study, his famous treatise on "strong-holds," of which more later.

Next day brought Katie Cave, and took away Wingate, who had much to do in connection with Mike's fly-in. How glad I was to see Katie! Wireless communications had not been good over the hills, but we had become almost telepathic in default of it: he to know my needs, I to realise his difficulties. We had a great gossip together; the place in the long procession to be occupied by Brigade was still some hours ahead, and we had much to talk over. I resolved to effect a temporary exchange of signals officers: to send Tommy Moon, who had been walking, out to Imphal, so that he could see how Rear Headquarters signals were functioning; and to take Douglas Kesting with us as far as the Uyu, to show him our troubles inside. I knew there were paddy-fields in plenty on the Uyu, and had no doubt that I should be able to build a light plane strip there, where I could swop them round again. Douglas Kesting's face was a picture of woe at first, as he got the idea that he was being punished for some shortcoming: nothing was further than that from my mind. All the same, it was good to see the spruce Douglas, from outside, who thought he had only come in for a joy-ride, ruefully donning Tommy Moon's enormous pack and hoisting Tommy's rifle on to his shoulder, while the bearded Tommy skipped gleefully along to the aircraft, for a week's rest in Imphal.

One of the Queen's columns, which had taken especial pains with its river-crossing training in India, set up an all-time high record this day at the Chindwin, crossing all its animals and men in two hours and ten minutes. Then Colonel Dick Cumberlege of the 45th Recce arrived, ahead of his column, to see the form. He confessed that his men were tired, as indeed they were bound to be. Just as the men at the tail of a column are always bound to be the weariest, so also the fatigue endured by the last columns of a long line is far greater even than the fatigue of those who are blazing the trail. One is always striving to catch up; and one lacks also the exhilaration of knowing that you are seeing something new, something which the others have not seen. I explained to him how I wished I could change the order of march at the River; but it was just not possible, without losing four or five days while columns passed through each other.

Jim Harman also came to pay us a visit that day, and we heard his rather negative adventures. It must have been a nervous task that I had set him, but he had accepted it eagerly, and I believe that he was sincerely sorry not to have had what he always called (to my irritation) a "duffy." Jim had had three holes knocked in him the previous year and had walked three hundred and fifty miles to safety despite them; I had been loath to bring him in again, doubting his ability to stay a course demanding long endurance; and I had compromised, by putting him with the light planes, intending to use him for short excursions only.

He had seen no Japs, but he had had one lucky escape, from his own handiwork. He had put booby-traps, not only on the track, but also on all possible detours which might be made around them. The second morning, going round his traps, he saw that a piece of paper which he had stuck on a bush as a decoy had fallen down. Forgetting the very purpose for which he himself had put it there, he walked towards it to pick it up; and had (I think) been honestly surprised to set off a trip wire and blow one of his own mines. Jim's leg has often been pulled, but it can seldom have had a bigger twitch than it got from us all when he told us this story with an aggrieved air.

More than half of the Brigade was now across the "Jordan." The decoy from The Black Watch had done its part, and the Japanese from Hkamti had gone hurtling down the river to see what they were at. The officer commanding The Black Watch patrol had the misfortune to break his ankle on landing, but he and all his men got out safely, after leading the Japs no mean dance on their own side of the Chindwin, before withdrawing into the hills. It was a perfect example of the innate gullibility of the Japs: the old Bulldog Drummond trick of saying: "By gum! Look behind you!" It always worked with the Jap, who was by no means so guileful as Carl Peterson. I have the greatest respect for the Japanese as a courageous fighter; and I have been as uncomfortable in Burma as most people; but there are two schools of propaganda about the war in Burma which everyone should distrust. The one is represented by the man (sometimes in high places) who says that the Japanese is cunning; the other by the man (usually in low places) who talks about the jungle as a " Green Hell." Both are nauseating, and both wrong.

Two or three hours before dark we had a last cup of tea and prepared to move off. The crossing had seemed thoroughly unreal; it had resembled Blackpool rather than the Upper Chindwin. It looked pretty certain that the whole Brigade would get clear across without a hitch, as it actually did. The Leicesters' leading column was streaking away to the southward, and moving fast: they had already caught an unsuspecting courier and his mate, bringing up the mail to Hkamti from Mogaung via the Uyu Valley.

My own mind was at rest in so far as the present and the immediate future were concerned, but it had flicked a long way from my surroundings. For in the mail which had reached me at the Chindwin I had had the news of the death of my old nurse at home. As we hauled ourselves, reluctantly after our two days of rest, up the monstrous path which John Fraser had carved for us on the cliff-face, my thoughts were in a far-off Scottish nursery, and on a tiny figure in old-fashioned grey flannel. I thought of being taken down to tea at the head forester's, or to call on old Mrs. Barton at the Lodge; of the statutory daily sweet after the midday dinner; of the twopence a week pocket money on Mondays; of the scratchy woollen gloves that irritated one's finger-nails; of feeding the ducks on the Serpentine from a bag of breadcrumbs. The same war which had driven her with its bombs from her cottage on the outskirts of Crewe, back to the nursery where she had brought up my brothers and me, had just sent me across the Chindwin for the second time. When I rolled myself up in my blanket that evening a few hundred yards south of Ninghkau Ga, I was still thinking of her, and of the new grave in the orchard cemetery at home.

IV

" Turn ye to the Stronghold, ye prisoners of hope ! "

It was Orde Wingate's wont to end his operation orders with a text from the Bible suitable alike to the operations with which they dealt and the temperament of their recipient. But the quotation from Zachariah set out above came not at the end but at the beginning of the treatise on strongholds which Orde Wingate brought in to me at the Chindwin on the 29th of February. It flared across the top of the first page and blazoned itself on my mind; its comforting rhythm and heavy beat fitted my step along many miles of jungle-path. Finally it resolved itself in a poem, which I scribbled out in pencil on a page of my notebook, to give to Wingate the next time I saw him. This was on the rising foundations of my own Stronghold two hundred miles farther south; I gave it to him as he sat in the light aircraft that was to take him away. Twenty-four hours later, his Mitchell flew into the side of a mountain near Bishenpur; and Orde Wingate, the supreme prisoner of hope of all time, had come at last into the Stronghold from which his whole life had been a gallant sortie.

I asked him, that last afternoon, whence the text derived; and he pretended horror that I, a Presbyterian, should have had to use him, a Plymouth Brother, for a Cruden. Whether deliberately or not, I do not know; but he tricked me by saying " Isaiah," wherein I sought it in vain. Bill Smythies, one of the two Forest Officers who accompanied me as representatives of the Civil Government, had also been greatly struck by its vivid phrasing; he read Isaiah through twice over in an effort to find it. I suspect that if I had seen Wingate again and told him that I had not found it there, he would have bidden me seek it in Jeremiah; and finally told me that it was all part of his plan for making me more familiar with Holy Writ. Such would have been characteristic of the fashion in which he used to pull my leg.

Of all the voluminous training notes which Wingate issued during the two years that I was with him, those on the Stronghold were by common consent the most striking. His writing of English was always magnificent, and it is a tragedy that he never put pen to paper, except in one article on his Sahara travels for the Royal Geographical Society. But Brigadier Derek Tulloch, his devoted Chief of Staff, has a complete set of his issues in 1943 and 1944, which he hopes one day to publish. Both in style and in matter they are fine stuff, that inspired the reader as much as they instructed him. *O si sic omnes!*

To the Chindwin he had brought nine copies of this latest treatise—one for each column of my Brigade and one for myself. These treatises, he said, must not go one pace nearer the enemy than we already were. Their contents must be mastered before leaving the River, and then they must be destroyed. To my reminder that several columns were already clear across and speeding south, he answered that they must be told of the contents by myself or another when next I caught up with them.

John Marriott, my Brigade Major, and I were thus able to have a copy each—I that of Brigade Headquarters, he one of the copies destined for a column which had gone on. Both of us were too busy to read them while we remained at the Chindwin. When at last we took stock, we found to our dismay that each had destroyed the copy which he held, trusting to read that held by the other. I had thereafter, deceitfully and in despite of Wingate's orders, to send a clandestine signal to my rear Headquarters alongside his own, and order another copy to be brought in secretly, by Tommy Moon when he came back to us. This we studied, mastered and duly cremated somewhere near the Uyu River.

I had known the idea when it first burgeoned in Wingate's brain, but in nothing like the clarity in which it now blazed from his triumphant paper. The conception was masterly and daring; the very word "Stronghold" was typical of his taste for the challenging and romantic word; his sense of drama, his unashamed and flaunting use of archaic phrases invested what might have been a drab life with a sense of history. The Army, on the Burma frontier as elsewhere, proclaimed the virtues of a "firm base"; how much more inspiring and invigorating is a sally from a stronghold than an offensive movement pivoting on a firm base!

Sometimes wrong in small things, never in big, like all Wingate's projects, the paper had one or two solecisms. Curiously for a man with such a wide knowledge, he advocated the growing of rice around the Stronghold in terms which made it evident that he thought it grew as fast as mustard-and-cress. But in the main it was a grand plan. It preached the art of selecting, setting up and defending, in the heart of enemy-held territory, an impregnable fortress from which to dominate a countryside in the manner of a Norman baron. He spoke of the "demesne," the surrounding district whence the fortress would draw its supplies and its information, and which its commander would administer; of the "keep" which would be its inner core; I think the word "seigneurie" also came in somewhere. The Stronghold must be self-contained in water; it must be dug, ditched, wired, mined and strongly defended; it must cover, if it could not safely include, a Dakota strip twelve hundred yards in length from which fighters could also operate on occasion; it must have secret exits and entrances known only to the defenders; it would have its garrison of West Africans, its artillery of Bofors, Oerlikons and 25-pounders; its hospital, its dispensary, its centre of propaganda for the local inhabitants. Finally, it must invite attack by the enemy; for all the world could see from our experience in Arakan that one's enemy should be offered provocation in the shape of something which he must attack (in Arakan it was Akyab), so that one could smite him as he approached and as he deployed. In addition to the garrison, we were to have " floater columns" hanging around the approaches, gathering intelligence, watching for the enemy, and buffeting him as he struggled through the jungle towards his objectives.

It was desirable, therefore, that the Stronghold should be only with difficulty accessible to the enemy, and that his approach to it should be limited to certain routes. Best of all would be a place to which he could not bring his train without elaborate road construction, in the making of which he would be mercilessly harassed.

On the 12th of March, eleven days after leaving the Chindwin, I received a signal from Wingate, slightly elaborating his previous operation orders for my approach to my objective. This was still the town of Indaw, around which as a hub we had operated the previous year, and which Wingate rightly appreciated was the key to Upper Burma. It was the last and northernmost centre of communications possessed by the Japanese. Roads radiated from it north, south, east and west; the Myitkyina railway ran through it from south to north, and the subsidiary spur line to Katha on the Irrawaddy took off from the main railway at Naba, two miles to the north-east. Around and in it was a cluster of important dumps, supporting the whole force opposing General Stilwell in the north, and capable also of supplying the divisions opposing our army on the Chindwin. My orders were to capture Indaw with its twin airfields. Originally I had been bidden to pass it, and then to swing back and storm it from the south-east. My new signal bade me make for it direct, "establishing Aberdeen en route."

This was the first mention of Aberdeen by name, but I knew at once that Wingate meant my Stronghold. I was sorry that the choice of a name had been taken out of my hands, for I had been pleasantly turning over in my mind a selection of possibles, for the last two hundred miles. I had thought of calling it after my own home; after Her Majesty the Queen, the Colonel-in-Chief of my regiment; or by some other appropriate designation. But the choice had been made, and I settled down with my map to look for a likely place wherein to hoist my flag.

The 1200-yard Dakota strip looked like being the biggest difficulty. In the thickly populated and highly cultivated lands near the railway I should find plenty of flat country suitable for airfield construction; but the Japanese held the railway in force, and even if they gave me time to set up my defences they could pin me down and insulate me wholly from the war. There seemed a likely place thirty miles or so south-east of me near Maingpok: a circular hollow in the hills, some five miles across, all routes to which ran through the friendly country of the Kachins. But this was at least a week's march from Indaw and the communications which I hoped to harry, and much too far for my offensive purposes. It would be as well to know the potentialities of Maingpok for future reference, now that I was so near it; and to this end I despatched a reconnaissance party with two officers to spy out the land, with orders to join me at a rendezvous a hundred miles to the south. They carried out their reconnaissance successfully, but unhappily ran into trouble within a mile of finding me two weeks later; both the officers and three of their men were killed. They lie in a quiet glade beside a stream twelve miles from Indaw.

When I got Wingate's signal, I was moving along the Uyu Valley in considerable strength. I had despatched nine hundred men under Dick Sutcliffe to seize the town of Lonkin some forty miles north-east of me, to carry out my side of the bargain made with General Stilwell six weeks before. I had with me close on three thousand men and four hundred animals, still moving in single file as they had done since early February. We were expecting to meet small Jap posts or patrols, but the scanty local inhabitants knew little about their movements, beyond vague tales of occasional patrol visits. Nevertheless, about the same hour that I heard from Orde Wingate, I heard also from my leading column (still the Leicesters) that they had bumped a patrol in the little riverside village of Sezin, and caught a prisoner. They reported that they were constructing a landing strip from which to fly him out, along with a few sick.

I had got myself into a bit of a mess just then. Before leaving India I had been furnished with particulars about a certain track reported to exist in these parts, which I resolved to find and follow. I was anxious to get myself and my brigade on to a broad front and out of this ridiculous single file, which the nature of the country and the rarity of tracks had forced on me for so long. I had already set up an all-time record for marching a brigade in single file, and I had no wish to become the laughing stock of the military world by deploying on to my battlefield in the shape of a sixty-mile crocodile. So I had led Brigade Head-quarters and the Queen's off the track and into what seemed to be good-going teak jungle, in search of the miasmic route they had told me of in India. Half a mile or little more had brought me into a country of vertical hill-faces and thick, broken-down bamboo, through which for the whole of a hot and dusty day we had been cutting a rough mule track. At one moment we were on the point of giving up when we were encouraged to persevere by reaching an area where the bamboo had been trampled flat by gambolling elephants. Although they had either not gambolled long enough, or not been quite heavy enough, they had at any rate done the spadework; and we continued to push on. Even with their help, the going was slow, and we had done no more than four heart-breaking miles when night dropped heavily on us—mercifully just as we found water.

This stream ran westward back to the main river at Sezin, which, had I not been lured away from the main track, I should have reached by noon that day. I cut my losses, resolved to make for Sezin, and wirelessed to my light planes, at their base at Taro, to have one ready for a reconnaissance to the south.

In the course of the next day we reached Sezin and found it a beautiful little place, perched on a knoll and overlooking the broad and shallow Uyu river. Below the village, in the paddy, was the strip which the Leicesters had built to fly out their prisoner. He turned out not to be a Jap at all, but a Gurkha survivor of the first year's Expedition, who had been pressed into the service of the Mikado. Shot in the leg, he had subsided cheerfully on to the ground, beating his chest, smiling and shouting: "77 Brigade! 77 Brigade!"[1] A less lucky Japanese in the same patrol had been killed and I saw his grave just outside the village. Over it the troops had put up (of all inappropriate symbols) a bamboo cross and on it the words:

UNKNOWN JAPANESE SOLDIER
HE DIED FOR TOJO

To this strip came a light plane, bringing Jim Harman as passenger and a stranger, Serjeant Sutton, as pilot. By this time I knew pretty well all my light plane pilots, but Sutton was newly arrived. What part of the States he came from I cannot now remember, but he had one of the slowest voices I have ever heard. He chewed incessantly, and on the back of his head he wore a black and red baseball cap. (It fell into Japanese hands some weeks later, and Sutton was lucky not to be inside it when it did.) I flew several times with him later on, and on one occasion we had a sticky trip when the top fell off our petrol tank on a flight to the White City; we trailed precious petrol over five

[1] The official title (Codeword LONGCLOTH) of Wingate's Force in 1943.

miles of Burma before, leaning perilously from his place, he managed to stuff the hole with a handkerchief.

I explained to Sutton where I wanted to go on the map, but he didn't seem greatly interested, despite the fact that this was his first operational trip. Apparently he didn't go much on maps.

"Kin yew show me the way?" he drawled.

"I can," I said.

"An' back here again?"

"I guess so," I said. (I find it catching.)

"O.K.," he said. "Let's go."

We went; Sutton in front, John Fraser and I in the back, lying on our bellies. My signal had been misinterpreted (the light plane force didn't go much on codes) and they had sent a stretcher-carrying plane instead of the dual control article I had wanted. We rose in the air, and saw below us the little figures of my men collecting supplies from a drop we had had that morning. To the south was the great mountain of Taungthonlon, on whose summit dwells the spirit worshipped by all the Shan-Kadus for miles around. To the south-east, with a pang of grateful recognition, we saw the Kachin hills, that sanctuary which had taken John and me and my thirty weary men into its bosom last year, and given us rest, comfort, food and encouragement when our fortunes were at a low ebb. These we saw over the shoulder and the black and red cap of Serjeant Sutton, and felt god-like and splendid compared with the tattered ragamuffins we had been when last we beheld them.

Southward we went, till Taungthonlon was on our beam, and then on our quarter. Below us now was the deep gorge of the Meza River, and I pointed downward to show John where we had crossed and bidden farewell to our last two Kachin guides. To the westward, below us like a model, yet prominent on its hill like a city of Palestine, lay the village of Pakaw, which had so befriended us, and towards which I shall ever feel like a much-benefited godson.

We swooped down to the first possible stronghold which I had chosen from the map—the village and paddy area of Hkaungtonsi. Flanked on three sides by Kachin hills, it was the northernmost Shan outpost on the Nami Chaung, which ran into the Meza near the Banmauk-Indaw road, and which was to play an important part (though we did not know it) in our forthcoming operations. Hkaungtonsi looked all right, except that the potential Dakota strip ran across two or three streams which would have to be bridged, and was dominated by no particular feature. We followed down the Nami to the next big paddy area of Nama-kyaing. This looked far more promising, in that the paddy area was three miles long and without interruption of any sort; but here again there was no worthy site for our defences, and we could see broad, dusty tracks leading east, south and west to link it with the Japanese world. Even the friendly hills did not crowd about it as around Hkaungtonsi. In the end, as it proved, both villages were under the enemy's thumb and heel; but both seemed possible at the first view.

Up and down we flew at Namakyaing, a few feet above the ground. A group of water-buffaloes gathered their cumbrous dignity into a laborious gallop; a few old men hobbled into the shadows of the teak-woods behind their nimbler grandchildren and daughters-in-law; Sutton, chewing, looked thoughtfully over the side at the ground, scudding below us five feet away at ninety miles an hour, and then nodded slowly as he pulled back the stick. That meant that he passed it as a potential airfield.

Westward. Over the dry and waterless teak-clad hills to the Meza Valley. I craned my neck to look southward to Indaw, twenty miles away, but it was lost in haze, tobacco blue. We slipped sideways from the Valley, at the point where it escapes from its black glen into the first green paddy at Budaung. Hitherto it has run through uninhabited forests; here it escapes into the sunlight and turns placid for its last fifty miles to the Irrawaddy. We flew down the valley, Sutton's head nodding approvingly at the paddylands of each village as we passed it, registering perhaps two or three nods a mile.

I pulled myself together suddenly, to realise that we were almost on top of Banmauk, which was usually garrisoned; so I tapped Sutton on his shoulder, and jerked with my thumb over mine. He shut off his engine and glided a moment to make it possible to speak.

"Yew wanna go back?" he said in his slow voice; it must have taken him a full ten seconds to say it.

"I want to take a look at that valley which comes into this

one from the west about ten miles back," I replied; and we turned round, and skimmed back up the Meza.

This was the valley of the Kalat, which runs into the Meza at Kalat village, near the much bigger village of Manhton. There is a whole group of settlements near the confluence including Taungle (which should be pronounced Towng-lay, and we all laughed at Roy Lane, R.A.F. squadron leader attached to my Headquarters, for calling it Tongle, until, to our horror, we heard General Wingate call it that too). As soon as I saw it, I said to John Fraser, "There's our stronghold!"; Sutton nodded; and there it was finally established, although the detailed location was afterwards shifted a mile or two by Wingate himself.

It had much to commend it. On three sides were high hills, inhabited by Kachins to the north-east, where we could form them into a sure warning screen to guard against surprise from that quarter, and to pass to us the gossip and tittle-tattle of the railway valley. On the east lay the waterless hills we had just flown over, coming from Namakyaing; we could have guessed they were waterless from the look of the teak, had we not been told of it already by Maurice Taylor, my other Forest Officer, who knew these parts of old. On the west, save for one pass at the head of the valley, leading to the reputed garrison of Mansi, there was the thick jungle of the Chaunggyibya Reserved Forest. Only from the south, from the main Banmauk-Indaw road, could the enemy move against us in force; and there, if he could be confined to that route, we should have him on the hip.

We flew back northward to Sezin; and as we circled the strip, after a flight of nearly two hours, we saw another column coming in along the river-bank. As we dropped, I took a quick look at the southward, and saw the shadows drawing swiftly across the land; that of the Taungthonlon stretched like a claw across the Meza forests, and the lower slopes of the Kachin hills were already black.

Seven days later, accompanied only by Captain Alan Sheppard, my Orderly Officer, I reached the top of the pass into the Kalat Valley about half-past ten on a hot March morning. Brigade Headquarters was an hour or more behind us with the Queen's; the Leicesters half a day ahead. I had sent the Leicesters a signal to prepare a strip at Taungle, for I had trysted to meet General Wingate there the following afternoon. We were now once more in country familiar from 1943. Last night I had slept at a village called Letpan, which I had been at pains to skirt with John Fraser a year before when we were being hunted; I had recognised a shrine just outside the village as being the very spot at which we had dodged across the track. The day before also I had made enquiries in another village, Nanaw, for two men I lost there in a skirmish that year, but with no great result. The countryside was full of memories, some of them sad; and yet it was fine to be back with a grand army of first-class troops, cocking my beaver in the face of the enemy, and patronising like a great warlord the same villagers whom I had been at such pains to avoid the previous year.

John Fraser I had despatched on a goodwill mission to the stout Kachins of Pakaw and Kaungra to thank them for their former help and to tell them I was come back with my new army. With him had gone Captain Chet Khin, a gallant Karen officer who had won the Military Cross with No. 1 Column in 1943 and was now commanding one of the Reconnaissance platoons of the Queen's. I had arranged, after our crossing of the Chindwin into safety in April 1943, for these devoted allies in the Kachin hills to have supplies of clothing, and other necessaries which they had long been lacking, to be dropped on them from India. I had been assured on high authority that this had been done, and John's mission was intended as an additional thank-offering from us. I was therefore indignant to learn when he rejoined me that I had been misinformed, and that until they saw John they had known nothing of our safety, nor received any drop. This is a thing that I shall always find it hard to forgive.

From the top of the Letpan Pass I could see little, except the great sugarloaf of the Kalat Taung towering out of the trees on my right hand. This fine hill was to be the landmark which brought all our fleets of aircraft to our help: the Dakotas, flying in nightly from India with stores and reinforcements, and out again with casualties; the Mitchells and the Mustangs, streaking in to our aid from their far-off airfields in Assam; and the light planes, bringing home our wounded to Aberdeen, or returning from reconnaissance or liaison missions. In time, we came to suspect that the Japs also used it for the same purpose.

At the top of the pass I noted a little spring of water bubbling out of the hill and leaping away down the slope towards the valley. This I marked as the water supply of any post I might deem it necessary to establish here, in case of invasion from Mansi and the Upper Chaunggyi Valley. Half-way down the hill we met a yellow-robed priest toiling up it, followed by two heavily-laden acolytes who were toiling even more. He carried only an umbrella; they were bent nearly double with fruit and vegetables and rice and a dozen other forms of goody. I addressed a few words to him and got more out of him than my sketchy Burmese would warrant; he was coming from Manhton and going towards Mansi, so I improved the occasion by telling him all about my magnificent army, of which he had already seen the Leicesters on his way. I would have pitched it stronger, only I didn't know the Burmese for "thousand." Tall stories in the neighbourhood of Mansi could do nothing but good. When John Fraser finally rejoined me, I found that he had met one of the two coolies returning from his trip; and what he told John Fraser about my Burmese, let alone my personal appearance, was distinctly ungenerous. I don't feel that John should have led him on so.

At the bottom of the hill we came out into the open paddy of Lé-u village at the top of the Kalat Valley. I found myself gasping at its beauty. For close on two months we had been living in the dark jungle, where the branches closed over our heads. Only occasionally had we emerged into full daylight, on the little paddies round forest villages, or when crossing a river or a *chaung*. Here before me stretched a smiling valley, of which I was now at the head. Kalat Taung stood guard over it; but in the valley were pretty homesteads, in well-kept gardens, with peaceful noonday smoke rising above the roofs. The houses were well-built and comfortable; the watchmen's huts were not tumbledown affairs of wattle, but rather resembled orderly summer-houses on English lawns. Truly Burma was a lovely country; and as I looked on this valley, over which I was to establish my benevolent despotism, wherein I was to set up my fortress against the enemy, I resolved to take the people under my protection and be good to them.

In high spirits, I took possession of my domain. I created Alan Sheppard there and then Marquis of Manhton; on myself I conferred the titles of King of Kalat, Grand Duke of Meza, Lord of Lé-u and Baron Budaung. Thus aggrandised, I stalked down the valley, and found the junior column of the Leicesters under Major "Dafty" Daniell a mile short of the confluence on my right-hand side.

That afternoon Wingate arrived by air with Clint Gaty, cantered away on a horse in the direction of Manhton, and came back having chosen my Dakota strip for me. Twelve hundred yards north and south it ran, with a nasty hill admittedly at its northern end, but a good run in and out at the southern. And on to that strip, when completed, were flown something like seven hundred sorties, from the first, on the 24th of March, to the last, the second week in May. It would be wrong of me to claim that the pilots liked it. When I lectured to 117 Squadron some days after I eventually came out, and asked the time-honoured query at the end, "Any questions?" the first of all was, "Who chose Aberdeen?" They did not fancy the hill at the end, which made it tricky for the pilot who wanted to change his mind. The aircraft usually came in by night and could not see the hills around them; they landed blind on a flare-path. Wing-Commander Millington told me long afterwards that when he saw the strip by daylight for the first time, and realised where he had been landing all unknowing by night, he came near to having a fit.

Clint Gaty set to work at once to build the airfield. He slept that first night not a wink; he was supervising the clearance of an area where the gliders bringing in the construction equipment were to land. Dafty Daniell had taken on his column to join the other Leicester Column in the Auktaw Reserved Forest, near our objective of Indaw; and the preliminary work of preparing for the gliders was being done by the Queen's. It consisted of the process (with which we had all become familiar, in connection with the light planes) of stripping from off the paddy fields the little banks, nine inches to a foot high, which divide each section from its neighbour, and act as retaining walls to the water which induces the rice to grow; these banks are known as "*bunds*" in India and "*kazins*" in Burma. During the months of the dry weather they become almost as hard as concrete; the best comparison for a dweller in these islands is the state of a grassy bank frost-bound in the winter. They take a lot of moving, and the best tool for the purpose is the native mattock.

Early in the morning of the 22nd March I was down on the glider ground. Six gliders were expected; and soon after dawn, at about six o'clock, five of them arrived, each in tow of their parent Dakota. The tow-ropes were cast off, the gliders circled and alighted. Out of one of them stepped a huge, uncouth, rather stout pilot, who said:

"I'm going to chu'ch in future!"

"Indeed?" I said politely. "Why?"

"Over the mountains the goddam tow-rope got around my goddam wheel; and I said out aloud, ' If that comes off, goddam it, I'm going to chu'ch.' And it came off. Say, is there a chu'ch around here?"

I said, "Not as yet."

He said, "O.K. By the way, the name's Coogan."

One hardly expected to meet a well-known film star in the hinterland of Upper Burma, flying a glider over some of the worst country in the world. But so it was.

The sixth glider turned up an hour later, when Clint and I were having a cup of coffee, and speculating where it might have crashed. It had got lost and been for a jaunt over China somewhere. Already the contents of the other gliders, bulldozers, jeeps and carryalls, were at work on the airfield. Engineers, chewing as ever, were nonchalantly driving them up and down on their various tasks, as casually as if they were back in the States instead of 150 miles behind the enemy lines. Thirty-six hours later, we were ready for Dakotas. Flare-path lights were down, a control was set up complete with radio, and we were an established airfield.

Thus came Aberdeen into being, and for the next six weeks it buzzed with activity. Primarily my property, I based all my operations on it and was ultimately reponsible for its maintenance and defence; but it served other people as well. At least three other brigades had their agents there; two brigade headquarters

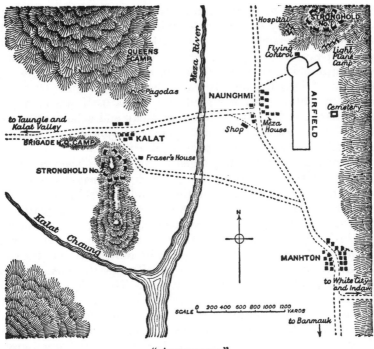

"ABERDEEN."

and six battalions, complete with animals, were flown into it;
two light plane squadrons were stationed on it; it supported
Brigadier Mike Calvert's White City Block; it was a staging-
place for the evacuation of most of the wounded of the whole
Force; it was the usual venue for Force conferences; it was the
principal clearing-house for Intelligence and for propaganda for
all sources except the Kachins; and it handled the interests of
such Kachins as dwelt west of the railway. Except from the air
it was never subjected to attack; for the Japs had so much to
worry about elsewhere that they could never amass a ground force
strong enough to take it on.

I propose, in defiance of chronology, to complete the story of
Aberdeen in this chapter. The six weeks of campaigning which
followed its establishment will be described later on.

Aberdeen did not fully meet all the requirements of a Stronghold as originally laid down by Wingate. In the first place, it was highly accessible to the enemy, had the enemy ever undertaken an expedition against it. But from our point of view it was admirably sited, and its location fully justified the apparent boldness of its selection. It was only fourteen miles from the important Banmauk-Indaw road, and Indaw itself was only two days' march away; the railway but a day and a half, although the need for caution on that particular journey sometimes extended the necessary time to two full days.

Its situation can best be judged by considering the letter "Y." The Meza river ran due north and south, but may conveniently be taken as the main stem of the Y and the right-hand upper arm; the Kalat being the left. Aberdeen was at the junction of the two. The strip was on the east side of the river and dominated by a hill at the northern end. Here the permanent garrison was established, surrounded on three sides by minefields. On the east side of the strip were one or two gunsites for the A.A. and the little gully where the light plane pilots lived, close under the stronghold. On the west, between the strip and the river, was the village of Naunghmi, a pretty place with good houses and gardens and all the appurtenances of a prosperous community. The southernmost house we more or less took over for conferences, since it was handy to the strip and easily reached by visiting officers; and as our visitors always came at night, and the raiding Jap aircraft usually only by day, it was both safe and handy. The first occasion when we met we spoke of as the "Meza Conference," as a sort of cross between Mena and Stresa; and thereafter the house was known as Meza House.

We had several such conferences, and they always followed the same line. I would become aware of their imminence during the preceding day; and would warn either John Fraser or Bill Smythies, one of whom was always present in Aberdeen, even if the other was away on a good-will mission in the district. It would then be his job (Bill's or John's) to warn the owner of Meza House that we wanted supper; and when the guests arrived, on the first Dakota of the evening, they would come to Meza House, climb the chicken-ladder to the door, and be invited to squat on the floor for their meal. (They were expected themselves to contribute the liquor in the shape of a couple of bottles of rum from India.) Then the meal would be served: steaming rice on blue china dishes belonging to the village; chicken cut into tiny mouthfuls, with the bones in awkward ambush; curry and sweet potatoes and gravy in a big central dish. After that, we would proceed to business; John Marriott would produce the maps, and we would discuss strategy. Then at last, the business killed, we would scoff the remainder of the rum, escort our guests back to the strip, and retire to bed, dismissing the sentries who had guarded our valuable persons from improbable assault.

Katie Cave, who though a last-war pilot, was a bit of a Jonah in the air, missed one of these conferences owing to the inability of his pilot to find Aberdeen, in spite of Kalat Taung, radio-telephony and other aids. The pilot, an American, was in touch with us all right on the radio, but was nevertheless adrift in the wilds of Asia. We had thought he must be somewhere in the neighbourhood, and asked him if he couldn't see our river, the Meza, silver in the moonlight, often served to guide errant aircraft into our ken.

"Can't you see our river?" we asked him impatiently.

"Sure I can see a river," he replied with equal petulance.

"Then fly up it," we said.

He flew up something for half an hour, and gradually his voice changed from petulance to something like plaintiveness.

"Got to go home now," he said. "I got no more gas." And Katie himself counted no less than four major rivers on his way back to base. We calculated that, reading from left to right, they must have been the Chindwin, the Irrawaddy, the Salween and something that nobody has ever seen since Marco Polo. Katie got no chicken and rice that night, and I cannot think what he did with his rum. Another night he crashed on landing.

Naunghmi village we thought best to empty of its inhabitants, since the Japs showed a taste for bombing the strip, and the strip ran close beside its easternmost edge. (Radio Saigon proclaimed one night, as the main item of its news, that our "barracks" had been totally destroyed by waves of dive-bombers; the real score amounting to a bottle of rum and nine eggs.) At the south-western edge of the village was an abandoned watchman's hut

which we used as the premises of the Aberdeen and District
Co-operative Society Limited. This was an establishment of
which Bill Smythies was Chairman, and Serjeant Mya Dein, of
the Burma Intelligence Corps, Managing Director, at which we
sold *loongyis* and other luxuries, specially flown from India, to
the inhabitants of the valley. It operated on a sound economic
basis, in that only Indian currency was accepted, and the only
potential customers with such currency were those who were
working for us and drawing pay at our hands. Jap money was not
legal tender, and thus those who wouldn't work for us couldn't
go shopping. We left the Manhton district the best dressed in
Burma.

West of the shop was the river, in which there were usually
dozens of men washing themselves and their clothing. Beyond
the river lay several areas in use as bivouac sites. The Queen's
used to bivouac round a fine old pagoda on a little hill five hundred
yards west of the village, and two hundred from the river;
Brigade Headquarters owned another hill south of them; south
of that again was another, in a state of defence, which was
occupied at various times by Pat Hughes's Nigerians and Dick
Cumberlege's English. At the bottom of this last hill was a
capacious hut which, at the time of our arrival, belonged to a
family of tobacco-growers, from whom I used to buy local leaf,
which I liked to smoke on occasions; its purchase gave me
pleasure, and I used to kid myself that I was buying from my
namesake's shop in the Sandgate in Ayr, as of old. But they
leased it to John Fraser and Bill Smythies, who there set up house
and their intelligence centre. I used to drop in sometimes for a
meal, when I would find them esconced in chairs borrowed from
the Manhton Rest House. Chairs, damn it! Long, comfortable
chairs with foot-rests, and that sort of buckshee arm designed to
swing across the paunches of fat planters as they lie, to support
their *burra pegs*. I had been so long away from chairs that I had
forgotten how you used them, and had genuine difficulty in
folding myself in the right places to sit in one; I had forgotten
where the dotted lines ran behind my knees *et cetera*.

They fed well, did John Fraser and Bill Smythies; and around
their little house flitted The Three Naidus (as John's personal
bodyguard of Red Karens was known), the Managing Director

of the Aberdeen and District Co-operative Society Ltd., two or three Kachin hangers-on from the hills around Pakaw and Kaungra, a couple of ex-forest rangers from Kalat and Chaung-gyibya, an opium smuggler from the Mu Valley, and other contacts, some of them ephemeral. It looked like a gypsy encampment, and the *cuisine* was as varied and as good. There was always the chance of a bit of news to enliven the evening; for John and Bill sent their scouts far and wide, into the very camps of the enemy, whence they brought back titbits of information to surprise and confound the experts far away in Assam and India. Faithfully and well those men worked for us, giving the lie to those who despise native sources of information, and whose ears flap better than they hear.

I must have spent an aggregate of three weeks in Aberdeen, and I grew fond of the place. Each of my units in turn spent a period of rest there during the first weeks in April, and my head-quarters were there all that time. Using light planes, I visited all my columns in their advanced bases, and carried out many reconnaissances to the south and east. During these flights I flew over many of the places we had visited the previous year. I saw the Bonchaung bridge, of which the blowing had given us such pleasure fifty-six weeks earlier; the little clearing outside Kyaik-in village where I had had to abandon John Kerr[1] and his men; the village of Seiktha on the Shweli where I had tried an abortive crossing and found Japs on the opposite bank; and many another spot of good or evil memory.

All day long the light planes would fly in and out, carrying reinforcements, liaison officers, stores and so forth, on their outward journey, and returning with wounded men. All night there would be the endless drone of Dakotas coming in from India and flying out again. The first would arrive as soon as possible after dark, and the last must leave before daybreak. Occasionally, in moments of crisis, they would come in by day; but there was always a risk in this, since Jap aircraft were faithful visitors. We averaged two raids a day for a fortnight, and on our peak day we had two proper raids and three single-machine intruder efforts. Only once did they actually manage to intercept,

[1] Lieut. J. M. Kerr, The Welch Regiment, and four men of No. 5 Column were left wounded in Kyaik-in on 6th March, 1943—only Kerr survived his captivity.

and on that occasion a Zero made two passes at a Dakota, shooting bits off it at each try. The pilot finally got down on to the strip, with his lights blazing, the leads controlling them having been shot away, and without any brakes. He was saved from a nasty pile-up by the baffled intruder himself who dropped a bomb on the strip right under the Dakota's nose, blew it into the paddy at the side, and brought it up all standing. The aircraft was a write-off, but the only damage to its passengers was one bullet through the chest of a West African askari. He had never flown before, and he appeared to accept this misadventure as a normal concomitant of air travel, since he made no fuss about it whatever.

Several times the Zero foxes nearly got in among the Dakota chickens. I recall one evening when they gave the strip twenty minutes of bombing and strafing. Our barrage was superb that night; the Bofors and the Oerlikons, which had been flown in from India, were pumping stuff into the sky in fine style, making an elegant sound like a bassoon concerto. At last the enemy aircraft drew off to the south-east, and they had hardly disappeared when droves of Dakotas appeared from the west looking like a lot of duchesses going to court. From all round Aberdeen I heard the troops giving that incredulous whistle which a lucky escape elicits.

There was another night when the first Dakota was due, and an aircraft came droning in from the right direction at the right time. Control told it to switch on its lights; it complied; the flare path was switched on; and our visitor, making as if to land, dropped a bomb instead. The bassoons opened up, the intruder went away into the night, we searched the strip, found a small crater, and kept the first Dakota circling for fifteen minutes while we filled it up. We did not tell them the cause of the delay, though: we feared they might go back to India without delivering their loads.

Our A.A. was superb: they claimed a good many damaged, but they never achieved a really spectacular shoot until the last two days, when they shot down three and four respectively in full view of the cheering garrison, and took one pilot prisoner. He was a chatty creature, this pilot; and once he had recovered from a misunderstanding with the butt of a Nigerian rifle.

which made contact with his mouth, he produced a lot of useful information.

There was a period when the strip was denied to our use for a couple of days by prolonged enemy air interference. It was adjudged unsafe for the lumbering and vulnerable Dakotas until the airfield in the far south, from which the Jap fighters were operating, had been sought out and walloped. Unhappily, this happened during an especially busy week, when we in Aberdeen were cumbered with an extra large number of wounded. Bill Lehacka's light planes were each doing up to eight or ten sorties· a day to fetch in casualties, not only from my own Brigade (who were at that time engaged in only minor operations), but also from Mike Calvert at the White City Block, who was being attacked nightly, and from Tom Brodie, who numbered among his battalions my own Regiment. The wounded piled up quickly and no Dakotas were coming in to take them out. The capacity of the hospital which we had set up, under a Medical Officer of Gordon Upjohn's Nigerians called Elbert, was only designed for a few men; and even the normal and regular flow of wounded coming off the light planes by day and awaiting transhipment to the Dakotas by night, put an undue strain on our resources. These men used to lie in a dry ditch at the northern end of the strip, near where the light planes landed and the Dakotas turned round. Here they were handy for water; and the local villagers, to earn money for spending at the shop, had built rough shelters to keep off the hot midday sun and the chilling night dews.

Each time the Dakotas started in, they were turned back either by thunder-storms over the Chin or Naga hills, or by the news of enemy air patrols; until at last I had over two hundred wounded lying, suffering not only from their original injuries, but also from lack of doctors, orderlies and drugs. Several operations were carried out, skilfully but under immense difficulties; and a few who died, despite the valorous efforts of Elbert and his assistants, might have recovered had they been able to reach a decent hospital. I saw many friends of my own brought in there in parlous case. When at last the Dakotas were able to come, we managed to clear the whole lot off in a night. But I was determined not to be caught that way again; and I was able with this new argument to induce the authorities to send me in an advanced surgical team, and a copious supply of blood plasma.

The first consignment of plasma unfortunately went missing, and every effort failed to disclose its whereabouts. I told the Nigerians (who among many other duties had to find fatigue parties to unload incoming planes) that since they had presumably unloaded it, the responsibility for finding it must also be theirs. After a lapse of an hour or two, their commanding officer came back with a rueful face to report that he had discovered what had happened to it. His Nigerians, mistaking its purpose, had spread it on biscuits, and scoffed the lot !

Lane and Gillies, two of my airmen, were mad keen to have some Hurricanes at Aberdeen, for purposes of local reconnaissance and strafing. I acquired two after much difficulty; but both were old and weary; and on two consecutive days of tragedy first Gillies and then Lane were forced down by engine trouble. In both cases the abandoned planes were found from the air; but nothing has ever been heard of those two gallant and eager pilots.

When I first came to Aberdeen, I had summoned the headmen of the five principal villages and addressed them through Bill Smythies at a special meeting held for the purpose in Kalat. I explained to them how I was formally taking their district back into the protection of the British Government, and told them what I wanted them to do for me. Among other things, I told them how in return they would get various benefits from us, both as a reminder of happier days under the benevolent British Government, and also as an earnest of good days coming back to them shortly. Food would be flown in from India, the Aberdeen and District Co-operative Society Ltd. started, and medical attention would be free for all, three days a week, outside the house of the headman of Kalat. Full advantage was taken of this last offer, and a stream of sick folk was always being tended by the Medical Officers of whatever columns happened to be in Aberdeen at the time.

One man who came to join us from the outside world was a Shan from Mansi, who had at one time worked as a cook for some British official in that area. He arrived to offer his services in that capacity, for me and my Headquarters. I was not con-

templating quite such a permanent establishment as all that, so
I sent him to Elbert at the hospital, who took him on most
gratefully. Our new recruit then produced from the bundle of
clothing which he had brought in on his shoulder a suit of
butler's uniform, complete with white turban and green cummer-
bund, which he donned once more in full conviction that British
rule, with all its conventions, had returned to Upper Burma.

Many and varied were our visitors at Aberdeen. Some were
old friends. One was Major Bertie Castens, an intrepid British
Forest Officer and an old ally of 1943. He had spent most of the
period of the Japanese occupation wandering around the country
with a wireless set, telling India what was going on. It was he
who in 1943 had found for us the so-called "Secret Track" which
we used to slip through the Jap defences east of the Pinlebu road.
He came in one night by arrangement, with two companions,
one a fine Anglo-Indian called Webster and the other a Kachin,
all three in tattered uniforms. Then there was an ex-Naik of the
Burma Rifles, who had guided us at one stage in our troubled
pilgrimage of 1943. He joined John Fraser in one of his patrols
in the Kachin Hills, and returned eagerly to the colours. Various
others, who had known us at some point on our last year's route,
also turned up to assure themselves that it was us indeed, and to
remind us (we needed but little reminder) of our debt to them.
Villages from far away sent us valuable news of possible threats
and—more welcome still—possible targets; some even sent in
the names of informers, and on one occasion at least they pinched
a spy who was watching the work on our airfield and handed
him over to us. One had to be careful about accepting such
evidence, for it was all too easy to denounce some personal enemy
as an agent of the Japs; and I was most careful never to convict
without strong corroboration. Even when it was forthcoming,
I merely took the man (or woman, sometimes) into custody, sent
him out to India, and thanked, but never rewarded, those
responsible for his apprehension.

I had other visitors, not always welcome. I made it plain to
our Headquarters in India that nobody was to come in without
my permission. I took it very ill when a cult developed of para-
sitic staff officers, who flew in, so far as I can make out, for no
better reason than to boast in Calcutta or Delhi that they had

been "inside Burma." With journalists I have always been friendly and indulgent; but when four came in against my express orders I was cross, and in a strong position for indicating my displeasure to them. Bill Vandivert of *Life* was a welcome visitor, and so were others; generally speaking, troops in the forward areas welcome visitors from behind, and it is good for them to see that interest is being taken in them; but such visitors must be sensible; must come only when they will not be in the way; must bring their own food and kit, and not expect to be waited on hand and foot when they arrive. I had to deport two separate staff officers who conceived it to be their duty to talk to the troops and make an estimate about the state of their morale; one of them, a captain in some such branch as the field security police, had the impertinence to write a report saying that the troops thought highly of their officers. A modern army, it seems to me, encourages more cranks, educational, psychological and otherwise, than is healthy.

But some visitors are always welcome. Katie Cave, my second-in-command, came regularly and did us all good; so did Brigadier Derek Tulloch and Colonel Henry Alexander from our Force Headquarters; and Peter Fleming, whose knack of getting into uncomfortable places is only equalled by his skill in getting out of them. He went to see Mike Calvert in his block, at a moment when all was quiet there; and his arrival sufficed to make war break out again in earnest. I had occasion to go over and see Mike next morning, and brought Peter away in my aircraft. He had already had a forced landing in a glider somewhere, and walked a hundred miles back across the Chindwin the previous month.

On the whole, I am glad that Aberdeen was never attacked other than by air; for though we should have given a good account of ourselves, I should have hated to see all the friendly villagers of Manhton, Kalat, Inbauk and the rest lose their homes and suffer punishment from the Japanese for all their goodness to us. They worked hard through all those six exciting weeks; Robbie Robinson, who was reponsible for the sapper work, handled them well; and Bill Smythies, my official Civil Governor (a grandiloquent title which I conferred on him) ruled them as a benevolent despot. When, after General Wingate's death, I was ordered to abandon Aberdeen, I was thrust into despond; after all my promises to the locals, that they were once more under British protection, and that we were come to stay, we were to march away and leave them to the tender revenge of our common enemy. One of the two conditions under which I had taken service under Wingate for the second time had been that we should not again, as in 1943, abandon to the Japs territory where we had caused the people to compromise themselves on our behalf. But such things happen in war. I was sad and remorseful; Bill Smythies was furious. He reproached me with having led his people up the garden path, and made to them promises which I had not seriously intended to keep if I should find them inconvenient. I found myself using to Bill the very arguments which had been used to me; but there cannot have been much conviction in my voice, for I agreed with all he had to say. In the end, when the last Dakota left Aberdeen; when the A.A. gun crews flew out flushed with their final success; when our once busy Stronghold, fortified with such high hopes against an attack that never materialised, was abandoned; when our dusty airstrip which I had so often used was left bare; when only our refuse and our graves marked our lapsed and fallen tenancy; Bill Smythies refused to come out, and stayed some time longer with the simple, loyal and likeable folk whom we had unintentionally deceived. Luckily, neither he nor they came to harm, and he is still alive and available to play his part in running the country of which he is so devoted a servant.

V

INDAW

I HAVE TOLD the whole story of Aberdeen; I must now tell of the operations which it supported. It was designed as a fortress from which to make sorties against the enemy; but the first time we sallied out, it was no more a fortress than the walls of Rome were walls when Remus jumped them in order to take a rise out of Romulus. He wouldn't even have had to jump at Aberdeen.

But the outlines of the stronghold were marked out. Old Robbie Robinson was bustling around designing the defences. His physical exertions in the Patkai hills had brought on a temporary collapse, and I had flown him out, protesting, to India from Sezin for a rest; but here he was back again, bright as a button, as Chief Designer of Fortifications, Aberdeen—the same giant of enthusiasm and energy as he had been on Saya Bum and Robbie's Steps. And Colonel Clint Gaty with his airfield engineers was carving out the landing strip on the flat acres east of the Meza and of Naunghmi village. He had expressed to me his uneasiness in being thus left without protection: I had soothed him with an assurance of troops ready to fly in as soon as his work was done, and I rashly promised him a dollar for every shot fired at him while I was away. (I had to pay him five in the end.)

At Aberdeen also were John Fraser, with his three Red Karens and two Kachins filched from one of the columns; Bill Smythies, so happy at being back in Burma after two and a half years' absence that he was oblivious to everything else; and Pat Hughes, commander and one-man advanced party of the 12th Battalion of the Nigeria Regiment.

Before leaving India, I had been told to select one battalion out of the 3rd West African Brigade as garrison for my Strong-hold when it should be set up; and I chose the 12th purely because Pat was commanding it. We had been at Sandhurst together, and had never seen each other since; but our friendship was of the quality that can pick up the threads after thirteen years of interruption. I had asked for Pat to come on ahead of his battalion so that he could spy out the ground, and be able to insert his men when they arrived, without delay; now they were standing by until Clint's airfield was ready to receive them.

These five individual officers comprised most of my garrison, except for some thirty sick and sorry men dropped by columns on account of sores, fever or other disabilities. To leave Aberdeen thus lightly defended was slightly risky; but it was only for a few days. Pat's battalion should be there in twenty-four hours; another Nigerian battalion, already landed at Mike Calvert's Dakota strip seventy miles east of us, was on its way across the railway valley to reinforce; and Wingate had told me that he intended to fly 14 Brigade to Aberdeen as soon as Pat Hughes's battalion was in situ. This was a new project; hitherto 14 Brigade was to have been held back for another couple of months; but those outside influences which were destined to alter the whole course of our campaign were now beginning to show themselves. The accelerated introduction of 14 Brigade was their first fruit.

On the 24th of March, the day I left Aberdeen on my way to assault Indaw, the general situation was as follows. Mike Calvert's Brigade, which had landed by air at Broadway, forty miles east of the railway, had successfully established itself athwart the road and railway a mile north of Mawlu, in the Block made famous under the name of " White City." The enemy's frenzied attempts to dislodge him had already failed, and he had tightened his grip to such an extent that it would take a major offensive to rock him. Joe Lentaigne was also in, with part of his Brigade streaking across to the Bhamo-Myitkyina road, and part making westward to the Mu Valley. The stage was set exactly as Wingate had planned it; but the Japs, after months and years of inactivity, had suddenly moved. On March the 15th, a week before I left Aberdeen, they had crossed the Chindwin at several points, attacked the 17th Indian Division under General Cowan at Tiddim, and were making in strength for Imphal and Kohima.

This thrust was potentially dangerous. IV. Corps was spread over a huge front, and its lines of communication ran north and south along the grain of the hills. The Jap offensive was at right angles to IV. Corps. Kohima, for instance—the northernmost point threatened in strength—was sixty miles north of Imphal and a hundred and sixty north of Tiddim. If the Manipur Road was cut at Kohima, IV. Corps was throttled; and if the Japs exploited that success, and also cut the railway through Assam to Ledo, then Stilwell's army was throttled too. Until the strength and direction of the enemy thrust was clear, the High Command was reluctant to commit more troops to the Chindit effort in the interior of Burma, partly because they might need the troops to help fight a defensive battle and partly because they might need the aircraft required to supply them for air supply to beleaguered divisions in Manipur, if the Manipur Road were cut.[1]

Wingate told me all this at Aberdeen on the 23rd of March, and confided also his fears that the situation might affect his famous Plan. Already, he said, he was being urged to keep his two remaining Brigades, the 14th and the 23rd, under his hand, in case they were needed to help repel the Japanese advance. This he was determined not to do. His was an offensive move, as opposed to the defensive strategy to which we had so long been thirled, and which irked intolerably his fiery spirit. Rightly or wrongly (and his shade would stoutly urge that he was proved to be right) he foretold that the Japanese effort would overreach itself, and that *pourvu que ça tienne*, the Jap armies would eventually starve. To remove his remaining Brigades out of reach of the High Command, he proposed to commit them both forthwith, before his right to do so had been abrogated.

14 Brigade was to come in first, as soon as Pat's Nigerians were installed at Aberdeen and they would co-operate with me against Indaw, working south from Aberdeen and then threatening against Indaw from the west. 23 Brigade would follow, but Wingate had not made up his mind where to send them.

That was the outlook as I knew it when I left Aberdeen on the forenoon of the 24th of March and toiled up the hill out of Manhton village. The weather was now hot and sticky, and the sweat poured off us. Behind and below us, Aberdeen looked

[1] See, however, the Introduction.

inviting and deceptively secure, the villages peaceful and pleasant in the valley. Such few misgivings as I had, I quelled with the thought that Pat Hughes's battalion would be there in a couple of days, and the other Nigerians, marching from the east, in four or five; and that Tom Brodie's 14th Brigade would be pouring in very soon. Attack, they tell us, is the best defence; and I hoped to keep the Japs so busy at Indaw that they would have nothing available to detach against Aberdeen. So certain was I that all would be well, that I had ordered the Light Planes from Taro to fly down to Aberdeen; and they were going to settle in at Taungle (code name "Dixie") pending the completion of the main strip. To maintain communications with me, I left an R.A.F. wireless set at Aberdeen under an amusing Canadian Air Force officer called Stick Harris.

I never know why the expression "trying to be wise after the event" is used only in a contemptuous sense. Not to be wise after the event is stupid: not to try to be, criminal. Only by such wisdom does one learn; and after a campaign one should rehearse and recognise one's mistakes, for the profit of others as well as of one's self. I once spent a week in attendance on a general who was showing a party of officers over a battlefield where he had conducted a moderately successful, though costly, campaign, against an enemy inferior in numbers. He ascribed mistakes in plenty to his corps commander, his neighbouring divisional commanders, and to everybody else concerned; but he never admitted to a single mistake, error of judgment, or misappreciation on his own part. I had heard much good of him, and I liked him; but this particular trait seemed to me thoroughly unsound.

I made at least three mistakes at Indaw. One was in not insisting on a rest for my troops before we assaulted. One was in failing to assess accurately, after all the practice I had had, the Jap reaction to the news they must have had of my approach. The third, and the least excusable, was in losing touch with my columns. There were good reasons for all three, but all three were bloomers.

The plan was made with Wingate in Aberdeen. I had only three battalions to play with, since Colonel Dick Sutcliffe's two gunner columns were on their way south from their successful

jaunt to Lonkin,[1] and could not arrive in the area for another
ten days or more. I had always intended to use the Queen's and
the Leicesters to bear the brunt of the assault: both had plenty
of experience in fighting as Infantry, whereas the Gunners and
45th Recce, recent converts to the Infantry trade, had none. But
my order of march made this impossible. The Leicesters were well
in the lead, and were already in the forests north of Indaw and
east of Aberdeen: they were well placed for the assault, and had
managed to snatch a day's rest while the rest of us were catching
up. The Queen's were second, at Aberdeen itself; while the
Recce were miles behind, separated from the Queen's by the gap
which had once been occupied by the Gunners, and which they
had never been able to make up. Their march had been further
delayed by some filthily bad supply dropping. The last column
being always the weariest, the Recce columns were even more
sorely in need of a rest than the others.

The agreed plan was for Indaw to be attacked from the north
with four columns, while the remaining two held the ring. Of
these two odd columns, one was to block the road from Indaw
to Banmauk, to prevent the Indaw garrison from being reinforced from the Mu Valley; the other was to sweep right round
to the south of Indaw, moving roughly via the Meza Valley, and
to come in on to the objective from the south. I did not dare try
to synchronise their attack with the main one so far ahead of the
final assault; but they were to reach a stated position in the jungle
south of the town, ready to be whistled in when I wanted them.
The enemy was almost certain to get news of their march, and,
I hoped, would be looking over his shoulder as a result.

45th Recce was obviously the favourite for this employment,
so that I could use the Queen's with the Leicesters in the main
assault. But the detour would take time and I could not wait for
the Recce to come up; even when they arrived, they would be
too exhausted to undertake such a forced march, and still be fit
to fight at the end of it. So the Queen's had to be given the two
independent tasks, and the Recce to fight as the second infantry
battalion in the assault proper.

[1] The Jap garrison of about 300 had fled before, and for a loss of less than half a
dozen killed they occupied the town and destroyed valuable dumps and stores.
General Stilwell sent us a message of warm congratulation.

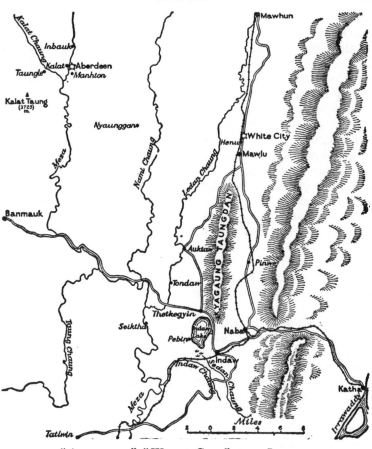

"ABERDEEN," "WHITE CITY" AND INDAW.

The main blow was planned to go in along the crest of a hill
called the Kyagaung Taungdan—the Kyagaung Ridge. This is
an isolated range separated from the main hills by the railway
valley, and itself separating the railway from the Indaw Lake.
From the lake to the railway is two miles. The top of the ridge
is so narrow that it is a question of moving along it in single file;
its sides are split every two or three hundred yards by deep little
gullies, running down to the railway on the east side, and to the

lake on the west: the western slope is steeper than the eastern. Indaw town, and the better of the two airfields, both lie at the south-western end of the ridge. If we could reach its crest, and move along it without interruption, we hoped we might descend into the town and on to the landing ground without encountering any of the main defences. It was Wingate's plan, and I accepted it: if I had stuck to it, we might have pulled it off.

As regards our weariness, I did suggest that we should fight the better for a rest; but Wingate argued, and reasonably, that we could not hope to linger in the area for a week and still enjoy the blessings of surprise. He had news, also, of reinforcements marching up the railway to Indaw from the south; the Indaw garrison was said to amount already to a couple of thousand or three thousand troops. Events on other fronts were moving rapidly, and the famous Plan was doomed unless we could show results quickly. With this reasoning I was in full agreement. The main assault upon Indaw was therefore carried out by four columns, amounting to 1800 men, who had just completed an arduous march of four hundred miles without so much as a day's rest.

The track over the hill from Aberdeen was a good broad trail of the category known as *asoya-lan*, or Government track. (As a matter of interest, it had been built many years before by Bill Smythies's uncle, who had been, like Bill, in the Forestry Service.) It did not follow the route shown on the map, but brought us down into the valley of the Nami Chaung, after some six hours of marching, at a village called Nyaunggon. There we bivouacked beside a slow and pastoral stream, a tributary of the Nami; and I walked into the village with Corporal Carroll of the Burma Intelligence Corps, a nice lad, with a Yorkshire father and a Burmese mother. The headman was away trying to buy some rice for the community, over at Namakyaing; but we found an affable middle-aged man who had been a minor forest official in the days of the British.

The villages of the Nami Valley run in a string towards Indaw before the stream turns south-west to meet the Meza River; and I hoped to pick up some gossip about our objective. But our new friend's first remark, after preliminary courtesies were over, proved a bombshell. I caught something about

"British" and "Indaw," and pricked my ears; I expected to hear something about bombing raids, which usually constituted the opening gambit of any conversation with locals.

But Corporal Carroll, when he turned to me to interpret the first exchange of his conversation, had something very different to announce.

"He says, Sir," he began, in his precise English, "that nine hundred British troops passed through here two days ago on their way to attack Indaw."

Who could these be? The Leicesters, I knew, had not come this way; and even if they had they would not have announced their intention like this. I told Carroll to ask him to describe the troops, and to say what made him think that they were bound for Indaw. In due course came the answer. From the description they were certainly British: two lots each of about four hundred and fifty men, and seventy animals; wearing hats like ours; coming from the east; moving south and south-west; asking many questions about the routes to Indaw, and the Japanese dispositions there. With a sinking heart I recognised the description of the troops as of two Chindit columns, and the description of the interrogation as the old technique of selling a dummy to the Japs by asking the locals a string of questions about a false objective.

It was easy to see what had happened. Two columns of some other Brigade, heading probably for Pinlebu, had crossed my front, using an imaginary attack on Indaw as their cover plan. They had presumably not been briefed that my Brigade was, in fact, going for Indaw, and that what was an admirable cover plan for them was the worst possible from the point of view of my own task. I confirmed, long afterwards, that this was precisely what had happened. It was another example of the old business of excessive security defeating its own object; the concealment of the main plan from subordinate commanders resulting in its chances of success being compromised. There was nothing to be done about it; I could not postpone the attack; it was too late to change its direction; I could only hope that my luck in other respects would hold. The Japs would probably be getting conflicting reports, and perhaps this new one would only muddle them further.

I thanked my friend, but disclaimed any particular interest in Indaw. I was bound, I said, for the railway near Pinwe (looking round me to make sure that we were not overheard): what could he tell me about the enemy's position there? He said that all the railway stations were garrisoned and fortified from south of Mawlu right down to Meza Station and beyond, and warned me to be very careful how I attacked them. Had the enemy many troops, I asked, from which he could reinforce Pinwe when I attacked it—from Indaw, for example, or the two airfields? In Indaw, he replied, there were between two and three thousand men, not mostly in the town itself, which had been badly bombed, but chiefly in the villages round about, and mostly on the south side. In Thetkegyin, for instance, the village nearest to Pinwe, there were about a hundred; although in Auktaw, about the same distance from Pinwe, and four or five miles north of Thetkegyin, there were none so far as he knew.

When I got up to leave him, he asked if I had a doctor with me, as his son, who had been working in Mawlu as a coolie, had a bomb splinter in his shoulder as a result of the early fighting there (Mike Calvert's). I bade him bring the boy along to my bivouac and we all walked back together. Jim Donaldson got out the appropriate instruments, and the boy, a lad of seventeen or eighteen, crouched nervously before him, sitting on his heels. The splinter was somewhere below the shoulder-blade, and Jim's probing must have been sore; but the lad never winced, nor showed any signs of pain, other than biting his lip. Jim decided that it would do no harm where it was: the wound was healed, and Jim thought that to dig out the splinter would do more harm than good—advice which Carroll translated into Burmese with much eloquence, without appearing to convince either father or son. It was not till I told them both that I, too, had a splinter in the side of my hip, which had been there for a year and gave me no bother, that they accepted Jim's professional advice, though rather doubtfully. An English cigarette apiece pleased them better.

But now I had two worries on my hands which were new since leaving Aberdeen that morning. The first was the two days' warning which might reach, and probably had reached, the Indaw garrison which was the subject of my intentions. The second was the apparent scarcity of water on this side of the Meza. From the Chindwin to the Uyu, and from the Uyu to the Meza, it had been plentiful; but during the whole of to-day's march we had not seen a single stream with water in it until we reached the one on which we were now bivouacked. I had asked my friend in Nyaunggon about water prospects ahead of us, and he had said that there was plenty in the Nami and plenty in the Ledan; elsewhere none. I remembered that Maurice Taylor, weeks before, when I had first reconnoitred from the air potential sites for Aberdeen, had said that east of the Meza was a dry country; and indeed I had seen it for myself from Serjeant Sutton's light plane; but with the need for stealth in this, our final approach, I was not too keen on marching along either Nami or Ledan, since they constituted the obvious approach routes to Indaw.

Once across the Nami, there was no water but the Ledan. There were plenty of other streams shown on the map; but the fact that all the villages, with the sole exception of Nyaunggon, were on either one or the other, was a strong indication that all other streams were dry at this time of the year. If this were true, and my friend had confirmed it, the concealed approaches to Indaw were dry entirely.

Had Maurice Taylor been with me in Aberdeen, when Wingate and I were discussing the plan, this discovery would have been less of a shock. Maurice had long been stationed in the Katha district; it was for this reason that he had been allotted to my Brigade; he knew the area better than any living man. But unfortunately he had developed some infection to the eyes soon after we crossed the Chindwin, which was threatening him with total blindness, and I had had to fly him out.

Staring at the map until my eyes were nearly as inflamed as Maurice's, I thought over this infernal water question. If my fears were well founded, and there really was water only in the Ledan and Nami Chaungs, my final assault must be launched from the Ledan, the nearest water to my objective. Its nearest point to the Indaw Lake, before it turned away to the westward, was at Auktaw, five miles from Thetkegyin and nine from Indaw town. It would be unwise to go into Auktaw, where the enemy was certain to have either scouts, or informers, or both: say we started on the final march from one mile north of the village, that would be ten miles to the objective. Yet even so one could not go direct without encountering fixed defences; we must make a detour of at least four miles, so as to get us on to the Kyagaung Ridge well before we came to the Lake. I reckoned that I was faced with an advance of no less than fourteen miles without water, with the prospect of having to fight for it at the end of that time; and I didn't like it a bit.

I had had experience earlier in the war of fighting without water. In Syria, in 1941, I had seen a company of Punjabis pinned to the forward slope of the Jebel Madani, south of Damascus, in the month of June—a hillside studded with lava, and throbbing in the sun. Fourteen men had died of thirst on that day. With this memory behind me, I was determined, whatever else I did, to make sure of a firm hold on a water supply; and, if necessary, to get a footing on the Indaw Lake before anything else.

Meanwhile, I sent out orders by radio that the two columns of 45th Recce, and two liaison officers from the Leicester columns, should meet me the following evening on the Ledan Chaung, at a point, conspicuous on the map, where the *chaung* had a sharp double bend. This feature, which we called "the crook in the Ledan," was to become a well-known landmark during the next few weeks. The Ledan proved to be a pleasant little stream, eighteen inches deep, with a hard sandy bottom, broad beaches, and fifteen to twenty yards wide from jungle to jungle. There we lay next evening, handy enough to the water, but far enough away to avoid being spied upon by enemy patrols or dubious villagers. The Recce columns arrived a few minutes after us. They were keen as mustard despite their weariness; they had never been in action, but they had waited four years to break their duck, and the prospect of doing so at last was meat and drink to them.

I explained how the problem of water was affecting the problem of the attack, and declared my intention of using the Recce columns to get a foothold on the Indaw Lake. The Leicesters were fresher than the Recce, and with them I would try and bring off the original plan, of working along the Kyagaung Ridge and down on to the fringe of the airfield. Indaw town seemed to me of secondary importance compared with the airfield, and I had a vision of finding myself in the town and wondering what the hell to do with it. The airfield was the Bull; the town was merely an Inner, or a Maggie. So I directed the Leicesters on Inwa, a small village on the mouth of a stream which was shown on the map as perennial, although only a few hundred yards long. At Inwa they would have the water of the stream; they would be almost on the Lake as well; and they would be on the northern edge of the airfield. Once there, they should try and establish contact with the Recce, who I hoped would by then be on the northern shore of the Lake, and who should also try and push patrols out round the east shore to find the Leicesters. The distance between them would be about three miles.

The information brought in by the Recce columns and the liaison officers from the Leicesters tallied closely with what we in Brigade Headquarters had managed to glean. Garrison of Indaw, upwards of two thousand; dispositions, mostly outside the town; actual site of defences unknown, as local labourers had not lately been allowed in the area.

Time programmes in jungle seldom succeed. To synchronise an attack involving approach marches from two different directions, you must allow ample time; so much time, in fact, that you must accept a long delay on the start line, and the consequent risk of the enemy finding you there and busting you off it. I determined to achieve one more concentration before despatching the Leicesters and the Recce on their respective tasks. The nearest point to the objective which I dared select was a point near the Ledan in the jungle about a mile north of Auktaw; and I ordered a concentration there for 13.00 hours the next day —one o'clock in the afternoon.

We now know a lot that we didn't know then. The Japs had duly received and acted on the news from Nyaunggon: that Indaw was going to be attacked from the north. They realised that the battle would be a battle for water, and made their dispositions accordingly. They reinforced Thetkegyin, and denuded the southern defences of Indaw to do so. They put four hundred Burma National Army troops into Auktaw together with a few Japs as a stiffener.

I marched down next morning to my rendezvous on the Ledan a mile north of Auktaw, with one Recce column ahead of me and the other behind me. I had just halted; the second Recce column was passing me to join its sister column; both column commanders had just come up to speak with me; the Leicesters, I knew, would be arriving in a few minutes from the other side of the Ledan. All seemed to be going well, and it looked as if our long march from Ledo was going to culminate in a successful concentration, when firing broke out a few hundred yards away, where the newly arrived Recce column was just halting.

To hear fire break out just when and where you have planned that it should is the most heartening sound in all warfare. To hear it break out where it shouldn't, and to know that your plans have gone agley is hateful; and that sudden outburst of mortars and grenades at Auktaw was a bitter moment. A minute later, firing began on the far side of the Ledan, almost in Auktaw itself; and I leapt to the conclusion that this was the Leicesters, who had perhaps overshot the rendezvous and stumbled into the village. It proved, however, to be the luckless reconnaissance party I had detached from the Recce a fortnight ago to have a look at Maingpok; reaching Aberdeen, and hearing that the battle for Indaw was imminent, they had hurried on to join in the fun, and walked straight into the enemy. Both officers were killed, and three of their men.

The gaff was now well and truly blown, and I could no longer wait for a leisurely conference. If the Japs had a force so far out in front, they would quickly have warning at Indaw, and there was no time to be lost. I told the Recce columns to do a Rugger hand-off on whatever was opposing them, slip round it, and go flat-out for the Lake.

"Off you go!" I said, and within twenty minutes the two columns, after a rapid watering, were saddled up and on their way. The shooting on their front had become desultory, but now there was more noise from beyond the river. This time it really was the Leicesters. In a short, sharp action, they dissipated the opposition, killed thirty and got one prisoner whom they sent over to us with a liaison officer. I took the prisoner; I told the liaison officer to get back to Colonel Wilkinson and tell him to go for Inwa and the Lake by way of the Kyagaung Ridge: I would follow.

The prisoner proved to be a rather miserable and very frightened Burmese, an ex-Post Office sorting clerk from Sagaing. He wasn't a bad little chap, and he told dismal stories of the lost livelihood which had driven him into the Army, and the lost self-respect which had followed. He could tell us little or nothing about the enemy at Indaw; his unit had only arrived from the south a couple of days before, and they had been thrust straight out to Auktaw, and told to expect an attack. They had all been Burmese, except for one Jap liaison officer, and a few henchmen who had bullied them and beaten them: our prisoners hoped they'd been killed, as so many of his own friends had been.

When the fighting started, and the departure of the Recce had left me exposed, I had rather ignominiously withdrawn Brigade Headquarters half a mile. A Chindit Brigade Headquarters at that time (I modified my own as a result of my experience in this battle) was a horribly unhandy affair—too clumsy to attach to a column, and too vulnerable to take a chance on its own. It had over sixty animals, and less than two hundred men; most of whom were muleteers, signallers, cipherers and other specialists; its means of defence were two platoons, and the problem of defending an airship with peashooters would have been easier to solve. To be involved in a scrap meant losing mules and wireless sets; to lose these meant dumbness and helplessness. I was loath to embarrass either the Recce or the Leicesters with our presence, and not at all keen to get involved in a scrap. Peter Dorans' platoon, spread meagrely over a wide front, was giving us what protection it could.[1]

What I should have done was to have taken one additional wireless set, and gone in person with the Leicesters' Liaison Officer, leaving the main body of my headquarters tucked away in the jungle as a clearing house for messages. I should then have been able to witness the Leicesters' action and to direct the main battle from there.

That is with post-event wisdom. At the time, however, I was far from sure that the Leicesters would succeed in their task; and I had visions of myself fighting a hand to hand battle by their side on the top of Kyagaung, unable to exploit the success which might have come the way of the Recce. In Chindit fighting, the

---

[1] 2753451 Serjeant Dorans, P., D.C.M., The Black Watch, born and bred on the estate of a kinsman near my own home, and my batman and henchman from 1931 to 1944. Now a keeper at Kilkerran.

Brigade commander cannot skip nimbly from battalion to battalion in a jeep, nor canter from column to column on a horse, nor tour his front in an armoured car. He can stay put with one unit or another, or at a command post, and chatter on his wireless. But here we had another slice of bad luck. For the next three days and nights, we had continual thunder-storms; we were virtually deaf and dumb.

Those days were of unrelieved gloom.

"I bet you wish you were commanding a column again, don't you?" said John Marriott; and indeed I did. If a column commander lost touch with his parent brigade, his job was still clear-cut; but a brigade commander who had lost touch with his columns is in a clove hitch. We were sitting on one or other of the spurs running down from the Kyagaung Ridge to the Indaw Lake. Somewhere below us, a mile or two away, we heard intermittent fighting which was presumably the Recce; somewhere towards the south-west we could hear the battle of the Leicesters near Inwa; but except for brief periods we could get nothing on the air, beyond one triumphant signal from the Leicesters that they were in Inwa, surrounded but quite happy.

I cannot now recall, and I have no notes to remind me, the order of events during those days; but I can reconstruct the main story. The Leicesters reached Inwa without casualties, surprising the Japs as they came down off the hill and seizing the water in the *chaung*. They held the village for two days against several spirited attacks, using their air support with skill and killing numbers of enemy. At one time they made a little progress on to the edge of the airfield; but it made their perimeter larger than they could safely hold, and they had to withdraw in the face of counter-attacks to its original limits. These embraced the *chaung*, the village and that portion of the ridge, some six hundred yards from the Lake, which most seriously dominated their position. They were all right where they were, but until I could get reinforcements to them, they could not exploit.

For the two Recce columns, on the other hand, things went wrong from the start. They found the Japs dug in at Thetkegyin and all along the Lake. At its northern end, it was separated from the jungle by a wide strip of paddy, which was swept by fire; and the Recce men could not get out of the jungle. They

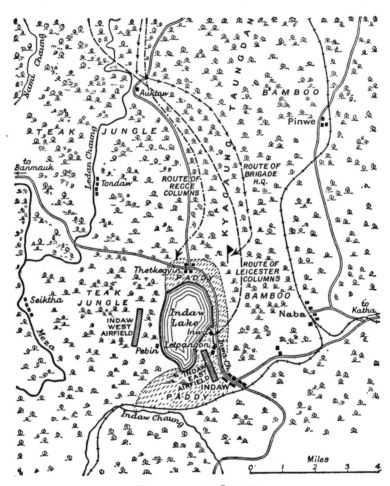

ENVIRONS OF INDAW.

had various subsidiary disasters: a mule carrying fuel for the flame-throwers had its tins set alight by an explosive bullet, and in its frenzy ignited a temporary dump of packs, mortar bombs and ammunition; it went off in a big bang. Many mules had been killed by a small party of Japs who infiltrated right into the gully where they had been hidden under guard.

Except for one or two platoons more lucky than the rest, these columns went for two and a half days without water. I could get no news whatever from the battalion commander with the senior column, and I afterwards discovered that his wireless set was lost to the enemy. For a long time I could get no signal from the other column either; but at last a message came through in clear, itself a bad sign, to say that it had had thirty per cent casualties, had lost touch with its sister column, and was compelled to disperse in order to seek water. On getting this signal, the first coherent news for two days from either Recce column, I realised that for some time at any rate I could get no help to the Leicesters from that quarter.

The woes of 45th Recce were not yet at an end. Working desperately westward to the Meza to find water, they were harassed all the way there by the Japs; and when they reached it, they found the Japs dug in there also. Many of the mules, smelling the water, broke away from their leaders, and galloped towards the river; and some of the men, maddened with thirst and caring for nothing else, were killed as they too dashed across the paddy to slake their thirst. These columns had already had a good many casualties, but they suffered more here. Theirs was entirely a battle for water, and the water had not been won. It was the fight which became known in the British press as " The Battle of the Water Bottles."

Next came bad news from that column of the Queen's which had been directed round the western flank, to come in from the south. They got a message through to us during another patch of good communications, when the screams on the radio became reduced for half an hour or so to a mere angry growl. They had been caught by lorried infantry at an awkward moment, and had almost all their mules killed or dispersed; they had no means left of carrying their heavy weapons; their colonel was wounded; they could produce nothing heavier than small arms fire. They could no longer take a major share in the storming of Indaw, so I signalled to them orders to "make your way to the nearest road in use by the enemy and be bloody."

Thus, out of my six columns engaged, three had lost their power to strike; two were fully committed; the only one intact was the second column of the Queen's under Terence Close which was blocking the road between Indaw and Banmauk, at the twentieth milestone from Indaw. Only from this column was the news good: they had beaten up a Jap convoy, and killed thirty Japs for the loss of one officer and four men. But this was a very minor item for the credit side of the ledger, against the debits already entered; and they were too far away to affect the main battle. Nevertheless, I summoned them to hurry east, as being my only reserve. The Gunners were still more than a hundred miles away to the north, floundering south through the Kachin hills from their successful raid on Lonkin.

It never rains but what it pours. News from the outside world, in the occasional snatches which we got between thunderstorms, was as bad as it could be. Not only could I get no news about the arrival of 14 Brigade: I could get no spark of communication out of my rear link at Aberdeen. From Rear Brigade at Imphal a message had come to say that a "considerable number" of Japs were marching on Aberdeen. This was followed by another saying that three hundred Japanese were reported at Taungle, and that the light planes had taken off for Taro. Then a sudden breathless signal came through, still from Rear Brigade, that they had been ordered to get out, and they were moving. This message broke off short, with an addendum hastily passed in clear by the operator to say: "Closing: closing: no more: moving." Tommy Moon, with a set face, got on to the key himself, and tapped out in clear many times: "What is happening? What is happening?" But there was no answer, and we were left wondering if the Japs had actually burst into the Signal Office.

For twenty-four hours we could get no news whatever from Rear Brigade or Force; and then, next evening, a set opened up very faintly on Rear Brigade's frequency. They had apparently moved all the way to Sylhet in Assam, and this was a 22 set operating until the big sets were ready to resume work. That looked as if the situation at Imphal was pretty bad; and I immediately began to wonder if 14 Brigade had not come in after all.

I wondered that still more when Rear Brigade reported "Position Aberdeen obscure." I couldn't get a word out of our set at Aberdeen; and, remembering the paucity of the garrison which I had left there, I began to fear the worst.

It was now four days since I had marched out of Aberdeen with such high hopes. I had done all that I could with my own resources and I was failing. The Leicesters were like a fat cheque that I couldn't cash: they were in a good position at Inwa, but I couldn't keep them there indefinitely, and I couldn't exploit their presence there without reinforcements. The only reinforcements in my own hand were the one column of Queen's, who were coming from the direction of Banmauk as fast as they could; but even when they arrived they would be physically tired and numerically insufficient.

Wellington was not more impatient to hear of Blücher and his Prussians than I to hear of Brodie and his British. I was hoping hourly to get news of them, and I sent personal signal after personal signal to Wingate, explaining my position and asking about 14 Brigade. But none of these signals were answered; perhaps he himself was still in Imphal. Then I started signalling Katie Cave, whenever the atmospheric conditions would allow: following up with rude signals in clear to ask why the others were not being acknowledged. Even then I could not get replies. I couldn't make out what was the situation of 14 Brigade, nor what had happened to Pat Hughes's Nigerians, nor the other Nigerians who were supposed to be marching on Aberdeen when I left it. There seemed good reason to believe that Aberdeen had been overwhelmed; and that the strip had fallen into enemy hands. In that case, 14 Brigade could not be in; Pat Hughes must have been chased out, either with or without his battalion; and the new Nigerian battalion would have arrived to find the Japs in possession. Their then colonel was called Day; and I remember sending a signal in clear to say: "When is Day dawning?"

The third day was pretty miserable. We had managed to get a rather dashing supply drop the night before, including some water in metal containers which would keep us going for a bit.

I was worried about the Leicesters' food supply, which I knew must be running low, and it was unlikely that they would be able to get a drop in their tiny restricted perimeter. (Had I only known it, they were feasting on captured Jap foodstuffs, and living better than they had done for months.) I resolved that unless by nightfall I got some news, about 14 Brigade or anything else, which would justify me in counting on a change for the better in the course of the next three days, I would pull out. Further delay might lose the Leicesters. Having made this provisional decision, I borrowed *Lorna Doone* off Bill Dixon the Transport Officer, and forgot my sorrows in that. Doone Valley seemed a trifle more secure than Aberdeen.

That night I issued orders to move to the southern fringes of the Kachin hills, some thirty miles to the north. With no news of Aberdeen I reckoned I must find somewhere which I could hold with the barest minimum of troops while the others rested. The Kachin foothills, which I knew, would be ideal for this purpose. They were only two days' march away; they held ample water; there were few routes up into them, and those were easily held; the population was fiercely partisan against the Japs, and would keep us well informed; we should be handy for the return march against Indaw; we should be fairly near Mike Calvert; and we should be two days nearer to reunion with the Gunners. I ordered Terence Close's column of the Queen's (the one which was hastening back from the Banmauk road) to cover the withdrawal of the Leicesters near Auktaw in case they were followed up, and we settled down to get these orders out over the wireless to all the columns with whom we were still in touch. From the Recce columns we had heard nothing for twenty-four hours.

Wireless conditions that evening were still bad. The Leicesters' orders had to be transmitted over thirty times before they were cleared, and Tommy Moon himself sat at the key to do it. By the time they acknowledged it, it was too late for them to move that night without reconnaissance; they managed to pass back a message to say: "Any diversion would help." But alas, there was none I could lay on. It must be up to them to do the best they could for themselves with their air support. That was a dark moment.

Next morning we heard their call for air support. The thunder had gone in the night, and we could hear the aircraft talking as they came, and the Leicesters' R.A.F. officer directing their attack, and saying, "Oh, *beauty*!" We felt the ground shake as the Mitchells put in their bombs, and the air was alive with their machine-gunning. It went on for an hour, and soon after came the Leicesters' welcome signal: "Withdrawing slowly owing to wounded."

There was a cheerful signal also from Terence Close, to say that he had arrived with his column near Auktaw and found a rear element of the Leicesters which Colonel Wilkinson had left there before going down to Inwa.

Now the nightmare began to fade, as the news got better and better, and more and more plentiful. Aberdeen was secure! There were no Japs there, or anywhere near it. Pat Hughes's battalion was arriving. The other Nigerian battalion from the east had been badly mauled in the railway valley and had casualties, but was now arriving also. The first battalions of 14 Brigade were already in, and the last two coming: but they were being directed down the Taung and Meza Valleys, and nowhere near Indaw.

To say I was relieved would be an understatement; but I was also damned angry. Why the panic at Aberdeen, and why the silence about 14 Brigade, and why had its job been changed without warning? All that I could thrash out later, but meanwhile revised orders were indicated. I was still out of touch with both the Recce columns, but I was pretty sure that in default of other orders they would make their way to Aberdeen. I told Terence Close and his column of the Queen's to find a secure bivouac in the jungle north of Auktaw, to set up a patrolling screen between us and Indaw, and to take pot-shots at any congenially easy targets which might offer. The Leicesters I ordered to find and lie up in another secure bivouac north of Terence, have a rest, and be prepared in due course to do the same as he. The other half of the Queen's were miles away to the south-east of Indaw, and all on their own: I told them to slip across the Katha-Naba railway and so into the Kachin Hills east of the main Myitkyina railway; across that, north of White City, and so to Aberdeen. It was thirty or forty miles farther than the direct route, but much safer, with more cover and better water. At Aberdeen they would refit.

Brigade Headquarters would go to Aberdeen, and direct the reorganisation from there. It was very clear—and I sent a signal to say so—that the Brigade must have some rest and some decent food before it functioned again. They had had a hard battle on top of a hard march of seven weeks, carried out on short commons and culminating in several days of insufficient water. They were tired and weak, and I reckoned that they must have at least a fortnight before they were called upon for another major effort.

My orders went to Queen's, Leicesters, Gunners and Rear Brigade during a noon halt. At the same halt there came in another signal, which explained some of the perplexities of the last few days, and which at the same time made the events of the last few days sink into lesser importance. It told of a loss which affected the whole war in the East. It brought the news which sent the Japanese in Rangoon into ecstasies of joy, bursting into the jail at Mingaladon to shout to the prisoners, so many of whom had served with him, that the enemy whom they dreaded most was dead.

Wingate was dead. His aircraft had flown into the side of a mountain near Bishenpur, and he had been instantly killed; but the signal did not tell us that. It said only that he had been missing for five days, and was believed killed; and that Joe Lentaigne would take over command of the Force when he could be flown out from his own Brigade.

Had I known earlier that he was missing, I might have guessed what was in fact the case: that the plan devised at Aberdeen for the use of 14 Brigade had never reached Force Headquarters. Thus none of my signals addressed to Wingate about 14 Brigade had been understood by his staff; and that Brigade's task had remained unconnected in any way with the Indaw battle.

Wingate was dead, killed at the very moment when his Brigades were poised for the stroke which he had so long been planning; and the bottom had fallen out of the campaign. The Japanese grip on the Manipur plateau was tightening, and the defensive battle was quickly ousting the offensive battle from its place in the British strategy. Wingate was dead, and his Plan with him.

VI

ANTI-CLIMAX

IT WAS a hot and dusty day when, at the head of the little Brigade Headquarters column, I emerged from the jungle, and came out into the Meza Valley on the southern outskirts of Manhton village. There, where the hill track joined the main track which linked the villages of the valley, we met a European sergeant and a squad of huge Africans. As we passed through Manhton into view of the airstrip, we saw how much progress had been made in the development of Aberdeen during the week we had been away. The strip was completed, and smoke from the lunchtime fires was climbing into the air. The garrison had arrived.

We skirted the southern edge of the strip, passing nine new graves as we did so: they were of men who had been killed in an air-raid two or three days before. It was a poor spot to initiate a cemetery, where people were passing every day, and I gave orders for the graves to be moved to a more sequestered place, where they would not constitute a standing *Memento Mori*. By a quarter to one, we were established on Brigade Hill, and I was embarking on an informal enquiry into the Aberdeen Scare.

It proved to have been a good example of initial panic magnified by silence. It seems that a native had run into the Americans' camp at Taungle crying that the Japs were coming. This in itself was apparently an exaggeration of a report by the natives that some Japs were preparing to come. Some of the Americans had just been chased out of Broadway (Mike Calvert's version of Aberdeen) two days before, and were in a mood where the imminence of Japs was credible; their nerve, unrivalled in their own element of the air, was not at its best on the ground, and they made for their aircraft and took off. The story spread like fire in cotton-wool and within the hour had peopled Taungle with three hundred actual Japs.

Meanwhile, at Aberdeen, only two miles away, John Fraser, Pat Hughes and the rest only knew that the air had suddenly darkened with light aircraft flying north. When they heard that Taungle was full of Japs John grimly went to see. The Kalat Valley was as peaceful as ever; there were no Japs, nor any news of Japs, except a vague story that the garrison of Pinbon was showing a tendency to be restless and might be sending a patrol over towards Aberdeen. But by the time that John Fraser and Bill Smythies (who, unlike the Americans, could speak Burmese) had traced and exploded the story, the mischief was done. Worse still, the solitary wireless set which I had left in Aberdeen chose that moment to succumb to one of those attacks of dumbness to which wireless sets are liable. There at Aberdeen sat John and Bill and Pat and Robbie and Stick Harris, powerless to kill the story, until at last they managed to raise Aberdeen.

This was the one black which the light planes put up during the whole campaign. Our debt to them is so great that this incident on their debit account is swamped by their incalculable credits. Phil Cochran dealt sternly with them, sacking their two senior officers, despite pleas by Mike Calvert and me that they should be reprieved. In their defence we urged that they had had a rotten time already at Broadway, and that their achievements had more than compensated for this one lapse; but Phil was adamant, and they went. I wrote to both of them, to thank them warmly for all they had done for us; but they had already left for the States. They were grand chaps, and we were all miserable that their association with us had ended in this way.

Marching back to Aberdeen, I had spent a night at the Crook in the Ledan; and there I found 54 Column, the junior column of the Recce—desperately tired and haggard, apologetic, but with their tails still up. They were the column which had still been able to signal me until fairly lately; but their wireless batteries were flat and they had lost their charging engine with its mule in the action. As I had expected they were making their way back to Aberdeen, not having known about the Great Aberdeen Flap. They were loud in praise of their doctor, who had performed great feats; and they were confident that they had killed quantities of Japs—a claim which was confirmed by subsequent patrols, who found many unburied bodies north of Thetkegyin. Still nearer to Aberdeen, I encountered one platoon of 45 Column, completely on its own, utterly ignorant of what had happened to everybody else, but completely happy in its absolute faith in its youthful commander, Tony Musselwhite. This young man, who had had a telling off at my hands more than once, had no inkling of what was going on, but was exhibiting complete un-concern to his men. We caught them up at a moment when they were halted at the side of the track, and as I reached the head of them, Musselwhite rose to his feet, a tall spare figure.

"Good morning, Musselwhite," I said.

"Good morning, Sir," said he, with a broad grin spreading over his face. "I will not deny, Sir, that I am exceedingly pleased to see you!"

"Well," I said, "I'll bet it's the first time you've ever been able to say that."

He was killed a fortnight later.

Back in Aberdeen we cast our accounts. The Recce columns had suffered worst; the Leicesters' losses were surprisingly light. Wilkinson and the Leicesters had had a good battle; but Wilkie had had his arm broken in two places at the preliminary skirmish at Auktaw, and was a write-off for the rest of the campaign. He and his wounded had been flown out from Auktaw, and had already passed through Aberdeen by the time I arrived. I put him in for an immediate D.S.O. and one of his serjeants for an immediate D.C.M.: and the news that both had been granted by His Majesty the King came through in less than three weeks, to give pleasure to the whole Brigade.

Dick Cumberlege of 45 Recce had put up a brave performance. He had put together a scratch platoon of his battered column and set out along the shore of the Lake to locate and join the Leicesters. Considering that he had had no news of the battle for two days and was utterly ignorant of its course, this was a soldierly act of a high order. He met the Leicesters as they withdrew. and returned with them to Aberdeen, sick and exhausted, but still indomitable. I sent him back to India for an enforced rest, but not without a struggle.

The day before I got in, I had sent a signal asking for a special effort to be made to give us decent food in Aberdeen. I proposed to grant each column a three days' holiday there, free from duty; and I was anxious to shovel really good and generous rations into every man during that period. My appeal met with a splendid response. Bully beef, bread, dehydrated potatoes, green vegetables, eggs and other luxuries were sent in to us, and every column in the Brigade renewed its youth like the eagle.

The death of Wingate and the irruption of the Japanese across the Chindwin left everybody in the air; and there was a woeful uncertainty about what we were likely to do. I sent two appreciations out to India, which I don't suppose anybody read. On the other hand, we read the Intelligence appreciations coming into us from India with a good deal of attention, and as much irritation at their irrelevance to the actualities of the situation.

I was naturally disappointed at my failure to capture Indaw, although less so when I found that it was no surprise to my colleagues or to Force Headquarters. Apparently even Wingate had said that he wasn't optimistic about it. Nevertheless, I had a nagging feeling that if I had stuck to his original plan, and put all my money on the Kyagaung Ridge, I might have pulled it off. We should have had a sticky time holding the objective after its capture, and we might have had difficulties over getting supply drops. Indaw had A.A. guns which could have interfered with them, and the open space over the Lake and in the paddy areas would have made the enemy's task of interrupting them fairly easy. The airfield would have been tricky to defend against attack from the south and south-east; but if the Japs could do it, we could also. A strong position, well dug, with plenty of wire and mines, is a good egg against the Japs, particularly if you have air support, and enough troops to enable you to keep plenty of strength outside the perimeter, where they can harass the enemy's preparations for attack. Wingate had preached this doctrine; Mike Calvert had proved it.

I saw a lot of Mike in those days. Sometimes he came over to me, sometimes I went over to him. Although it was the best part of two days' march from Aberdeen to the White City, it needed no more than twenty minutes in a light aircraft. First you climbed to cross the high range that formed the eastern side of the Meza Valley, you circled within the valley a couple of times to gain the requisite height, and then went off, skimming the trees, almost due east. "Tree-top height" was the permanent standing order for the light planes, since at that height you stood a good chance of not being spotted by enemy aircraft, and were past ground troops as soon as they heard the sound of your engines. The Nami Chaung would flick beneath you, with the familiar feature of the Konhka pagoda; then the Ledan, then some jungle; and finally three miles of open paddy before the White City itself.

The White City was so called from the many parachutes hanging in its trees, and in trees outside the perimeter. Its frequent subjection to enemy mortars and guns, and, less often, to bombs from tip and run aircraft, had stripped the trees of all foliage and most branches; but from the top of them some parachutes still hung rakishly. The perimeter consisted of four or five low hills separated from the main hills on the east by a few yards of pasture and at one point by a stream. On the south the Henu Chaung divided it from a half-mile width of paddy, beyond which lay the small town of Mawlu. (Mike went into its railway station once, and took a ticket to Rangoon.) On the west side lay the railway on its low embankment, and beyond the embankment a wide stretch of open paddy, interrupted by one long copse. But White City's greatest treasure, apart from the essential water, was the natural light plane strip lying between the low hills, which curved protectingly about it, and the railway embankment, so placed that when a plane was on the ground it was defiladed from all sides. This strip, and the planes that flew in and out of it, was the life-line of the White City.

Masses of wire, duly booby-trapped, protected it, and all the hills were honeycombed with keen digging: one night's mortaring in White City would make a digging enthusiast out of the biggest sluggard. Casualties from these bombardments were for this reason astonishingly light. A night of noise (and we could hear it distinctly from Aberdeen) would produce no more than half a dozen casualties.

From time to time the garrison would change; but within that small perimeter there were never less than fifteen hundred men of mixed origin. Gurkhas and Burma Riflemen; Nigerians and Hong Kong Chinese, old friends of Mike's rom pre-war days; South Staffordshires and Lancashire Fusiliers. Pat Hughes was there at one time; Malcolm Freshney, Burma Rifle Officer and old hand of the first campaign; Mike Calvert himself, with his Brigade Major Francis Stuart and his airman Bobby Thompson both old friends of mine. Francis had long been A.D.C. to General Auchinleck, and then had served in North Africa with his regiment, but had begged his way back to India to be a Chindit; he was Mike's shadow; once he said to me that he had never realised that being a Brigade Major merely meant following your Brigadier about with a bag of grenades for his personal use; and he showed me two bullet-holes in his trousers as demonstration of the result of being Brigade Major to Mike Calvert. Bobby Thompson was a Malayan Civil Servant in the R.A.F. Reserve of Officers; he had escaped out of Hong Kong after its fall; got to India via China; been with Mike on the first show, when he got an M.C.; was to get a D.S.O. on this one; and alone of all the original Chindits was to see the Burma war through to its end, and enter Rangoon. He was our expert on air support, having devised our methods from scratch with Phil Cochran's boys; in this science he was a pioneer, and I would back his knowledge of it against the world's.

Then there was Paddy Ryan, Japanese interpreter and Intelligence Officer, who used to crawl up under the Japanese positions and listen to them discussing whether or not they would attack again—one of the bravest men I am ever likely to meet. There was Taffy Griffith of the Burma Rifles, who drew first blood on the first expedition and who was to Mike what John Fraser was to me: Mike thinks better, I think not so good, so we are all four happy. There were many others, a cheerful, happy, confident lot, whose talk was always: "What fun it would be to do this!" and "Wouldn't it be fun to do that?" Now Bobby has gone to be Governor of Christmas Island, and hopes to find out in good time where it is; Taffy has gone back to Burma; Francis died from sudden and desperate illness in Calcutta a month after he got out of Burma; and Paddy died in Sylhet from the loss of a leg in one of those bombardments of which he affected to make so light.

White City is not my story, and I cannot tell it, except in so far as it concerns me; but I can pay tribute to its defence and its defenders. And during the month of April, 1944, the holding of White City was the main concern of the Force. It was still our hope that the Japanese thrust across the Chindwin would spend itself in time to allow of the old Plan, of flying troops in to the

Indaw area:[1] and although we could now bring troops in through Aberdeen, our strip there would not be usable in the monsoon; for it was built on undrained paddy, which would flood as soon as the rains began in earnest. (Now our trouble there was not water but dust: every aircraft that took off left a cloud of dust behind it that hung about for a couple of minutes.) So it was pretty certain that the Indaw airfields must still be captured; and it was essential to preserve the Brigade as intact as possible in anticipation of that stroke.

With my own threat to Indaw temporarily receded, the Japs were free to make another effort to dislodge Mike from the White City. They had already made several, and been thoroughly seen off each time. But they had now been reinforced by the Regiment (Brigade) which we had long awaited, and which had marched up the railway line from Wuntho to the south. Their advanced guards had helped in the attacks on the Leicesters at Inwa, and among the documents which were brought from there, filched from the dead by the Leicesters' I.O., had been a diary of one of their officers (not, incidentally, conspicuous for high morale). One of Tom Brodie's columns far down near Tatlwin had also reported considerable reinforcements coming up the road, the new road which I had stumbled on myself the previous year.

My columns were resting, two at a time, at Aberdeen. The others were being used in two ways, in the triangle Aberdeen-Auktaw-White City: they operated against the build-up opposing White City from the south, and they made the enemy apprehensive for Indaw by activity north of Thetkegyin. This process occupied most of April, and produced a number of skirmishes and minor actions.

There were a good many irritations about this time. Health had suffered a savage decline, and malaria was widespread. The Indaw area was particularly unhealthy, and the infection in many men's blood was so strong as to prevail over the daily intake of mepacrine in suppressive tablets. The Leicesters, who reported that the mosquitoes at Inwa were considerably more bother than the Japs, were particularly hard hit; and in one highly successful excursion which Dafty Daniell led to the railway, he could only amass about two hundred men out of the two

[1] See, again, the Introduction.

columns fit enough to cover the country in a really agile fashion. Many of the less tough men were considerably under the weather, which was now abominably hot; and any attempt to march during the three hottest hours of the day resulted in widespread collapse. Watching reinforcements stepping out of Dakotas at Aberdeen was like watching something from a far-distant past; it was like attending a play in eighteenth-century dress: the newcomers would hurdle the paddy-kezins for fun where we dragged our feet over them, and we dimly remembered that we ourselves, long ago, might have felt like that.

From far away in India there came other annoyances. In Long Range Penetration you are your own best source of local Intelligence: and the stuff that comes in sealed envelopes from behind is not the best source of information about your own area. We were told that there were two thousand Japanese in Hopin; we politely queried it; we were told, impolitely, not to; we sent a patrol there to find out, and there were thirty; we were told that our patrol must have been somewhere else. Then we were told that the road Pinlebu-Mansi and Pinlebu-Pinbon were the main supply routes supporting the Japanese thrust into Manipur. They were, indeed, the obvious routes; only they weren't being used. They had been, up till the beginning of March; quantities of stores had passed along them, but they were now as deserted as General Wade's road over Corryarrack; Major Sandy Dickie's Gunner Column, arrived from the north, was sitting four miles from Mansi and watching it; but our information on this point was resolutely ignored. We would not have minded had it not been that each new appreciation coming in from India took into account the "facts" which had been exploded. There were still a few dumps along the roads in question, and occasional guards; but nothing like the surge and flow of a line of communication such as was pictured in India. In point of fact, the Jap thrust, at least so far as Kohima was concerned, was entirely supported by the contents of a few dumps built up by the beginning of March, and the pious hope that they would capture, with the fall of Kohima, whatever else they would by then be needing.

I visited all the columns as often as I could by light aircraft, and reconnoitred by air until I knew it like the back of my hand

all the country around Indaw. Various of the column commanders did the same. John Fraser made several expeditions into
the Kachin hills, and organised supply drops of rifles, ammunition
and clothing to our friends of the previous year. Conferences
took place almost nightly in Meza House. The Japanese paid us
frequent visits by air, without doing much damage—although
while we were away on our first attempt against Indaw they
killed the nine men whose graves we passed on our way back in.
New clothing, stores and equipment were flown in; new boots;
new mules, complete with brand-new comments from the pilots
bringing them. Aberdeen was busy all that month. The Dakotas
came in and out each night, and each day the light planes answered
the summonses coming from the columns to fly out to some
hastily hewn strip in the jungle, and bring in the wounded with
the yellow, bloodless faces, or the more than ordinarily sick. The
first light plane would go out soon after dawn, and the last
would come home when the shadows had climbed to the very
brim of the glen; and between times the pilots had flown many
weary sorties, and risked their lives in each. Whatever blame had
attached to the panic at Taungle had long since been washed out
in the hundreds of lives that had been rescued. Those pilots were
brave.

Each column in turn, coming for its rest, was shown where to
lie, and then left in glorious peace. There was only one fatigue
for it to do, and that was to go and collect its food each day from
the dump on the air-strip. I had brought in one of my staff-
captains from India to deal with the problems of issuing food and
equipment, and also (what was nearly as valuable) a Jeep and its
trailer to help hump things about Aberdeen; for we were dispersed fairly wide. Except for collecting the food, watering the
mules, cooking and reading mail and newspapers, the men were
free to lie about and rest, and most of all to sleep, which they did
all day long.

I went and spoke to each column for twenty minutes or so, on
the progress of the campaign and the form generally. They were
keen to know all that was happening, the situation at Imphal
and Kohima, the news and prospects from the White City—which
we all knew had become the main battlefield for the moment.
For so long as Mike's people lay athwart the road and railway at

the White City, nothing could reach the Japanese 18th Division and other odd troops facing General Stilwell in the north; and the Japs had put so much into their trans-Chindwin thrust that they had little to spare against us in the central area.

There was one awkward question, however, which was raised against me at every one of these visits. The Secretary of State for War announced in the House of Commons that every man with five years' service overseas was on his way home. This was the result of a most unfortunate slip on somebody's part, because in point of fact I had four hundred men in the Brigade with over five years of foreign service, and a good number of men with more than six. The announcement was made one of the first days in Aberdeen, and was blazoned in fat and juicy type across the first crop of newspapers which reached us there; it could hardly have happened at a more unfortunate moment. I sent a signal off to India asking for an amended statement to be supplied, to be given the same publicity, both in the House and in the Press as had been afforded to the first; but nothing came of it. Somebody, somewhere, lacked the guts to confess to a bloomer.

Various doctors came in to see us, to report on our physical condition; and most of them pulled longish faces at our emaciation. I was worried about the men's weariness myself, but I thought we probably had another major show in us, provided it didn't last too long. I was a great deal annoyed by a supercilious major, who had never been in the field in his life nearer to the front than a divisional headquarters, who came in to see me, and who bade me recollect that all victories were won by tired armies; I damned near kidnapped him and attached him to a column. There was a doctor, also, whom I didn't take to at first sight, but who endeared himself to me in the end by making a bamboo splint for the under-carriage of a light plane in which I had sent him out to an advanced strip where wounded were being loaded; the undercart had collapsed on landing.

The doctors thought we had had enough, and they were probably right; but it seemed a sad business to pack up so soon after we had arrived in the area which had taken two months to reach. However, the minor expeditions and outings in which the columns were now engaged were not so arduous as a set-piece battle; and working from advanced bases and hidy-holes it was possible to lighten their loads a good deal, and to send them out with haversacks instead of packs. The trouble was in finding suitable advanced bases in the small triangle which I have described. It was very small, and except for one or two odd pools elsewhere, there was only water in the Nami and the Ledan, which were easily watched by the Japs, or by informers on their behalf.

The Recce columns were certainly the hardest hit: they had had far the worst march, followed by far the worst battle, and their columns were much under strength. Mike Calvert was chafing at having so many men locked up in the White City, and was anxious to get more garrison troops in, so that he could get more of his own men out. His troops were fresh; they had only had four or five days' marching from Broadway, where they landed, to the White City; and although they had had plenty of fighting there, they had mostly been stationary ever since they had come in a month before; we had been marching for ten weeks. So it was suggested that I should lend the two depleted Recce columns to Mike for a spell at White City, together with one of my Nigerian garrison battalions—Pat Hughes's. This left me with only one of the two Aberdeen forts defended, with Gordon Upjohn's (formerly Day's) 6th Battalion; but as the Japs were showing only an aerial interest in Aberdeen, this risk seemed acceptable.

So Pat and his Nigerians went across to the White City to take over part of the garrison; and a day or two later the Recce columns, now down to some hundred men each, went out in their turn. The City was clear at the moment; some ferocious sorties by Mike, and some hefty air strikes by Phil Cochran's boys, had induced the Japs to withdraw for a bit, as they sometimes did, to lick their wounds and think things over. There was therefore a reasonable hope of changing over the garrisons without bother. Pat Hughes got in all right; but at that moment the Japs showed themselves again in one or two villages south and south-west of the City, and it became apparent that something was brewing. I flew over to see Mike, and found him on the point of leaving the City himself, to lead in person a sweep round the jungle beyond the western paddy.

He had halted the Recce columns, who were already under his orders, at a point some three miles north-west of the City, where he already had something of a striking force in readiness. He had not fully grasped that I had lent him the Recce columns for static use only—in fact, for a rest; but to have insisted on it now would have ruined his project, and I did not do so. He told me his plan, I wished him luck, he borrowed my plane, and he flew away with Francis Stuart to join his little army. In due course the plane came back, and I returned to Aberdeen.

Unfortunately the Japanese concentration in the jungles south and west was much stronger than we had thought; they had been thickening up by a new route, east of the railway, and outside the purview of my patrols in that area. Mike succeeded in clearing several villages, though not without loss; and then one morning, soon after dawn, trying to get back into the City from higher up the Henu Chaung, he met the Japs, in force and in good positions. The Recce had had losses in the opening actions of the sweep, and on this occasion they happened to be leading. In the course of a fight lasting nearly an hour, they suffered heavy casualties, and ended with something like seventy wounded on their hands, the very devil in our sort of fighting. But they had managed to knock seven bells out of the Japanese, who had lost considerably more than they. Mike sent them up into the Kachin hills east of the City for a rest, but even there they had two or three rearguard actions to fight on the way up.

Their first campaign had been a bloody one, and their losses had been woefully heavy, including a high proportion of officers. Six months before they had been a highly trained mechanised regiment, who had never been in action, and never been on their feet; all that was far behind them, and they had shown themselves tremendous in making their first history. But they were so weak now that they could muster less than one column; and I got permission to send them on through the Kachin hills slowly towards Broadway.

The Leicesters had been having it all their own way round about the railway. They had brought off some decent ambushes, and had one first-class scrap where they induced the Japs to attack them completely without method, with satisfactory results. In

five days they counted ninety-five Jap dead for the loss of two
men died of wounds; and this figure was not one of your fanciful
ones, so common on many fronts, but a proper body-counting
check. Terence Close had a minor fight or two, and so did one
Gunner column at Pinwe—Pinwe, which had a tiny railway halt
and consisted of ten or twelve houses; which was described in a
communiqué, when finally reoccupied by a British division, as
"an important rail centre."

While these minor skirmishes and scoutings were going on,
we had found and were playing a new game. From talking to
coolies who had worked for the Japs at Indaw, we amassed a great
deal of information about where the Jap dumps were. Indaw had
long been a stock target for air action; but, being a hundred and
fifty miles across the Chindwin as the crow flies, little had been
known that was accurate about where the worth-while targets
were. This was just what the coolies could tell us. Their stories
were long and involved, and not unlike the baffling directions
given to motorists in rural England: "Where U Tin's pig was
found after it was carried away"; "Two furlongs beyond Maung
Oh's tobacco patch." But with patience the answer would
emerge; and thereafter a tree-top flight in a light plane would
confirm what had been said. By such means, and by a system of
target indication to be described elsewhere, we were setting to
work to destroy the whole dump system of Indaw; and we had
some gratifying results, including ammunition, rice, and a
highly spectacular dump of 8,000 gallons of petrol near Naba.
After Rangoon fell, we learned that these supplies had been
intended for the trans-Chindwin thrust, and that their destruction
had materially affected that campaign.

Meanwhile we had been giving thought to our organisation.
I was determined not to take the field again with such an un-
wieldy Headquarters as I had taken to Indaw at the end of March,
and I had cut it as much as I dared. I had further introduced what
I called the "cloakroom idea," developed from a bright idea of
Wilkinson's before we lost him to an Indian hospital. To a
greater or lesser degree, every column had with it more than it
wanted for actual fighting; and so we devised a plan whereby
it dumped its soft parts two or three miles short of where it
hoped to fight, in a secret hiding place, somewhere near water,

with an adequate guard found from sick and sorry. From this guard a party would seek out a potential landing strip, and cause it to be built by local labour, a process which did not take more than a couple of hours. The wounded would walk or be ridden on mules back to this point, and thence evacuated to Aberdeen.

At last I got my orders to move once more against Indaw. This time I was to go for Indaw West airfield, on the opposite side of the Lake to my former stamping ground; and Tom Brodie's 14 Brigade, which was sculling about down south of Indaw, was to come in against the town from that direction. Derek Tulloch, the B.G.S., came in to see me, and gave me an order, very difficult to observe, that I was to be on the air to Headquarters, in person, at least once in every two hours. I pointed out that I should be on the move, at which he suggested that I should run the battle from Aberdeen. I was determined, however, not to lose touch with my troops again; and we agreed on a compromise which suited me well from every point of view: that I should let the Brigade move out on its own, somewhat as Mike had done with his striking force, and join it at the last moment before deployment.

The terrain this time was completely different to the country over which we had fought on the previous occasion. Whereas the country north and east of the Indaw Lake was hilly and thickly forested, the country this time was flat; and the nearer we came to our objective, the closer together flowed the Nami, the Ledan and the Meza itself; and the more plentiful became the paddy-fields. There was thus an ample choice of potential light plane strips; and indeed a good many existed already, from the various ploys of the various columns over the past three weeks.

I had selected a paddy on the Nami at Tondaw to be my advanced base on this occasion. The Leicesters were now the least fresh of the three striking battalions still left to me, and I selected them to be my reserve, located near myself. Gordon Upjohn's Nigerians held the fort at Aberdeen. The Queen's were to have their cloakroom base at Seiktha and the Gunners to have theirs at an ill-defined point on the Ledan. All these could be reached by light planes. I joined the force by air at a village a few hours short of Tondaw, and there also a few hours later Bill Smyly arrived to join my Brigade, a successful result having been reached after months of string-pulling to get him. The other battalions were marching parallel to us; for in that flat teak country you can march where you will. It was desperately hot by now at any time from ten-thirty onwards; and a lot of the men were dropping from heat-stroke or fever. We passed Auktaw, and the graves that marked the scene of our scrap there a month or more ago; the Gunners had been there for some time, using it as their base in the triangle with complete impunity: I had visited them there by air a few days earlier. All of us were expectant and optimistic about the outcome. Jim Harman was having his leg pulled, because I had given him a new and very odd job. Determined not to run out of water again, and knowing that this time we should have ample tracks to play with, I had made Jim drive the Jeep and trailer all the way from Aberdeen, purchasing earthenware pots in villages on the route. My idea was that he could drive water forward when wanted and bring wounded back when applicable. In the end he did neither; but at least he had the satisfaction of having blazed a remarkable trail.

Yet this second approach to Indaw was an anti-climax, and for two reasons. First, just before we went in we were told that even if we captured the airfield of Indaw West, no troops, no divisions would be available from India for flying in: all hands and the cook, it seemed, were tied up in the great battle for Manipur. We were to capture the field for two or three days and then to abandon it.

Secondly, it was early apparent that the birds had flown. The Queen's got right on to the airfield without a shot being fired; and only the Gunners succeeded in discovering any Japanese at all—a small party in a stockade north of Pebin village, of whom they claimed to have killed eighteen. There we were, in a slightly ridiculous situation, with nothing whatever to be done about it. From our Rear Brigade came the order, relayed from Headquarters, to stay where we were for a couple of days, and then pull out.

Then came detailed orders. We had finished our campaign; we were to fly out to India. The Recce columns were already reaching Broadway. Brigade Headquarters and three columns were to go there also; the other three columns were to go to

Aberdeen, and fly out from there. Our fly-out completed, both Aberdeen and Broadway were to be abandoned, and their garrisons, together with the remaining Brigades, were to move north to help General Stilwell from nearer at hand. Even White City was to be given up in a week or two, but this we did not yet know, although I guessed it. That was to be sad news for all, but especially for Mike and his fellows: for without doubt the setting up and defence of White City was the finest feat of arms of the whole Burma campaign of the year.

I sent the Leicester columns and one of the Gunner ones to fly out from Aberdeen, and led the other Gunner lot and the Queen's out to Broadway. The journey took six or seven days; we never saw or smelt a Jap the whole way, and were quite pleased not to. At one point, near the railway (which we crossed with considerable caution on account of its wide stretch of paddy) I asked from very shame permission to seek and engage some reported enemy; but was told to lay off. In point of fact, everybody was on their last legs; and the struggle over the Kachin hills was hard work, necessitating frequent halts. At one point I crossed my track of the previous year, but failed to find any of my former benefactors.

The hills, as usual, were loud with rumours; and as usual most of them were false. For all his great warrior virtues, the Kachin is a pessimistic broker of rumours; and he would scorn to pass one on without having first embroidered it. Yet I love him, and was deeply sorry to pass through Pumphyu, the last Kachin village for the year—and, as it has turned out, the last I have been in at all. Some day I must go back; meanwhile I can do no more than commend that gallant race to my countrymen, who are mostly unaware of its heroic and unsupported war against the Japs. To carry on their own, independent way of life, they will need our protection and help for many generations to come, like that other splendid race the Karens. Let us see that they get it, for we owe them a lot.

The day dawned, of which we knew that the evening would bring us to Broadway. Already we were in the curious basin of flat and uninhabited jungle in the centre of which it lay. It is a country of thick and stunted forest, through which there runs one solitary and sinister river, the Kaukkwe Chaung. I had never seen it before, but I had heard much of its inordinate depth, quite out of keeping with its thirty yards of width.

In 1943, homeward bound, I had crossed the Irrawaddy some miles below the Kaukkwe's mouth; but those who had crossed upstream of it and found the Kaukkwe still between themselves and home, had had trouble in getting across it. No. 8 Column, under Walter Scott, had been caught by the Japs in the very act of crossing, and suffered casualties there. However, Mike Calvert, speeding from Broadway to the railway at the beginning of March, on the way to establish White City, had found a ford at a place called Moko Sakan, and I had been warned to make for that.

I reached it at about half-past ten in the morning, after a march of five or six hours, of which the last hour had been along the Kaukkwe bank. It was odd country, with many stretches of grass. There were also broad lagoons separated from the Chaung by only a few yards on which there were innumerable duck and cranes: I longed for Bill Smythies to tell me what they were, and then wondered how Bill was getting on at Aberdeen.

At Moko Sakan (*Sakan* means camping-ground) we saw some huts on the far side, of the type which fishermen build as occasional shelters. We plunged into the water, and found it more than waist deep.

"Never mind," we reflected. "We shan't get wet many more times."

It was damnably hot, and I resolved to rest as soon as we were across. There were only another six or seven miles to go to Broadway (always provided it was where I thought it was); the track was in regular use by troops going and coming between there and the White City, and we could average three miles an hour with ease, an unusual luxury. We could spend the heat of the day where we were and still get in before dusk. As I rose like Venus from the waters of the Kaukkwe (but not very like Venus), I found waiting for me on the far side, a patrol of the King's Regiment, under a young captain. He said that Walter Scott, the former commander of 8 Column and now C.O. of the King's, was waiting for me four miles along the track, and had sent this patrol on ahead to see if they could give me any help.

But I was determined to have our midday halt in shade and comfort. One of the Gunner columns was ahead of me and was probably halting on the next water; the two Queen's columns were a day behind me; there was no hurry; I would stop where I was, where the cool waters of the Kaukkwe were tempting us all to swim and wash. So it was not till half-past three that we pushed on.

At five o'clock Scotty popped out of the bushes on the left of the track, and fell on my nasty, dirty neck. And what do you think? He had a mug of tea ready for all the hundred and eighty men in my headquarters, and an extra one for me. In a life which has been blest by much kindness from many people, I never met the like; and I hereby thank him again.

Another hour's marching, and the last moments of daylight brought us into Broadway. We emerged suddenly on to the open expanse of trodden grass and gazed about us curiously as we marched for fifteen hundred yards along the fringe of that famous airstrip. This then was the scene of that remarkable exploit, Mike Calvert's fly-in. Here Walter Scott had landed in the first glider; here over forty men had been killed when their gliders struck teak-logs concealed in the grass; here Colonel Claud Rome, Mike Calvert's second-in-command, had beaten off the two hundred and fifty Japs who had tried to occupy the strip, and deny its use. We had heard much of Broadway, and it was interesting to see it at last.

For the last time Alan Sheppard the Orderly Officer blew his whistle to signify "Halt." We need walk no more. The long months were over, and the second Wingate Walk, so far as we were concerned, finished. Claud Rome, the Laird of Broadway, appeared to welcome us; I went to his command post, and we pledged each other in rum. I met a lot of friends I hadn't seen for many months, and was introduced to a lot of strangers. I suddenly felt very tired.

A most efficient embarkation staff had been flown in from India, and there was nothing to be done by my own officers in the way of arranging our departure. There were Tannoy equipments all over the place, which broadcast notices and ordered forward details to their aircraft. The first Dakotas arrived just after we came in, and the Gunners, who had been marching through Burma two hours before, found themselves climbing into aeroplanes already. It was hardly credible. Brigade Head-quarters and one of the Queen's columns would go out the next night, and the last Queen's column the night after.

There was a slight feeling of anti-climax. We had walked a hell of a long way, but we hadn't much to show for it. The results were falling mostly to the other Brigades: they deserved them, but we should have liked a share in the dividend. We had had a lot of trudging and pioneering, and not much honour and glory; but we had put our best into it, and must be satisfied.

All that night the Gunners were flying out. Next day I awoke at the usual time, when the dawn was beginning to "net the flushing mountain spires" away to the west; and a great joy surged up in me at the thought that there was to be no walking to-day. Broadway was busy; for Claud Rome had orders that as soon as we were out, Broadway was to be abandoned, and all troops to march to the north, towards Hopin. Bill Smyly, still fresh, came to me eagerly to ask if he could sign on with the Gurkha battalion which was acting as garrison in Broadway, but was now girding up its loins to go fighting: they were two or three officers short, he said, and were more than willing to take him. I gave him my blessing, and he skipped away beaming.

I borrowed a light aircraft from Claud, together with a pilot —an R.A.F. officer, not an American—and went off to have a look at Myothit, where Japs had been reported with some cir-cumstantial detail by the Kachins on my way through the hills. Knowing that the second Queen's column would not be flying out for another two days, I had diverted them to Myothit, which was a mere ten miles off their route, to see what they could find. We circled the village for twenty minutes, and peered into *chaungs* and other likely camp-sites without result, and then flew back to Broadway for a midday meal. In the afternoon I flew again, to take my leave of Aberdeen—dear Aberdeen, whence the glory had departed.

Westward I flew, across the hills, across the battered railway. I passed south of Mawhun Taung, familar landmark of two campaigns. I saw abandoned light plane strips. I passed above many tracks and villages that I knew well. Everything I saw brought back some memory to my mind, of a bivouac, a skirmish, a dusty march or a grave.

Aberdeen was nearly deserted. The other Gunner column and one of the Leicester columns had already flown out; only a few of the last Leicester column remained. Gordon Upjohn and his Nigerians were preparing to march north, like Claud Rome, to join in the next phase of the campaign around Hopin. The last few light planes were still there, but they too were packing up. John Fraser was lying sick with malaria near Elbert's rapidly closing hospital, with Mya Dein and The Three Naidus looking after him. Smoke was rising from fifty bonfires where refuse was being burned. The villagers, as quick to scent departure in the air as a dog whose masters are going away, had already taken to the jungle for fear of the Japs. From the hospitable houses of Manhton and Kalat no smoke was rising into the warm May air.

Back at Broadway that evening, there was no news of any Japs for fifty miles around, and it seemed that nothing could go wrong. The next evening would see the last platoons out, and all the individuals bar a few animals. I had intended to be the last man out; but there was nothing for me to do at Broadway, there would be lots to do in India, and it seemed to me that to stay for the sake of a gesture would be an affectation. So I decided to fly out that night with my Brigade Major, and to leave a field officer in charge under Claud Rome for the last twenty-four hours.

We had all laughed the previous night at the adventure which had befallen some unfortunate gunners. Their aircraft had taken off and flown for an hour, when it developed engine trouble and returned to Broadway. The passengers had not realised that they had turned round en route; and when the plane taxied to a halt they jumped out and began shouting the good old soldiers' cry of "Charwallah!" thinking that they were in India. I hoped that no such undignified performance would mar my own journey.

The men were all being flown to Comilla, where some sort of reception camp—very poor, but allegedly the best available—was awaiting them. I was required at Sylhet, where my Rear Brigade and Force Headquarters were. The plane in which I was to travel there direct was coming in at about 10 p.m. I was so tired that I could no longer keep my eyes open; so I took my blanket down to the strip, and showed John Marriott where I was so that he could waken me when the time came. There for the last time in Burma I went to sleep with my head on my hat as usual.

I cannot remember waking up to get into the plane, although I have a vague memory of lying curled up on the floor of an aircraft and feeling chilly. The next thing I knew was a torch shining in my eyes, and the grinning faces of Derek Tulloch and Katie Cave as they woke me in India. It was two o'clock in the morning of the 3rd of May, and I was out just in time to celebrate my thirty-third birthday.

VII

SOLILOQUY

MY BRIGADE was out of the hunt. For the others, still in it, the fox had been changed. The main armies were fully engaged in Manipur, and there was no hope of any being spared to come in to us at Indaw. The enclave from which they were to have broken out was useless to us; and the object of our operations had to be exchanged for a more modest aim. The efforts of the remaining Brigades were to be directed to helping General Stilwell reach the line Mogaung-Myitkyina.[1]

The first step was to give up White City, a cruel blow to those who had held it so long. The Japs were still about it; but a neat little operation on the 8th of May[2] cleared them from their positions dominating the Dakota strip which Bobby Thompson had constructed on the paddy just west of the railway. That night twenty or thirty Dakotas flew in, loaded with guns and stores, and flew out again; the garrison stole quietly away in the darkness; the Japs were carefully induced to think that the Dakotas had, in fact, brought reinforcements; and this belief was driven home by several light aircraft landing and taking off the following day on the unguarded light plane strip as usual.

There followed nearly three months of hard fighting in monsoon conditions: Tom Brodie's 14 Brigade in the Kachin hills west of the railway and near the Indawgyi Lake; 111 Brigade, formerly Joe Lentaigne's, nearer the railway, with a detachment still over near the Bhamo road; and Mike Calvert's 77 Brigade biting stubbornly against the Mogaung position until at last it fell to him. When that day came, the B.B.C. in error ascribed its capture to the Chinese; and Mike broadcast a signal (copy to me) saying:—

[1] For the last time, see the Introduction.

[2] Anniversary of the fall of Corregidor, Myitkyina and Akyab and the eve of the Battle of the Coral Sea, in 1942: the date which may be regarded as the turning point of the Japanese War.

"Understand that Chinese have taken Mogaung. My Brigade now taking umbrage."

Of all that later fighting I have only a hearsay knowledge. By all accounts it was grim: casualties were heavy, and battle casualties were swollen by a heavy sick-rate with high mortality, especially from scrub typhus. The Black Watch in 14 Brigade finished their campaign with a dashing assault on the village of Taungni, played into battle by their pipes, which had been dropped by parachute two days before. The Japanese 18th Division had wasted away to nothing; the fall of Myitkyina to Americans and Chinese marked the virtual end of the war in Upper Burma.

It is my own conviction, put forward in all humility, that we should have continued to hold what we had—the hills north of the line Bhamo-Katha-Indaw-Mansi. These hills would have been easily held throughout the monsoon by stationary forces, and it would have been possible to build decent huts against the weather. A ready-made intelligence service existed in the Kachin tribesmen; and, high above the rotting valley-bottoms and monsoon swamps, health could have been kept moderately good. Two objections were made to this plan which I and others urged. The first was the difficulty of keeping the force supplied during the monsoon: that objection answers itself, because the force was in fact supplied during the monsoon—a feat greatly to the credit of the air crews responsible. The second objection was political: that it was important that the American and Chinese forces farther north should see British co-operation under their noses.

The last argument is outside my purview. But it was a bitter blow to have to give up what we had won, and go north; it was bitter to see the British 36th Division started off, a few weeks later, from Milestone 0 at Myitkyina when we had already held Milestone 140 near Indaw, and toil slowly and grimly southward over what we had dominated long before. As a child, one was tempted to weep, when ordered to go back to the start at Snakes and Ladders or Grandmother's Steps: this was as bad, or worse.

Spilt milk is ill wept over, and I doubt if the Burma War as a whole would have been won any earlier had this plan been adopted. For that war was won, not in Upper Burma nor in

Central Burma, but in Manipur; not in 1945 but in 1944. It was lost by the Japanese as a result of their suicidal over-confidence, which led them to gamble on a British-Indian withdrawal in Manipur, and the winning of the British-Indian supply-dumps. The Manipur positions were held, and the Japanese starved, and their Army in Burma broken for ever. As a measure of that defeat within my own understanding, I heard from Denny Sharp, my R.A.F. officer in 1943, that over twelve hundred starved bodies were found on the ten-mile track from Thanan to Hwematte, by which we had approached the Chindwin on the first Expedition. The victory had to be clinched by generalship and hard fighting in 1945; but it was surely won in Manipur in 1944. Before the final round, Wingate was dead, and his beloved Force disbanded.

With the passage of time, it should be possible to begin assessing Wingate's importance in perspective. He is in danger of being thought of more as an eccentric and glamourised guerilla leader than as a serious military figure. I was myself solemnly warned against engaging under his banner, on the grounds that one's orthodoxy would be for ever suspect. A good deal of venom can be infused into the over-worked phrase "a private army." Through misuse it has lost what pungency it once possessed; and in any case if Wingate's was a "private army," I am proud to have belonged to one.

Both his Burma Expeditions have been criticised on the grounds that they failed to affect the main battle. But the cardinal fact is often forgotten, that both were designed as offensive rather than defensive. In both years his object was to help forward the great advance across the River Chindwin which was the ultimate object of all our plans. When he set off in 1943, he did so knowing that the offensive was postponed, but anxious to have a rehearsal for the day when it would come off, and to prove that he could do what he claimed. It is often said that the 1943 Expedition was not worth while. I can only say that when we were surrounded, and my private inner conviction was that the odds were 5 to 1 against our getting out, I still thought otherwise. In fact I told my two most trusted subordinates that, if I failed to get out, they must themselves seek out General Wavell and impress my view upon him that there was a future

in L.R.P. In the event, one of the two was killed ; and the proportion of my men to get out was precisely one in five.

In 1944, we had high hopes of a big offensive. The "main
battle" which we failed to affect in that year was not the offensive
which had been planned, but the defensive forced upon us by the
enemy.

As for Phil Cochran's "private air force," its allotment to
Wingate was interpreted by many as an assault upon the principle
that the allotment of aircraft in "penny packets" (another
horrible cliché) is a bad thing. Principles must not be confused
with axioms. In 1944 we were designed to hit hard and accurately
and our air force was our instrument. It had to be more closely
integrated with us than any air force in history had previously
been. The bombers and fighters trained with us until these pilots
and we were on Christian-name terms; we knew precisely each
other's capabilities.

My own Brigade set out before the bomber and fighter
squadrons had completed their concentration, and the period
during which we actually fought was short compared with that
of the other Brigades. Even so, we had some remarkable results,
notably with the Leicesters at Indaw. But they were nothing to
the results achieved by Phil's pilots in association with Mike
Calvert and Bobby Thompson, who had been more closely
trained with them before starting. Bobby, indeed, had much of
the responsibility of devising new methods of co-operation
between ground and air; and Phil's pilots were hand-picked
from the most experienced men in the Army Air Force and the
American Volunteer Group in China. Men like John Allason,
Oley Olesen and Bob Mahony were prepared to try anything;
and they took the view that the place for experiment was in the
field.

Their knowledge of us, our problems and our situation at any
given moment was so intimate that we were able to dispense
entirely with Air Liaison Officers. The R.A.F. officer with each
column briefed the pilots in flight. If when they arrived they
were in any doubt as to their target, they would make a pass at
what they guessed it to be; and the officer on the ground would
correct it until they got it right.

It would be hard to exaggerate the value of these R.A.F.

officers on the ground. The R.A.F. in S.E.A.C. was short of pilots, and took a lot of coaxing before they were made available. But so essential were they, that, as Mike Calvert declared on paper, we Brigade Commanders infinitely preferred to have three pilots on the ground and nine aircraft in the air, than to have twelve aircraft in the air. Pilots on the ground know exactly what it is reasonable to ask from pilots in the air; and pilots in the air have confidence in pilots on the ground. No non-pilot and no Air Liaison Officer, however good, can be an adequate substitute, and when these pilots reverted to flying duties at the end of the campaign they were far better qualified to afford air support to infantry than others who lacked their own experience on the ground.

I shall describe in a later chapter how we put the bombers on to their targets by means of smoke-bombs dropped from light planes; but this was not by a long chalk the only new-fangled idea, although it was a good sample of what Phil Cochran used to call "dreamin' somethin' up." Another of his tricks was what he called the "circle jerk," and we the "coicle joik": the Mitchells would steam around in a circle for an hour, peeling off in turn and hitting the target with bombs or cannon shells or depth charges or rockets. Too often we had found in direct air support how the safety margin between forward troops and the target allowed time for the enemy to pop up again after he had had his dose of fire. We got over this by two methods: by integrating our air so that our supporting aircraft were striking only a hundred yards ahead of us, across our front; and secondly by dummy runs, which were as effective in keeping down the enemy's heads as a genuine run. Never was there such air support as ours. And it could only have been achieved by an air force pledged to our support and ours alone. It should be noticed, in passing, that this method of ground control of air forces was in use with us many months before it was sanctioned elsewhere, and that if we had been working on the normal system half our tricks would have been disallowed.

Wingate's development of direct air support by these methods (which are now known by other names) and of air supply were wholly new contributions to military thought. They themselves may furnish an answer to those who think of him purely as a guerilla leader. He would have been equally ready with ingenious proposals in any branch of warfare—and equally intolerant of scepticism.

His conception of Long Range Penetration had travelled a long way from being a mere scallywag, raiding, sabotage performance. That could be better done, as he often admitted, by parties far smaller than his original force. But he saw and preached Long Range Penetration as something much bigger that that. He saw how in desert and in jungle, and indeed elsewhere, hard and costly battles had to be fought for objectives which had no intrinsic value and which when won left the winner with little advantage. Of what use to us, or to the Japs, were the many miles which separated our armies in Burma from our main objectives in 1944? This idea was nearly related to the island-hopping technique in the Pacific. Our purpose was to restore the overland route to China and to take Rangoon. If it were possible to leave the enemy in empty enjoyment of the useless territory between the Irrawaddy and the Chindwin, the way would be open for the capture of the Delta, and the overland route to China would eventually be ours as well.

Nothing enraged him more than to hear his Penetration Groups described as "detachments": he saw them as an integral part of the battle, and designed them as such. But on the whole he failed to convert contemporary military thought to his belief in deep penetration. He obtained permission and facilities for his two experiments, it is true. But the first was no more than a laboratory experiment on a minor scale, to show that he could fulfil his part when the great advance came off. The second was intended for a full-dress performance; this time it was as if the detonator had worked as it was supposed to work, but without a charge to detonate. Had the Japs not crossed the Chindwin; had it been possible to ante-date the campaign by two months; then the result might have been very different and the dividend high.

As it is, it has been said that the dividend declared was something like 5 per cent.—too small for the number of troops engaged. In terms of fact, that is probably a fair estimate; but to arrive at a fair assessment of the possibilities of Long Range Penetration, it is proper to consider what might have happened. 1944 was the year when the Indian Parachute Brigade fought on its feet, and the 2nd Division, trained for combined operations, fought six hundred miles from the sea.

Medium penetration, or the "short hook," found more favour; and the campaign of 23rd Brigade in the Naga Hills was quoted as evidence that the "short hook" was an improvement on deep penetration, in that it influenced the main battle. 23 Brigade, a first-class Brigade out of 70 Division like my own and trained as Chindits, did a most useful short hook under Brigadier Lance Perowne from May 1944 onwards, catching the Japs as they reeled back from their defeat at Kohima and cutting them up almost without loss to themselves. Wingate would certainly have passed this as a permissible L.R.P. operation, but he would have denied hotly that it was the standard type. He would have pointed out that it was being used in a defensive battle, even though in the closing and winning stages of that battle; and the defensive irked him: he thought always in terms of the offensive.

There are those who say that the days of Long Range Penetration are over, and that it will have no place in any future war. Anybody's guess about future wars is as good as anybody else's. Nobody would claim that L.R.P. in a future war would be the same as L.R.P. in this; but *mutatis mutandis* I think it will come again. For various reasons, including shortage of manpower, Wingate's Special Force was wound up before the 1945 campaign began; but, had even one Brigade survived, possible operations for an air-borne Chindit landing came into the view of the eager. For instance, when the remnants of the Japanese were escaping out of Burma through the Karenni Hills north-east of Rangoon, a Brigade dropped near the passes could have played the part of 23 Brigade in the Naga hills, only at a greater depth. The terrain was suitable; the local inhabitants were Sgaw Karens, warlike and fiercely anti-Jap; lines of communication were easy to cut; there was jungle, there was water, there were potential landing-grounds. But there were no Chindits, and the advance of the 14th Army was using every Dakota that could take the air; the project could only have been maintained at the expense of one Brigade out of the main advance. It would, nevertheless, have been a neat and exhilarating little operation, fully in the Wingate tradition, and declaring a dividend higher than the rankling and pedestrian 5 per cent.

W.G.E.   K

Wingate is buried near where he crashed, not far from Bishenpur. Lance Perowne's brother Christopher, the senior padre of the Force, walked there to bury him and the others who were killed with him, George Borrow and the rest. His place in the hall of captains is not easy to assign. Public praise of him was fulsome; military judgment prejudiced; neither was discriminating. Some of those who now whisper that he was not all that he was cracked up to be remind me of the mouse who has a swig of whisky, and then says: "Now show me that bloody cat." He was hard to serve, and difficult to command; but if I had a rope round my neck, to be jerked tight unless I recanted my allegiance to him, I would still proclaim that he was a great soldier. And what is more, he sought battle when many others were seeking excuses for evading it.

Those who served under him will like to remember Mr. Churchill's words in the House of Commons after Wingate's death, when he described him as "a man of genius who might have become a man of destiny." Those words are more than a fine phrase; they are a worthy epitaph, with which history will not quarrel.

PART TWO

VIII

JUNGLE TRAVEL

MAPS are my delight—my favourite form of doodling, at dull staff conferences. Better men than I have the same weakness. Some even go in for maps of imaginary places. Buchan: witness the sketch-maps in *John Macnab* and *Huntingtower*; Stevenson: although the chart in *Treasure Island* is a bit too fanciful to be convincing; Evelyn Waugh: the splendid map of the island of Azania in *Black Mischief.* (Our John Fraser's stock stumped badly in 1943, when he lost his pack, complete with the column copy of *Black Mischief,* crossing the Shweli River. It was the last book we had, barring one Trollope novel and the Bible.)

Lord Wavell has confessed to reconstructing a map of Xanadu from the data given in *Kubla Khan*. Monsignor Ronald Knox has compiled an excellent one of Barsetshire from its extant *Chronicles.* Ruritania, so far as I know, has still to be mapped. If these things be done in the green tree, what shall be done in the dry? If such satisfaction is to be had from maps of legendary places, how much more may be had from real?

Yet, as an Army, we are poor at map-reading. We consider ourselves accomplished if we can count road junctions from a fast-moving staff-car, and expert if we can do a beastly calculation called Intervisibility. That is about the dullest, and quite one of the least valuable, things to do with a map. The average reader does not learn one-twentieth part of the information which the kindly cartographer sets down.

At Sandhurst, map-reading was the most miserable of subjects. It was taught from a manual which gave one fair warning in its opening sentences of how dull it was going to be. From that platitudinous level, it droned on, through Vertical Intervals and Horizontal Equivalents, without a spark of liveliness or imagination. It was natural enough that in the Army we got only the standard of map-reading which we deserved.

If you put a map into the hands of the average man, and ask

him to describe in three sentences the country it portrays, he will
say something like this: "Well, it's hilly. There's a high mountain in the right-hand bottom corner, and a river just to the left
of it with a big town and a bridge. And there's a railway running
right across from left to right."

How much wiser are you? Or he?

The first thing he should do is to get a general idea of the
drainage of the country, the "tilt." Which way does it slope?
If it slopes more ways than one, never mind. Once you know
the way or ways which a country slopes, you have the key to a
knowledge of the communications; and all war, to a greater or
lesser degree, even with the advent of air supply, is a matter of
communications.

The less developed a country is, the more this applies. In a
primitive and undeveloped land, man settles where there is water
(that is, according to the drainage system). Where man settles,
villages spring up; between villages, tracks spring up; villages
become towns, tracks become roads, roads become railways;
until at last the country is developed. Even when this process is
completed, the discerning eye can still see, beneath the overlay
of modern communications, the original factors of nature which
dictated the manner of evolution.

There are, of course, cross-currents of influence which flow
across this simple primary system. Chief of these, especially in
an industrial country, is the extraction of various kinds of ore.
The rules which dictate where these may be found are less obvious
than the primary rules of drainage. In Burma, for instance,
there are tracks into the mountains in various areas which at
first sight belong to no system of communications based on the
grain of the country. But if, wisely taught, you look to see what
the cartographer has marked for you, you will find that this
apparent exception belongs to a recognised class of exceptions;
and that where the tracks seem to end without purpose in nasty
mountains, the words "Ruby Mines" or "Jade Mines" supply the
reason for their eccentricity.

Otherwise it is the river-system and the stream-system which
link the community. It was so in our own country. In Ballad
days we talked and sang of the great Lowland septs by the valleys
wherein they lived:

" March, march, Ettrick and Teviotdale!
    Why the de'il dinna ye march forward in order?
March, march, Eskdale and Liddesdale,
    All the Blue Bonnets are over the Border!"

Thus it was with us; and thus in Upper Burma one had to learn how the men of the Chaunggyi, the men of the Namkadin, the men of the Uyu, are divided from each other by the mountain ranges which separate the waters by which they live; and that rumours flying along the Meza might not yet have roused the men of the Mu.

Watersheds and water-systems are thus the primary source of information and deduction. There are, moreover, many complementary deductions to be made from them, relating to good or bad " going," the presence or otherwise of natives, and the presence or otherwise of water. The fact that a water-course is shown on the map by no means indicates that you will find water in it. Many spirits have been broken, and many plans gone astray, from that assumption. But you can, of course, be sure that if villages are marked on the banks of a *chaung*, that *chaung* at least will have water throughout the year.

A rudimentary knowledge of the language is helpful to map-reading, in that it helps you to construe place-names. We have got out of the habit in our country of making deductions from the names of places; it is no longer a useful practice in a land so highly developed as ours. In earlier days it may have been useful to be able to deduce that there was a bridge over the Cam at Cambridge, or that there was an eyot at Eton. But in Burma, to know that *Kan Gyi* means a big pool, or that *Kwin* means an open grassy space, may have a considerable bearing on your choice of a bivouac site, or a supply dropping area. This may seem a refinement of map-reading; certainly it is more important and more urgent that people should master, as so few do, all the conventional signs put on a map for their convenience.

Pity that poor cartographer. He stuffs his map with information, some of it unwittingly, till it almost squeaks; yet the average reader extracts the minimum from it. As our experience grew, we came to realise that not only our safety but also our success depended on a high standard of map-reading; and in the end we achieved it. We did not always bless the map-makers; when you are marching, striding along with a pack on your back for nine hours in the day, your mind becomes progressively more and more anti-social, and you curse the whole race of them. John Fraser used to prove by demonstration how the particular map-sheet on which we were working must have been compiled by a drunken Chinaman working by proxy on a Saturday night. I used to mouth a rhythmical curse on the officers whose names appeared at the bottom of the sheet, and I am glad that I have heard of no sudden deaths in the Surveyor-General of India's Department to strike me with remorse. In fairness it must be conceded that the standard of cartography in Burma was reasonably high, particularly when one takes into account the inconsiderate habit of the Burman of moving his village to pastures new every fifteen or twenty years, and taking the old name with him. It suits him for agricultural reasons, but on the maker—and user—of maps it bears hardly. When a village is shifted, its local track-system naturally shifts as well; and we learned to rely on natural features such as hills and rivers, in preference to man-made features such as villages and tracks.

We worked chiefly off half-inch maps, which covered an area some thirty-five miles square. When training men in map-reading, we used to issue identical sheets to the students on the scale of one between two, so that they could put their heads together and consult as to their answers. A good student, asked to describe a small area of country from the information given on the map, might say something on these lines:—

"The tilt of the country is eastward. The big *chaung* has a lot of villages on it, and paddy runs along it on both sides. Some of the tributaries might have water. Most of them have steep banks. The track down the big *chaung* is a cart-track, and possibly motorable. There's a monastery in this and that village. The jungle is bamboo. There should be a pond at Kangyi. The gossip of the countryside probably goes to Banmauk, via the motor road, and also to Pinlebu. (These were two places usually garrisoned.) You could travel by the Forest Boundary going north, and then along the watershed to the east. The jungle is thick in the *chaung* bottoms, but it looks fairly sparse in between them. Nearest motor roads are at Blank and Blank, and you are ten miles from the railway. Drainage finally into the Meza Valley."

Such a description is a useful mixture of fact and deduction, and everything in it would be of value to any one contemplating a journey in the area. We used to do a great many "map exercises," giving a situation as it might reasonably be known to us, plotting enemy garrisons, producing "locals" for interrogation, and then setting problems about cross-country marches, the setting up of road blocks, the organisation of supply drops and so forth. Always one would begin with these exercises in map-reading for a few minutes before tackling the problem proper.

There are exceptions to the rule of building villages along the river-banks. Where the inhabitants have achieved some measure of settled living, they live thus so far as possible, so that they may have water for themselves and for their agricultural needs. But in wilder country, where the inhabitants are Kachins or Nagas, more warlike than the Burmese or Shans, the villages are perched on the hill-tops. This is hard on the tired European, who has scrambled painfully up a nearly vertical path to his night's rest. But the Kachin or Naga woman speeds blithely down the hill to water, and up again nearly as blithely, despite her load of brimming water-pots. It makes one sick to see her.

To be a successful guerrilla fighter, you must understand the system of the bush-telegraph and its workings, both when it is working for you and when it is working against you. You must be able to assess the area of each gossip system; and to understand how the gossip system in each valley is insulated, to a greater or lesser degree, from the next. The degree of insulation depends on the degree of isolation; and this depends on the efficacy of the barrier dividing the valleys.

Therefore, when planning a cross-country march from the map, it is wise first to establish the "tilt" of the country, and then to look for the watersheds. They not only define the boundaries of gossip-systems; they usually afford the best route to travel. If for some reason you cannot use the tracks, the best going is to be found along the watersheds. There the jungle is always thinner; and along the top of them there is always some form of game-track. In cross-country marching, the most heart-breaking fate which can befall you is to find yourself travelling

across the grain of the country. I first learned this lesson vicar-
iously. In 1942, not long after the Japanese first occupied Burma,
a party of Gurkhas, under a British officer called Roberts, was
parachuted into Upper Burma to investigate conditions there,
and to return by way of Fort Hertz. It was not a very useful
expedition; and it was surrounded by a degree of secrecy ludicrous
to any one who had not been hopelessly bitten by the security
bug, which at that time infested the world in general and India
in particular. But Roberts, when he returned, wrote an excellent
and light-hearted report which went far to de-bunk his own
expedition; and two sentences out of that document often came
into my mind during my years of walking. The first was a
reference to a water-buffalo which watched his descent by parachute with a supreme indifference; the second to the fact that,
every time he came to the top of a crest, he saw countless other
crests ahead of him which he knew he must scale. Had we known
then what all of us know now, he would have been dropped somewhere on the same grain as that on which lay his destination;
and not on a range several scores of ranges west of the place to
which he was bound to make his laborious way.

I have often made a detour of as much as two days in order to
reach a suitable range for my journey. The same principle
applies to a short march. It is better and speedier to travel round
two sides of a square than to go direct from an ill-sited A to an
ultramontane B. Even on minor crests, separating two miniature
chaungs, this will often save minutes; and usually on the top
you will find a game-track of some sort. To this rule there are
few exceptions.

Sometimes it pays to travel along the bed of a *chaung*. This
is particularly so in flat country, where the *chaungs* tend to be
broad and sandy, and where the jungle trees cannot link their
branches across the intervening space. There are two main snags
to this. First, your footprints show up unmistakably British,
and proclaim to the world until the next rains come that you
have been this way. Secondly, sand makes heavy going; and your
delight when you first break out of the forest on to a *chaung* is
soon swallowed up in a yearning for solid ground that does not
overwhelm your ankles, nor fill your socks with grit.

Permanent disillusionment is one of the chief features of jungle travel. You are always wishing for some other form of "going"; and yet whenever your wish is granted, your satisfaction speedily vanishes, and you find yourself once more longing for that which you have lost. Take teak. Teak abounds in virtues. It is almost the only jungle where you can travel in any direction you like without large squads of "slashers" cutting a path before you. The undergrowth is restricted to teak seedlings two feet high, whose stalks are so soft that you can trample them as you go. Visibility is ideal; it extends to a hundred yards, at which distance the thick tree-trunks have become numerous enough to hide you, your fires or your smoke from all eyes. There are no branches to be cut from the tree-trunks; teak branches do not take off from the main trunk until a good twenty or thirty feet above your head.

Teak forests, on the other hand, are dry: you may travel ten or fifteen miles without water. Late in the dry season, the leaves come off the trees, exposing you to a merciless sun, and a choking dust that fills your throat and penetrates inside your sweaty clothing. As you move through the rhubarb-like leaves of the undergrowth, you make a noise as though you were trampling through broken china. You feel that even bamboo would be preferable to this.

Try bamboo. Green bamboo has its virtues too. You can find water in its hollow stalks. You can cook in it, and make water-bottles, rafts, anything you like, out of it. Your mules will eat it, and cease clamouring for oats and *bhoosa*. It makes splendid bedding. The clumps are often wide enough apart to enable the infantryman to run, only slightly bowed, swiftly to and fro between them. Over your head the branches meet, and conceal your presence perfectly from the air. But the arches are just too low for your mules to pass under, and must be cut. Cutting bamboo makes a noise that seems to echo into the far distance; and once you cut the key branch, the whole bamboo system falls in an exhausted heap at your feet. Then you must start cutting in earnest; each branch is entwined with a dozen neighbours; and when at last you have ploughed your way through, you see the next clump waiting to embrace you like an octopus ten yards on. Dead bamboo is even worse; it has few of the virtues of green; and it is already collapsed at your feet, offering you not even a sporting chance of being able to pass underneath it. And ten strokes at dead bamboo blunts the best edge of the keenest *dah*. Even evergreen, you think, would be better than this.

Evergreen offers no prospect but blood and tears, toil and sweat. That cynical officer, John Fraser, used to call it "Peter Fleming" jungle. There are so many leaves that you cannot see where the branches are; so many branches that, when you strike at one, a thousand shake and quiver, and help absorb the strength of your stroke. This is jungle so solid that it has to be cut out like the slice of a cake; half-a-mile-an-hour jungle; four-hundred-yard-an-hour jungle; cursing officers; sullen men; mules unloaded and column resting for an hour, then saddle up, move for twenty minutes, hear the slashing ahead of you, halt; off-load again. Give me teak.

Or indaing jungle, such as you find on red laterite, affording no shade from the sun, but beloved of red ants; prickly bamboo,[1] only negotiable by elephants; kaing grass, ditto (ten feet high, and solid); all these are beastly. Beware above all of optimistic estimates, beloved by distant headquarters, of your rate of progress across country. I once heard a responsible officer, of the breed which Wingate described as "clerical soldiers," say: "It's only six miles: surely it can't take them six hours."

I am bitterly against those who say that it is impracticable to embark on a fight by night; but I do say that you should never hope to march across country by night, even with the brightest of moons; and never try to march by night along a track unless with a good moon. It simply does not pay. Only for short distances is it worth while. If you must move at night, the use of torches should be forbidden: apart from making you conspicuous, every time you flash it on you are condemning yourself to some minutes of night-blindness thereafter.

We used to preach that there were four rules to bear in mind when making a decision as to whether to travel by track or across country.

Travel by track if you are in a hurry and you have reason to believe it safe; travel across country if you are in no hurry and do not want your presence known.

Travel by track if you do not have to linger at the end of

---

[1] Bill Smythies tells me that what I call "prickly bamboo" is really a species of palm.

your journey; travel across country if at the end of your journey you have to hang about.

Night is best for track-work, and day for cross-country.

Your aim is to achieve a sound combination of both.

With a few simple precautions, cross-country travel is absolutely safe. The jungle covers you like a mist, and you disappear from human knowledge. One of John Buchan's romances, *The Blanket of the Dark*, describes how an outlaw, for whom all England was searching, was able to submerge into a hidden England of gipsies and the like, and be lost to view for generations. This analogy was often in my mind.

For the average inhabitant of Burma does not willingly plunge into the jungle, any more than the average inhabitant of Britain normally chooses to leave the highway. You will never find a guide willing to go through the jungle; and in 1943, when we were tiptoeing home to India, one of our embarrassments was the way in which guides were always trying to lead us through the very villages which we had engaged them to avoid. The villager usually enters jungle only to find vegetables or to cut firewood; and the first indication that you are nearing a village is usually the thinning of the jungle, due to one or other of these activities. At about the same time, you may expect to hear the crowing of a village cock (not easy, until you are expert, to distinguish from the crowing of a jungle cock); the barking of a dog (not easy to distinguish from that of a barking deer); the sound of voices, laughter, or the chopping of wood. And there is a bird which imitates the last most skilfully.

There are other nasty noises. The chattering of monkeys, which echoes for miles; the thunderous buzz of a particular kind of cricket, which resembles the noise of a sawmill, and is accompanied by the falling of a saliva like rain; the sharp and unexplained crack of a dry tree. Twice, too, I have known troops deploy at what they thought was small-arms fire; the first time was a bamboo thicket on fire (and I must confess to having been deceived myself); the second a startled elephant galloping away through clumps of the same ubiquitous stuff. When bamboo is broken, or when it bursts in a hot fire, it makes a sound like the crack of a rifle; and any man whose fire emitted such a report, was immediately made to put it out, and to dine off cold food and water instead of a hot meal and that blessed beverage, tea. Bamboo splitting in fire had its own dangers: at least one man under my command, who had not learnt this lesson despite many warnings, lost an eye through a bamboo splinter out of a hot fire.

If you are moving cross-country, you do so probably from a desire to keep your presence secret. Only the nefarious-minded move in this way; and the chances are a thousand to one against your meeting anybody. There are few hazards. One such is a forest village; and the warning signs of this I have described already. Otherwise the chief tactical obstacles are roads, railways, open valleys and paddy. These are always worse in anticipation than they are in practice.

I have spent many hours gazing at such obstacles on a map. The longer you look at them, the less you like them. They are easily watched; and in addition they are usually lateral lines of communication in use by the enemy. One is sometimes faced with the problem of crossing a valley two or three miles wide without a shred of cover: you see it on the map two or three days ahead of you, and lose much sleep in wondering how you will do it. The answer lies in a moonlight night; and I remember crossing such valleys three nights in succession, marching by moonlight across uncannily dappled plains, and lying up each scorching day in friendly jungle. I once lay up for a whole day, just south of the Irrawaddy, with seventy men in a thicket a hundred yards wide, standing by itself in the middle of a treeless plain. Many escaped prisoners who have been on the run will know what that feels like.

When we were in weak parties, or when the need for secrecy was essential to success, we had to take great precautions; and the crossing of a road was an elaborate affair. A column, being four hundred strong, with perhaps sixty-five animals, takes ten or fifteen minutes to pass a given point; and when that point is in the open it becomes a nervous business. Once, in 1943, when we were green, I led my column across a motorable road between Pinbon and Sinlamaung, where the Japs had strong garrisons, which we were anxious to dodge: we were sneaking up to the railway, which we hoped to demolish; the process would take some time, and it was essential that our approach march should be secret. My tail-unit actually caught, as it crossed, a party of coolies carrying baggage; and this party turned out to be the baggage train of a strong Jap patrol which was ten minutes ahead of its coolies, and whose own tail I must have barely shaved with the head of my column. Thereafter, before crossing a frequented track, we used to close up just short of the obstacle, and cross it in a single wave, in groups of some thirty or forty, on a wide front; reforming again on the farther side.

That trick solved the problem of completing the crossing in the minimum time: there remained the problem of leaving no trace. We found, early on, that four men and two animals left virtually no trace whatever of their passage: an expert tracker could follow it, but the Japs are rotten trackers. From this there sprang the system of "breaking track": under which it was forbidden for more than that number to follow each other. On seeing the obstacle—usually a track running across one's front—the word would be passed back to break track. The column spread out left and right, a hundred yards; and then swept across the obstacle, more or less simultaneously, over a broad front. A small party, perhaps a section on either side of the leading platoon, would halt at the crossing place, facing away from the column as it crossed, looking up and down the track in case of interruption. When the column was across, it would obliterate the tell-tale footprints by brushing away the dust with handfuls of leaves, and then follow on. The only precaution that had to be observed was a five-minute delay on the far side of the track, to enable the scattered parties to close in again and form up for the onward march. I know of no occasion where this drill was properly carried out, on which the Japanese tumbled to what had happened.

If you ever had a hunch that you were being followed across country (for a column travelling across country leaves behind it a track as wide and trodden as any track in ordinary use) then once again the remedy was to break track. You halted; gave orders to each little group to turn right or left; gave out a compass bearing, whatever it might be; and ordered everyone to march on that bearing for five or ten minutes. At the end of that time, you halted and made contact with the various parties: then you set off again, confident that the Japs would have lost you. We did not often do this, but it was a comforting procedure at times when one had reason to fear pursuit.

In country where water was scarce, it was along the water-courses that the Japanese sought you; and so, on a cross-country march, it was advisable to cross a small stream in the same way, so that the Japanese, searching along the stream, could not find where you had crossed it. Otherwise your muddy feet, and the hooves of the mules, slipping where their brethren had muddied the banks before them, proclaimed to all passers-by that you had crossed their route. Where the *chaungs* were broad and sandy, concealment was more difficult, though it could sometimes be achieved by laying carpets of branches or leaves, and removing them when the column was over.

Going across country, the tradition is that the column commander leads. True, he may delegate the duty to some trusted subordinate, but normally he himself is in front of all except the "slashers," with his compass in one hand (elbow glued to his side) and his map in the other. All the time he is conscious of the "tilt" of the ground; he has an instinct for falling ground on this side, for rising ground on that, for a watershed yonder, for a *chaung* down there; he feels them as an experienced skipper feels the wind on his cheek or in his sails, hardly conscious that he does so. It is only a real expert, though, that has this sense developed to such a fine point that he can let his mind slip away from it altogether. Perhaps the nearest analogy, again from the sea, is of the skipper who, even asleep, is conscious of a turning tide, and of a ship that now streams at a different angle to that of a few minutes back.

Nor does the analogy of jungle-craft and seamanship end there. I have written elsewhere and spoken often of the strong resemblance of jungle navigation to the navigation of the sea. I compare it with navigation in a small boat in a thick fog, on leadline, chart and compass. You cannot see your landmarks, so you can hope for few, if any, "fixes." Your contour lines are your soundings; and except for them you must navigate on dead reckoning, by time and distance. If ever you are being steered in jungle by a stranger, watch him at the beginning of a stage. He will study the map before he goes, to give him an idea of what to expect; when the time comes to start, he will look at his watch, hold his compass in his hand, and look at it every twenty or thirty seconds. Every time he looks up from it you will see him fix his eye on some object a little way ahead, and know that he has chosen it to march upon. He will not move upon it slavishly, but generally; and in thirty seconds he will look at his compass again—a glance, and no more. Then relax, and think of something else, to take your mind from off your pack: for you are in good hands.

However thick or however thin the jungle, you should have a "slashing party" at the head of your column always. Every branch or twig plucking at your mule-loads reduces the life of the load; remember that every mule needs a five-foot path. Branches must be cut right back into the bush or tree, and saplings right down to the ground; otherwise the jagged stump projecting will wound an animal or a man.

Working across country is slow, and needs careful navigation; but it is almost always safe. If you run into trouble, you have either asked for it, or you have been extremely unlucky. The use of tracks is easier and quicker, and to some extent, particularly if you use guides, you are relieved of doubt as to whither you are heading. But they are liable to be watched by the Japanese, and if you use them you are almost certain to meet potential informers.

This naturally applies chiefly to the ordinary tracks between village and village, since they are the most frequented. They are usually marked on the map, although not always reliably. It is a pity that the maps do not distinguish between Government tracks (*asoya-lan*) and non-Government tracks: the former are all of a constant width and gradient, and are kept up by the villagers under Government orders. Under Jap domination some had been allowed to lapse; others were strictly maintained, and in addition to our own pre-war specifications the jungle on either hand was cut back several yards, presumably as a precaution against ambush. I have described how in 1944 Jim Harman drove a jeep and trailer some twenty miles out of Aberdeen and back, when for the second time we were operating north of Indaw. He broke a good few earthenware water pots in the process, and was not used—so to speak—in anger; but at least he proved the value of the *asoya-lan*, as a potential jeep *bahn*.

W.G.E.   L

We used to speak of a second category of man-made paths under the name of "jungle-paths." By these we meant tracks other than those between villages which nevertheless served the needs of villagers. Less well-trodden than the main communications, they were used for such purposes as cutting firewood and seeking vegetables, or for travelling to outlying paddy-fields and favourite fishing-pools. They were apt to lead one into trouble unless used with care; but they also provided one with the means of snapping up villagers, either for use as guides or as sources of gossip.

Then there were the game-paths, free of natives and often useful. They led along the tops of watersheds where the gradients were easy, and eventually down to water: game needs water as much as we do. The presence or absence of water could be deduced from the state of the animal droppings found on the track itself: old, dry droppings were a bad sign, fresh and dark were good. There were the timber-hauling tracks, easily recognisable from their width and from the deep corrugations caused by the heavy logs as the elephants dragged them along. These were also sure to lead to water: for, as all the world knows, the method of timber extraction in Burma is for elephants to drag the logs to a tributary of one of the great rivers, and to leave them there until the rains cause the stream to rise and carry them down to the sea. The Japs still practised extraction here and there, but only in a limited and haphazard fashion; so that only once in our two years of asking for trouble did we actually find it on a timber-track. Lastly there were the Forest Boundaries, shown on the map by a line of dots in pairs, and on the ground by special markings on the trees. These were always good going, as rides were cut along them to enable Forest Officers to go their rounds. These boundaries did not exist in the more remote areas, which had never been surveyed as Forests; but where they did they were a most useful adjunct.

We learned never to despise a track that was only just off our line of advance. If it ran within 20 degrees of the right bearing, it was well worth using. If you decide to use a track, it is as well to take the following precautions. Have a plan always ready in your mind, in case you walk into trouble; it will be too late to think it out when the bullets start to fly. A small point section should lead, far enough ahead to see round the next corner, but not so far ahead as to run any risk of taking the wrong turning. This party should, if possible, have a villager with them, to reassure any natives you may meet, since otherwise they tend to take to their heels; failing a villager, a Burma Rifleman in native dress is almost as good. In some ways he is better, since he can usually speak a little English as well as Burmese. In 1943, in a village in the Meza Valley, we picked up Maung Oh, a Karen Burma Rifleman who had hidden there, wounded, during the 1942 evacuation. His feet were hard enough from his year in native dress to go barefoot without discomfort, and we often used him to precede us, and to go into villages before us. He still had his Army Paybook when we picked him up.

Your leading men must watch the track carefully before they put their feet down to see whether it is in recent use. The Japs always wore a rubber shoe with a distinctive herring-bone pattern on the sole, quite different from the British. Boot-tracks were unmistakably British; elephant tracks or droppings, except in the Kachin Hills, were always sinister. When Burma was evacuated, all British-owned elephants were set free; but many were collected and used by the enemy. Only in the Kachin Hills did we see elephants still being worked by private owners; and Mike Calvert had a highly organised elephant train working for him in the hills east of the White City.

Even the stupidest private soldier became used to looking at tracks and speculating with fair accuracy who the last user was, and when he had passed that way. The practice taught one also to be circumspect about what tracks one left oneself; and sometimes we would put men to walk barefoot at the tail of the column to overprint our tell-tale boot-marks. The splendid villagers of the Kachin village of Saga, some miles east of the railway, saved my bacon for me in 1943 in this manner. I had come over the hills towards the railway; and, secure in the knowledge that the hill-folk were our devoted allies, I had taken no precautions to blot out our tracks. While we were buying rice at one end of the village, a patrol of Japs more than twice my strength approached the other. My party consisted of twenty-five all ranks, all tired, mostly weak, some sick and four wounded: we were in no state to fight if it could be avoided. The lieges of

Saga concealed us in the bamboos just outside the village; and later brought me news that the Japs were going to continue up the track down which I had just come. I immediately thought of our tell-tale footprints; but the villagers had thought of them already, and had despatched several men to block them out with their bare feet before the Japs renewed their journey.

According to those who had fought them on other fronts, the Japs were apt to put snipers in trees. I never met this at first hand, but we had to guard against it, and also against parties hidden on either side of the track. But when you are carrying a heavy pack, with the best will in the world your eyes drop to the ground and stay there. Watch a column on the move, standing five yards to the flank, and the odds are five to one that they will walk past you without spotting you, with heads bent and eyes down-cast like a Buddhist priest. It was necessary to detail a few men at a time to keep their eyes about them, relieving them every few minutes.

However much one studied the map before starting, to ensure that no unexpected feature on the ground took one by surprise, there were always many more tracks on the ground than there were on the map; and it was exceedingly difficult to decide which was the one you were trying to follow. When instinct, compass and map all clash, the rule is that the map is often wrong, you are sometimes wrong, but the compass is never wrong. If you are badly lost, don't go blundering on: sit down, smoke and think. Above all keep your sense of proportion, like the old Canadian bushman who was asked if he had ever been lost.

"No," he said, "I never bin lost; but once, for about three weeks, I was kinda puzzled."

Success in map-reading depends largely on confidence in one's own ability to read it. The results of such confidence are often surprising. There is a tale of a Gurkha, captured by the Japs in the fighting around Imphal, who managed to escape and make his way to the British positions. He was asked how he had found his way.

"Quite easy," he said. "I had a compass, and I had a map"; and he pointed out on his tattered map exactly how he had come. Here was this track; here was that nullah; he had dodged round the Japs here, and nearly been caught by a patrol there. The whole

story was convincing; the only surprising part of it was that the
map was a London street map, torn out of an old A.A. book;
but a little thing like that had not daunted the Gurkha in any way
at all. He had a map and a compass, and confidence in how to
use both.

You can get far more lost in a maze of tracks than you will
ever get travelling cross-country (that is, always provided you
have a map and compass). Guides certainly save time and worry;
they don't know a wide range of country, but within their
limited neighbourhood they are usually sure so long as they
stick to the tracks. You have to be careful where and when you
dismiss them: if they gossip, or fall into enemy hands, they may
bring you disaster. Unless you have been operating in a district
for so long that you know your strength is no longer a secret
from the enemy, it is worth going to some trouble to ensure
that your guides do not learn what it is. We used to pay them in
cash according to the amount of inconvenience to which we had
put them, so as to leave them with a good taste in their mouths:
this wasn't difficult, since their ideas of soldiery are Oriental,
and they are always agreeably surprised at non-Oriental treatment
of civilians, and at any payment whatever, except for services
involving treachery. They should never be told, when they are
engaged, where it is that you want them to go; and they must
never be dismissed until you have reached an area when they can
do you no further harm with their tongues. We often had a
string of disconsolate ex-guides trailing along at the tail of the
column, until they could be dismissed; they would come in
handy carrying the pack of a sick man. We usually parted friends
in the end.

On a Government track or on a motor-road, it is possible to
march two or three abreast; but marching on a motor-road is
not a habit in which we often indulged, and Government tracks
are as rare as they are welcome. At all other times, and for ninety-
nine hours of every hundred, we marched in single file—or, as
Wingate taught us to call it, "column snake." This formation
raises problems of intercommunication and control, but the
pros far outweigh the cons. It is a difficult target for the enemy
to attack; and if the leading platoon gets involved there is ample
time for the rest of the column to deploy and prepare for the

engagement. Non-Chindits used to be rather shocked at hearing that we had no system of flank-guards; but they were not half so shocked as we were at a certain division which afterwards started through our old stamping-ground at a snail's pace, owing to its insistence on flank-guarding every step of its advance. Good information is the best protection; and that we had in full measure from our trusty Burma Rifles.

The chief snag of the Column Snake formation is the fatigue caused to those well down the column. However steadily the head of the column tries to move, there are always dozens of minor checks, lasting perhaps a couple of seconds, perhaps eight or ten. These checks increase in time all the way down the column, and in the end, unless one is careful, large gaps occur; so that the men at the rear are always hurrying to catch up the front.

Say, for example, that I, at the head of the column, with compass and map in hand, am leading my troops along a track. A fallen tree lies across it—only a small one, diameter about ten inches, height above the ground perhaps a foot and a half. I step over it, checking for about two seconds, and carry on. John Fraser, just behind me (probably talking about food: he usually was), has to check a moment while I step over the tree; then he steps over it himself, and I am already five yards ahead. Toto the Terrible, his Karen orderly, checks in turn, and a few more seconds are added to the sum. After twenty men come the first mules, and each of them wants a couple of seconds to sniff at the obstacle before stepping over it. So the gap widens, and as there are thirty such checks in the course of an hour's stage, great gaps occur in the column, and the men at the rear are panting to catch up the next man ahead, who has just disappeared round a corner. At the end of the hour you halt for the statutory fifteen minutes; and when it is time to move off again, your tail is only just coming in to halt.

It needs constant watching: and however much care you put into it, the men at the tail are always tired. In an ordinary column, so far as possible, the order of march is varied, and the rifle platoon whose turn it is to march at the head dreads the morrow, when it will once again be marching at the tail. In a Brigade Headquarters, it is less easy to vary the order of march;

and when, at the end of the 1944 campaign, the doctors got at us in their zeal for scientific enquiry, they found that the accumulation of fatigue and nervous exhaustion was far higher in those sections which usually marched in the second half of Brigade H.Q., than it was among the leading elements.

Gaps were constant worries. In 1944 we had little portable wireless sets called "Walkie Talkies," in shape and size about the same as the cardboard box in which your shoes are delivered from the shop, with earphone and mouthpiece attached as on a telephone. These were distributed on a scale of six per column, and it was possible to call up the head of the column and report gaps as they occurred. In 1943 we had no such fancy aids, and the tracks were usually too narrow for a horseman to ride up and down. Our first effort to combat the problem of knowing when gaps were forming was to make the nearest officer to the gap blow "W" (for "Wait") on his whistle. That led to an absolute orgy of whistling, and the right to use one had to be restricted to three officers in addition to myself. Otherwise we were dependent on messages being passed up from behind by word of mouth; and these, as in the game of Russian Scandal, often became distorted *en route*. The classic case happened in a column other than mine, when the message: "There's a gap in the column," reached the leading troops as: "There's a Jap in the column!" It conjures up an enjoyable picture of the troops carrying on, looking stolidly to their front, not daring to look round, because of the fearful fiend close behind them treading.

If one knew the country to be Japless, then one was prepared to accept gaps, provided that they occurred between platoons and not within them. Each platoon then moved in its own time, halted at the end of the hour without bothering to catch up the platoon ahead, and moved on, still in its own time, at the end of its fifteen minutes' halt. The whole column was expected to be complete at the midday and evening halts. If on the other hand Japs were thought to be about, then one went to great pains to keep together, and accepted as graciously as possible the consequent reduction in speed.

Travelling cross-country seldom led to gaps being formed, since the going was always much slower; and in those conditions the irritating factor was not the constant galloping to catch up, but the standing about under a heavy load while the slashers in front completed the cutting of the track.

But so far as I was concerned, the most maddening element in jungle travel was the most trivial, so trivial indeed that I can hardly bring myself to confess to it. As one marched along at the head of the column, particularly at night, one was for ever blundering into huge and horrible spiders' webs, and getting a mouthful of web. It affected me as it might affect a hysterical schoolgirl; and sometimes I dream of it still. I have confessed my weakness: let nobody tease me about it.

Looking back on those months of incessant jungle-travel, I realise that we suffered from a form of agoraphobia. Our vision was always restricted, and a "view" occurred not more than once or twice a month. I suppose our outlook on the world must have resembled that of a rabbit in long grass, except that rabbits don't travel in Column Snake. Monkeys do, though; and we often saw long processions of them running nimbly in single file parallel to our line of march, and sometimes across it. Old wizened venerable monkeys; young, sprightly and rather bounderish looking male monkeys; arch, skittish and (according to their lights) soignées female monkeys; matronly, housewifely, harassed-looking mother monkeys with their offspring on their backs, whose pink hands had a good, hearty grip of the maternal topknot. They always got a cheer from the men as they galumphed past us, and usually a ribald cry of "There goes 23 Brigade!" Their discipline as regards noise was sadly lacking, but they certainly knew all about movement across country.

IX

BIVOUAC

I CANNOT HOPE to convey the utter boredom of a long march. When in 1942 we were training in the Central Provinces of India, Orde Wingate, in one of his many talks, said: "The first five days of a long march are the worst." A legend grew up that he had in fact said, "The first five months," and this figure was often wanly quoted.

For those marching near the head of the column, where the dust or the mud (as the case might be) was moderate, the process was barely tolerable; for those farther down the column it was sheer hell; for the muleteers, who not only bore the same burdens as the rest of us, but had to cope with their animals as well, it must have been the equivalent of seven or more very special hells. Duncan Menzies, my Column Adjutant in 1943, and I each led and looked after a mule for twenty-four hours on the Manipur Road to see what it was like; and we were both heartily glad when that short period was over.

For the ordinary soldier, life had few interests to relieve the monotony of marching. A Column Commander had plenty to occupy his mind; and he, like some other privileged folk, could at least vary his position in the long snake; but an ordinary soldier saw the same thing in front of him day after day in absolute slavery. For some, it was the back view of the same man; for some, the back view of the same mule: the same ears, the same load, the same rump, the same tail hanging down, the same flick of the same fetlocks every second of every hour of every day of every week of every month, interrupted only by halts and battles.

For two long years we used to amuse ourselves discussing the Victory March through London after the war, and deciding which of us—and which mules—should represent the Force. In the end, the question didn't arise, as the authorities ruled that the Force shouldn't be represented at all. I fancy that we hadn't marched far enough to qualify.

I imagine that most people evolved something of what psychologists call escape mechanism. I certainly did. I have described elsewhere how one used to daydream, or to recite, in the free and unenslaved recesses of the mind, long wads of poetry, Psalms and Paraphrases. But to offset the pleasure of these, little unwanted sentences, or snatches of tunes, used to come into one's mind and drill away like the torture of dripping water, until one managed to summon up a long narrative dream to exorcise them and drive them out. I remember one which derived from a story by Ian Hay of somebody rowing in a bumping race at Cambridge: it described how, at the end of the race, the hero slumped over his oar, oblivious "of everything save the blesséd fact that he need row no more." Those words were always with me, and I knew just exactly how he felt.

After each hourly halt, one swore one wouldn't look at one's watch until something like the hour was up; yet I always found that the first time I looked at it, no more than twenty minutes out of the hour was gone. And then one would set to dreaming. Sometimes, with a really good dream, one would become absorbed in it as in a really good book; almost to the point where one resented the interruption bound to come with the halt, when people would break in upon it. My own feelings then used to be almost those which I experience when, absorbed in a first-class novel, I notice that it is almost five o'clock, and realise with distress that in a minute there will be an interruption for tea. On such occasions as these (and I fear they were infrequent) you became almost reconciled to the rude whistle that summoned you to heave yourself to your feet, hoist your pack on to your shoulder, step off again—and try to like it.

One of the dreams that haunted me most, particularly towards evening, was the mere thought of lying stretched out full length. Such a posture seemed the ultimate luxury, and it was hard to believe that in in hour or two, this pleasure would actually be ours to enjoy for the whole long night. Yet, stirring at the same time, far back in memory, was a dim recollection of a joy even more precious, savoured long ago, and probably never to be savoured again: to lie in that same posture in the sleeping car of a train. I thought of that far more often than I thought of a bed: the wheels sweeping along smooth railway lines, and the long miles rolling beneath you as you lay: four hundred miles, five or six weeks' marching, covered in the span of a single night of sleep.

What a fuss there used to be before the war, and even during the war in other campaigns, about where one should camp for the night! We made none. We chose no site, we worried not at all the proximity of water, dominating heights or anything else. We marched until dusk, left the track, drew the secrecy of the jungle about us, and bedded down with less fuss than the dog who walks three times round before he settles. Our procedure varied little, except in special circumstances. In waterless country, for instance, when Japs were close at hand, we avoided camping near water, since that was where we should be sought. But normally we marched until it was near darkness, and then would bivouac, judging the time just carefully enough to get settled in before it was too dark to see.

Whether we were marching on an existing track, or cutting our own as we went, the procedure was the same. (I except those occasions when we knew for certain that there were no Japs for many miles.) The whistle would blow "Halt!" I would choose the side of the track where the jungle looked most suitable, and announce a compass bearing leading that way, on which all ranks were to march for five minutes. The whole column then turned in that direction, and "broke track." That is, not more than four men and two animals were allowed to follow each other; but each such party, moving parallel to its neighbours, would leave the track and plunge into the jungle on the bearing given. By this means, no trail was left which could be followed up by an enemy.

While most of the column was thus burrowing into the forest, parties of two men, known as "stops," would automatically be dropped from whichever platoon was responsible for that duty for the day: these would make sure that there was no pursuit.

("And the city, dusk and mute,
Slept, and there was no pursuit."

This was another little wisp of long-remembered verse that used to flutter into my mind, night after night, to be chased savagely away.) If for some reason we were halting some time before dark, and there was a possibility that we were being followed, more men would lead on down the track for half a mile, to lay misleading footprints; so that their sudden cessation where we had turned off would not betray our hiding-place.

Meanwhile the bulk of the column, swearing dumbly, was pushing with its shoulders into the jungle and parting the inhospitable vines with their hands, for the allotted five minutes. (We dealt in minutes as being surer than hundreds of yards, which were hard to judge in thick jungle.) At the end of that time, the whistles would sound for "Halt!" the column would turn to its front again, and find itself once more in "snake," albeit something ragged. Having ensured that all its pieces were duly articulated, I would move off again for a few yards, secure in the knowledge that I had broken my tell-tale track; and would lead until I was sure that a respectable chunk of jungle lay between us and it. By this means we were free to make fires and to indulge in quiet talk, without fear of being overheard by passing natives or pursuing foe.

We have gone far enough. I select my tree, "The Commander's Tree," and point it out to my Adjutant or my Orderly Officer behind me. That tree is sacred. Only I and my immediate staff may go near it, and nobody else may settle down within twenty yards of it. It is my command post, my office, my dining-room and my bed; my cell, my library, my country house, my ivory tower. Within two minutes my big map, unloaded from off its mule by the Intelligence N.C.O., will be propped up against it, so that I can go into a trance over the war situation if I wish. Better than a tent, or a flagship, or even the shell of a snail, this bivouac is my little kingdom; and when I say "Good-bye" to it to-morrow at dawn, I shall feel that I have dwelt here for years and years.

With the Commander's Tree as the centre of the circle, everybody knows where to go, and which is to be their segment of the perimeter: a staff officer points out the boundaries between each. My pack is already off my shoulders: it has slipped off, and, after a brief and blasphemous interlude while it has fouled the hilt of my *dah*, it now lies abandoned at the foot of the tree. The inside of it, where it has been against my shoulders, is greasy and black with sweat. Without it, I feel so light that I might be a barrage balloon, striving to soar above the treetops. I watch the men go past, bent almost double under theirs, and sweat making runnels down their faces and hanging in their beards, their bush-hats floppy and covered with little bits of leaf, legacies of their last few minutes of forcing their way from the track. Golly, do I look like that? I suppose I do. The men mostly grin as they trudge past, and some of the incurable crack a joke. I suddenly feel fond of them beyond the ordinary.

The officers have two or three minutes to get free of their own packs; and then, while the men are busy unloading the mules, the whistle goes for "Orders" and the officers come to The Tree. They, like me, are feeling suddenly as light as thistledown, burdened only with their maps and carbines, and perhaps their belts and *dahs*. I confirm our position; give out the rendezvous in case we get scattered during the night or the next morning's march; and say at what time we will move in the morning. Nine times out of ten, I add to this last the phrase: "Not having had"; occasionally it is: "Having had": the missing word at the end of each is "breakfast." For I like the cool hours just after dawn for marching, and I like to feel, when I stop for breakfast, that at least two hours of travelling are behind us; if we eat before we leave, we must pay for it by marching for four or five hours with no more than the statutory fifteen-minute halt at the end of every hour to look forward to, which is bad for mules and men alike.

Time was when I believed implicitly in the old legend that the British soldier must have his "gunfire," his early morning cup of *char*, before he does anything else. It was not until we were some fifty miles east of the Chindwin, in 1943, somewhere near the Nam Kadin, that Orde Wingate persuaded me to have a week's trial without it. I was highly sceptical, and my officers shared my view; but he proved plumb right, as he nearly always did: and since those days I have never allowed it to become a routine, but only a rare, special and genuine treat. The hours of coolness are too precious to waste, and so are the hours of darkness when a man ought to be sleeping; I never let them get up early to brew tea, and we soon got used to going without.

It was a recognised thing that fires were to be out an hour and a quarter after getting into a nightfall bivouac, except for the signallers and cipher operators, who might still be working, and who were richly deserving of any small privilege which it was in our power to give. So our only other orders of an evening dealt with our protection: how many listening posts we must have. Sentry posts or listening posts were all that was necessary, provided that the usual precautions had been taken of getting deep into the jungle and well off the track. Stand-to at dawn we never had.

To be caught in bivouac you must either have been very unlucky or very careless: it was a thing that shouldn't happen. Of all the people whom I have known to be caught, the only one who can be fully acquitted of carelessness was one who had been condemned by my own orders to remain for good reasons in a locality which was heavily overJapped and over-inhabited: natives denounced him, but he was able to beat off the attack, with the loss of one officer and one man who were outside the bivouac watering their animals, and a couple of men killed at their posts.

I shall tell in another chapter how one column in my Brigade got caught while going into bivouac with too few precautions: they took a chance which many people have got away with, which proved to be the hundredth time. In their case, they had the excuse of appalling fatigue, and a thirst which had not been slaked with a drink for thirty-six hours. A case with less excuse concerned a column (not, let me hastily say, one of mine) which, marching by moonlight along a railway line in close proximity to the enemy, decided to halt for a few hours' sleep. Instead of going deep into the jungle, they slept a mere fifty yards from the railway; and when they got up to move in the morning the enemy was around and among them. Many of them got back to India, but they had ceased to exist as a column. It is easy to find fault, but fatigue engenders carelessness; and one night in 1943 in a narrow glen not far from Pinlebu, I took an equally foolish risk: I got away with it, but I remind myself of it now as an antidote to pride.

At all events, when proper precautions have been taken, a couple of listening posts between one's bivouac and the track are good enough; and the "stops" could be called in, half an hour after dark, unless one has especial reason to be windy. And now the bivouac is devoted to a sort of weary joy. Fires have been lit; each little group of men has organised itself for cooking, and the flames are leaping up from dry sticks laid between long green logs, across which mess-tins and crash-tins are balanced. A crash-tin is a home-made cooking pot for brewing tea: it is no more than a round tin, the former container of some canned food, with a strand of wire twisted across its mouth; it hangs from the man's equipment, and serves both to shock the orthodox soldier and to bolster up the genuine soldier's morale. It is far better for brewing tea than any article of issue, and I would jettison my mess-tin before my crash-tin every time—quite apart from the fact that the mess-tin issued in India buckled and gave up the ghost after six weeks of moderate use.

The mules will have been watered at the last stream: they will not drink after dark or before dawn. The men were taught never to expect water at a bivouac: except where there was a real water-crisis, they were always expected to arrive in bivouac with full water-bottles. If a stream occurred within half an hour of going into bivouac, they were also given a chance to fill their *chagals*, a canvas bag capable of holding water for that length of time or a little more. If by chance a stream was near the bivouac, then they would be allowed (enemy situation permitting) to drain their water-bottles, and go down to the stream to re-fill; so that it was a normal sight to see a water-party setting off under an officer, each man with his rifle and a handful of *chagals* to fill for himself and his friends.

To sleep on top of your water was a bad plan. Apart from the fact that it was by water that the enemy would seek you, there was the further drawback that mosquitoes were usually more plentiful; and there is nothing more miserable, when you are settled down in your blanket and just dozing off, than to hear that triumphant little *z-z-zing*, needle-sharp, in your ear, which is the mosquito's way of conveying to you, "I've arrived!" and to his buddies, "Boys, look what I've found!" I used to sleep with my Balaclava over my head, and my heels drawn up under my behind, to leave as much blanket available as possible for tucking in the whole of my head except my nose; but it wasn't any good.

There was weariness in plenty in those bivouacs; but there was delight too; and utter joy in seeing one's blanket lying ready for one, the firelight on the bearded faces, and rosy on the tree-trunks and against the greenery overhead; the sparks flying up into the branches; and the thought of the long night ahead with nothing to do but lie, and sleep. There was delight also in the feeling of security, knowing that all soldierly precautions had been taken, and that one was snugly and Bristol-fashion on one's moorings. One always dreaded having to fight the last hours in the afternoon; the possibility of meeting the Japanese just before dreams of the bivouac were about to be translated into fact. More than once that trouble has befallen me at that moment, and it is almost more than one can bear. One longed to cry out: "O chivalrous Japanese, be a sport! We are *very* tired to-night, and we do want to go to bed. We are quite prepared to fight you to-morrow morning, but, dear Jap, please don't start anything now, *please* don't." I was never in action once in Burma, nor were any Chindits so far as I know, when we didn't go into battle absolutely and thoroughly exhausted before we ever began; and that breeds casualties more surely than any incompetence or ill luck. One reads with envy of people in other theatres being pulled out to rest before an attack, and I remember seeing troops moving up to the attack in Arakan carrying nothing but haversacks: but we had to attack with all our worldly goods on our backs, or to risk losing them.

So the leaping firelight was a joy; for it was the symbol of our peripatetic hearth, and where we ate we slept. We are often asked whether we were not afraid of our fires giving us away. There was not the slightest risk of it. The forest closed over one's head; it was secret as a cellar; and as for giving one away on ground level—even in teak, the most open of jungles—a fire cannot be seen from more than a hundred yards, since at that distance the trunks of the trees have closed in to make a timber wall. It was just outside that limit that we would place our listening posts. Smoke is far more likely to give you away than flame, and therefore night is safer for fires than the day-time. Even so, with training it is possible to make fires practically without smoke; and anybody who has flown over jungle will know how many columns of smoke rise everywhere above the trees from native fires at all times. There is mercifully no difference between smoke from a British and smoke from a native fire, unless it be that the native, with his clearer conscience, sends up a more generous column. I have remarked the same thing flying over the jungles of Equatoria and Uganda in an Empire flying-boat; and in Burma I have deliberately sought in vain the fires of my own troops at midday, when I knew them to be halted. I have in mind one day in particular, when I was looking in a light plane for two columns of the Leicesters somewhere near Pinwe. I marked and circled a dozen plumes of smoke, peering into the teak out of which they were rising, and found neither British nor Japs, but either scurrying, white-clad Burmans, or nothing at all.

Our normal availability of water and tea would run to a cup with the meal, and another just before we raked the fire out. Of the many statistics in my mind for which I shall probably never find a use again, there remains the relation between the contents of a water-bottle and the making of rice and tea: one water-bottle will give you a mess-tin of rice, a cup of tea, and still a little water left over for the morning. As for cooking, each man to his taste; but of all my pet aversions in the way of food, "biscuit burgoo" heads the list. All soldiers go in for it, apparently, except myself. In this imaginary bivouac of ours, biscuit burgoo will not be on the menu.

From behind my tree comes the sound of one of the wireless sets at work. Of all the hardships which the signallers have to bear, the most cruel is the loss of this happy hour in the evening, when men sit around their fires and sip their tea, spinning it out as long as they can, smoking one of their rare cigarettes with it, and gossiping. Signals and ciphers fare ill in this respect. I have always been lucky in the men given to me to discharge these all-important duties. I was lucky in 1943, with the indomitable Foster and White, who, after their wireless sets were lost, turned themselves into first-class infanteers for the trip home to India, and were mentioned in despatches. I was lucky in 1944, with the signal section which had been with 16th Brigade in every action since the war began, and in the Palestine rebellion before it: some of them had been well over six years abroad, and Tommy Moon, their commander, no less than eight. When we got into bivouac of an evening, and the others got down to making up their fires, Rudd and Welsh and the rest of the operators would start looking round for a suitable tree over which to fling their aerial, an elaborate process which involved tying it to a heavy weight and swinging it round their heads to the danger of all who passed that way. They were a cheerful lot, and the best bunch of operators I ever had or saw.

To and from the wireless set would go Jim Buchanan, the tall, burly, short-sighted, Glasgow cipher officer, and as cheerful a chap as ever concealed the fact with a gloomy face. The plague of his life was corrupt signal groups. One filthy wet night up in the Patkai hills he was bringing John Marriott, the Brigade Major, a signal which he had just deciphered, when he tripped on a root and let loose a horrid oath.

" *Jim!*" we all said, in mock-reproachful chorus.

" Sorry, Sir," he said; " I'm afraid that was another corruption."

The others would come along to The Tree, partly to report, partly to hear the gossip: the doctor; the Animal Transport Officer; John Fraser, to boast how much better a meal he had had than we, owing to some goody or other that his Burma Riflemen had scrounged in the course of their duties. Then perhaps I would haul myself up reluctantly for a walk round and a few words at each long fire, where the brew-cans were on for the second time, and the final half-cup of *char*; where the smell of wood-smoke pleasantly hung. Some of the men would already be rolled up in their blankets, doubled up two by two if the weather were cold: we had only a blanket each, and many of them preferred to sleep together for mutual warmth, and for two blankets instead of one. Of those thus early bedded, some might still be sharing in or listening to the talk; but most would be fast asleep, in a heavy slumber which nothing could disturb. We used to average nine hours of sleep a night, and it wasn't a minute too much.

Then one would stroll back to The Tree, and perhaps have a talk about " the form" before bed. This group would be Duncan Menzies and John Fraser in 1943; John Marriott, John Fraser, and Wilfred Kinnersley, the senior Intelligence Officer, in 1944. More tea, the last, spun out as long as might be; soon the signallers would report that reception was getting bad, and at last that it was hopeless. And so to bed, in that enticing blanket.

When I was a boy, and we used to camp out at Glowrie or in the Cowan Glen, we thought that the expert always dug a hole for his hip-bone, and religiously followed that rite ourselves. Not so here: a scrape with the *dah* at the leaves, a cut with the *dah* at the roots if there were any; and there was your bed for the sleeping in. There weren't many preparations to be made: boots off if there were no Japs about, on if there were; hat off, to make a pillow (the head fitted beautifully into the crown of it, and, with one's boots under it to give a little more height, it was a hundred per cent.). Balaclava over one's ears, heels drawn up to one's behind, blanket tucked in all round, nine hours' sleep ahead of one; nothing to worry about; look at the fireflies; smell the woodsmoke; hark at the crickets; nothing to worry about; sleep. . . .

" *Z-z-zing!*"

Mosquitoes were certainly hell, but one got used to them. Indeed, one was so tired that nothing could keep one awake, not even aches in the legs and across the shoulders. The only period during the whole two years when we suffered from lack of sleep was on the last two or three weeks of the journey out to India in 1943; and then the causes were threefold. First was undoubtedly the cold. We had no blankets and no groundsheets, having lost them in the various disasters which had befallen us; and it got very chilly after about two in the morning. Secondly, we were undoubtedly rather jumpy, and I for one kept waking up having dreams that we were safely out, to find with a nasty feeling in the tummy that we weren't. (After we got out, I kept waking up dreaming that we were still in.) Lastly, we were a mass of lice; and as soon as one lay down and composed oneself for sleep, the lice woke up and went for a constitutional. But except for that short period, I always slept like a top, and I think this was true of everybody.

Rain, to be sure, might keep one wakeful, if it came unexpectedly; but we were all weather-wise, and seldom to be caught napping. When we had groundsheets there was nothing simpler than to rig a waterproof shelter, lashing two of them together with lengths of cord if it was early in the campaign, or with parachute cord if it was later. The trick was to make the lashing tight, with a couple of rolls to the sheets where they joined, so as to cheat the determined jets of water which could otherwise be trusted to find their way through. The joint sheet would then be stoutly lashed to trees or stakes two to three feet above the ground: we would roll underneath them, and there perform prodigies of clothes changing. One precaution had to be taken which might not strike the greenhorn: a length of string must be tied taut across the middle so as to make a rooftree. If this were overlooked, a deep reservoir of water would collect over your head, with one of two results: either the whole edifice would collapse; or, if it were strong enough to survive that threat, the opposite would happen: the cavity would fill until its mounting waters lapped over the sides. The results for those sleeping below it did not greatly vary.

If groundsheets were lacking, either because of some disaster or because it was necessary to travel especially light, some form of shelter had to be built if the rain showed signs of being heavy. Several patterns were favoured. You could either build a lean-to against a big tree, semi-detached; or a fully detached house standing proudly in its own undemarcated grounds. Roofing material varied from grass, which had to be lavishly applied, to teak or plantain leaves, of which three thicknesses would be ample to keep out normal rain. These would be kept in place by crosspieces of stick laid lightly across the thatching, and by string of vine or bamboo. (Bamboo string is easy to make, provided that you take it from the green outside edge of the bamboo, and do not attempt tight knots or super-hard twists.) Bamboo leaves are also reasonably good for roofing, except that you need a good many of them, and they require more elaborate fastenings: you should also avoid the proximity of mules, who like bamboo leaves as an article of diet.

No pleasure is more unmixed than lying awake a little when the cruel hour of rising is yet far distant. When all was quiet in the camp, the very silence was worth savouring. If it were a moonlight night, there were bright galleries among the trees where little lumps of blanket lay like molehills; beneath them men were sleeping, but not even heavy breathing made the outline stir. If the moon were high, the shadows of standing mules were foreshortened and stumpy; if low, they were long and grotesque; and the same applied to their loads and the saddlery, lying on the ground near by them. The saddles would be standing on their noses, in a shape curious to the stranger but very familiar to us; near them would be the double line of loads, ready to put on in haste in case of alarm: the big, ungainly wireless sets, the boxes of mortar bombs, the Vickers machine-guns with their long and sinister barrels, the leather *yakdans* with miscellaneous stores. Seeing them so, and knowing that, in the black shadows beyond the moonlight, other loads and sets of saddlery were lying in the same orderly fashion and in the same state of readiness, soothed one into the knowledge that one could sleep with a clear conscience.

That knowledge was the sole essential sleeping-draught that the Column Commander must have. Once the fires were down and the lights out and the men sleeping, it was too late to wonder whether all was in order, and still to sleep at ease. I used to think of John Buchan's verses at the beginning of "Salute to Adventurers":

> "I sing of old Virginian wars,
>   And you have known the desert sands,
> The camp beneath the silver stars,
>   The rush at dawn of Arab bands. . . ."

The silver stars look down benignly enough on the soldier who has done his duty; but on the neglectful with a celestial reproach.

So, when we came into bivouac at night (or, as we often did when moonlight and a good track tempted us to march by night, in the welcome light of morning), all things were set down so that we could bestir ourselves and be ready; whether to fight, or to move at the first crack of a bullet or thunder-clap of a mortar-bomb; and the Jap thinks it stylish to open proceedings with a mortar-bomb whenever he can. When the mules came in, they were off-loaded in line ahead, in groups pertaining to their parent platoon. Each mule halted, was unloaded, and marched away, leaving his load in its two halves, on either side of where he had stood. The next halted short of him, and his own two half-loads set in line with the two first. Thus, when all twelve mules of the Support Platoon had been unloaded, their loads stood in a double line; so that next morning the mules marched into the space between the loads like a railway train between two platforms, and the loads had merely to be put upon the animals' backs—a drill as easy by night as by day. I often marched before dawn so as to keep us handy and practised in the art of loading up by night.

As for mules, so for men. They were taught, before bedding down, to call a mental roll of where all their property was. Even although their blankets and other necessaries were out of their pack for the night, each man's pack was to be shut up and fastened and ready to put on his shoulders in the same state of prepared-ness as that in which the Children of Israel ate the Passover. I can remember my own roll-call now, down to the last detail. The eyeglass which I wear, which normally trusts to luck (and, according to my enemies, to saliva), is reinforced in the field by some running rigging around my neck: at night, it was removed and suspended by the same running rigging from a branch sticking out over my head from the Commander's Tree. When I lay down, and before I allowed myself to think of sleep, I would run over all my possessions in my mind, starting with my eye-glass over my head, and finishing with my hat and my boots under it. The mental roll-call was therefore also a mental tuck-up.

Each man knew to within twenty seconds how long it took him to get up in the morning. Some platoons, those with many mules, rose earlier than others; but it still seemed fair that each platoon should be awakened only when it had to be. The Support Platoon and the Sabotage Platoon won on other swings what they lost on this particular roundabout: the job of duty platoon or of tricky patrols came their way less often than they came the way of the others. Thus, the sentries knew exactly when to waken each platoon—and exactly when to waken Me. I used to scowl at the sky for precisely one minute, thinking how beastly it looked.

Some masochistic instinct made it impossible for me to forgo this daily minute of self-torture. It was beyond a doubt the worst moment of the day. I used to think of the hundreds of miles behind me, and the hundreds ahead, and, more especially, of the particular hours ahead on that particular day. An utter weariness of muscle would set in, with all the aches of yesterday cramping the sinews of thigh and calf and shoulder; and another snatch of long-remembered verse, regular as ritual, from A. E. Housman, would flash on to the screen of my brain like a platitudinous subtitle in a film:

"... and all's to do again."

Then the sense that I, of all people, must never be late (and I never was, not once) would rescue me, roll back my blanket and get me on my feet.

Around me in the darkness, the camp, unhurried but busy, was alive. The restive mules, whose occasional movement had been the only sound in the night, were pawing the ground as they were saddled, in the mulish equivalent of my recent mood, while their bits were forced into their reluctant mouths. Teams of men were heaving their loads on to the elusive hooks of the pack saddlery. The last remnants of the previous night's fires were being covered over with leaves and twigs; for it was our boast that nothing but pressed-down grass where men had lain might mark the site of a vacated bivouac: pressed-down grass revives in a few hours' sun, forgets its shame and stands proudly once more. The only sound from the men was muttered swearing at the animals, and the suppressed clearing of throats.

I read somewhere lately, marked the source and straightway forgot it, of the sound of an army in bivouac clearing its throat in the early morning. It is true. It is also a euphemism. For an army in the field coughs like hell when it first rouses for the day. And this is a luxury which cannot be allowed to a guerrilla column in enemy country. I had a strict rule that anybody coughing within a quarter of an hour of getting up in the morning should have his cigarette ration docked, and only the stern enforcement of this order effected an improvement. I once promulgated a set of training rhymes based on Admiral Hopwood's classic *Laws of the Navy*, of which one verse ran as follows:

"Would'st hazard thy life for a gasper?
  Ye stand to lose more than ye gain.
If ye cough when ye smoke in the morning
  Be wise and beware, and refrain."

The life of a rabbit is forfeit
  If he hazard the gaze of a stoat:
More foolish the death of a Chindit
  Who dies from a frog in the throat."

Let us therefore say that in all the movement going on, nobody
coughs; or, if they do, that that section in Doc. Donaldson's
panniers (on what are so picturesquely called the "Medical
Mules") known as Medical Comforts, is richer by several days'
rations of cigarettes, mulcted by way of a fine from their original
owner.

In hot weather, the best precaution against thirst is a real
long drink first thing in the morning, before you feel the need
of drinking. If water was near by, or if there was a reasonable
prospect of a fill in the next hour or two of marching, all ranks
were induced to drink as much as they were able, and far more
than they wanted. Nobody wants to drink a whole water-bottle
full of water before dawn, but it is a wise measure; and the
benefit to be derived from it lasts long into the day, even after the
sun has been engaged for several hours on doing its worst. This
is a wise word, too often forgotten or not believed.

Ten minutes before we are due to move off, the first whistle
goes—the first signal of the morning applicable to all, the first
synchronisation of the day. I have from now ten minutes in
which to perform my toilet. It consists of having my blanket
available for my servant to roll up, so that he can complete my
loathly pack; I must put my boots on, if they are off, and lace
them up in any case; I must do up such buttons as I have undone;
I must put on my hat, which will need a punch or two on changing
its functions from pillow to headgear; I must (very probably)
spit; my belt must go on, with its various protuberances of
bullet-pouch on my left front, compass on my right front, *dah*
on my right buttock and pistol on my left buttock; then my
pack, with my servant pushing it manfully upward (Bob M'Clung
did this at every halt in five months); and last of all my map-
case to be slung over my shoulder. Towards the end of the
process the two-minute warning whistle has sounded; as it
ends I move to my place at the head of the column; and when
Dot-Dash ("A" for "Advance") sounds, I can step off, sure in the

knowledge that behind me, without fuss, bother or crisis of any sort, the Column Snake is uncoiling itself and stepping off in good order and military discipline.

As I move off, the first glimmer of tropic dawn punctually and precisely splits the night. The bivouac, so lately strange, is now a friend, and added to the long roll of ephemeral homes already in my memory. The jungle will swallow it again, and soon; but we have slept a night there.

X

FOOD, WATER AND HEALTH

FIGHTING in our fashion, our needs were surprisingly few. I put them down as five—food, water, information, ammunition and health. Of these, the greatest are food and water.

After our first Expedition, with scant propriety (as he did not fail to point out), I tried to make two conditions with Orde Wingate before signing on with him to enter Burma for the second performance. The first stipulated that we should not go in again unless we were going to stay in: we all hated to think of what might be happening behind us across the Chindwin, in the shadows of the Japanese occupation, to those who had helped us at the risk of their lives. Next time, I said, we must go in and stay in. My second stipulation was that we must fare better in the way of food. Both these conditions were accepted, although unfortunately the first was not fulfilled.

The worst feature of the 1943 Expedition, apart from having to abandon our wounded, was the lack of food. Only five aircraft could be spared us for our air supply; and of these two were Hudsons, which proved useless for the purpose. With so few aircraft, the number of missions they could fly was strictly limited; and it was ordained that we could only have one drop every seven days at most. This meant that we must carry seven days' rations; it meant also that those rations must be light; and we were further told that we must be prepared to make seven days' rations last for ten days, eking them out by local purchase and by hunting.

Hunting proved almost impossible. We were always in a hurry, and a marching column makes enough noise to scare away any game that might be about. We rarely saw any, and when we did it was either out of shot or we were tiptoeing owing to the presence of the enemy, and shooting had to be forbidden. I only once sent out a hunting party deliberately, and they returned with nothing but a minute tortoise, which doesn't go very far among three hundred famished men. Twice, however, in 1943, we managed to shoot water-buffaloes. The first occasion was especially fortunate, as we had had nothing to eat for three days except two tablets each of malted milk; I had already lost several men who were too weak to struggle on, and few of us would have lasted much longer had it not been for that lucky encounter. The second time we were not in such dire straits, but the beast was welcome all the same; she was grazing on the banks of the Chaunggyi River when my faithful batman, Peter Dorans, stalked and shot her. ¡Whatever virtues she may have embodied (good looks being ruled out), nothing in her life, I am positive, can have become her like the leaving it.

Local purchase depends on many chances. It takes time, and is a source of danger if there are enemy about; to feed a whole column you need a great deal of rice—probably more, even for one meal, than a village can supply at short notice: and there is little hope of finding adequate supplies of anything other than rice. You may get a few chickens or ducks, but nothing like enough to go round. Eggs are scarce, and the locals do not eat them at all; of any eggs you may get, fully half will be addled. Rice apart, you may find that, with luck, enough food may be forthcoming for the sick, but no more.

When, in 1943, we had lost our wireless sets, and with them all hope of further supply-drops, we were reduced entirely to local purchase and hunting. The Japs knew our plight and our physical weakness, and planted garrisons in all villages which they thought we might visit in search of food. Even when we got away from the areas where the enemy were thickest on the ground, we found it impossible to forage for large parties; and this was one of the reasons which induced most columns to split up. A reduction in our fighting strength was preferable to maintaining our ration strength.

There was a school of thought in the training world which used to contend that it was possible to "live on the country" in a narrower sense than this. Much time has been wasted in teaching the doctrine that a man who knows what is what in the jungle can subsist on edible roots. I have had rows with all sorts of academic and doctrinaire soldiers over this. It is conceivably possible in certain jungles at certain seasons; everybody knows of delicious plants which one can recognise and eat; but to live on such chances alone is a whole-time job. It is nonsense to suggest and wicked to teach that troops can cover their daily distance, carry out their job, and fight the enemy, on what they can find in the jungle.

It certainly adds interest to one's daily life if one can recognise and exploit chance foodstuffs in the jungle. I have no *flair* for it myself, but I have often enjoyed unexpected benefits from being with those who have. Some are easy to spot. There is a flower not unlike a geranium to be found in January and February which, when fried, tastes like a cross between mushroom and marrow. Bamboo shoots, in season for two or three months in the year, are like celery, but with less taste; they have to be boiled twice, and the bitter water which results from the first boiling thrown away. The water in which rice is boiled should, on the other hand, be drunk: it doesn't look good, it doesn't taste very good, but it has a high nutritional value. Rice, incidentally, if you aim at being a jungle Beaton or a Burma Brillat-Savarin, should be steamed for a bit after cooking: only so will you get each individual grain separate from its neighbour. Rice pudding is blasphemy.

We thought that five or six weeks on rice and nothing else was pretty good hell, and even that limited period was enough for some of the men to show signs of incipient beri-beri. But many of my men that first year were to live on rice for much longer; they had two years of it in Rangoon jail, while those caught earlier in the war had longer yet. Some got used to it, some did not. My own men did not tire of it, and after we reached India many of them refused to be parted from their remaining stocks, but brewed it up between meals as a snack.

Even before we became reduced to an all-rice diet our appetite for it was keen. In theory we were to count on seven days' rations every ten days; in practice my column only got twenty days' rations the whole expedition. And the so-called "day's ration" consisted of only two pounds of food. It was originally designed for the use of parachutists, and according to the rules they were not supposed to live on it for more than five days at a time. Its principal component was twelve excellent biscuits, of a type known as " Shakapura"; coarse as oatmeal and full of nourishment. Then there were two ounces of nuts and raisins, four of dates, one of cheese; a tiny packet of salt; tea, sugar and powdered milk; and a disappointment which was supposed to be chocolate, but was nearly always acid drops. And there were twenty cigarettes, of the infamous type known as "V," compounded from inferior Indian tobacco.

Of its kind, it was an excellent ration, ingenious and balanced; but it was woefully insufficient. The raisins and dates and acid drops gave us plenty of sugar, in addition to what we had to put in our tea. Whatever the doctors may say, I am certain that sugar is every bit as important as salt; in the extremities of hunger one does not crave for salt as one does for sugar. Of this I have written elsewhere; how it becomes almost tangible, and torments one with hallucinations, till one sees birthday cakes, coated with icing, growing on the trees. I described this experience in a paper read before the Royal Geographical Society in London, and no fewer than three distinguished explorers came to me afterwards to confirm it: one with Polar, one with Saharan, and the third with Himalayan experience. The American aviator Rickenbacker, who spent over three weeks adrift in a dinghy in the Pacific, also confessed to it when we swopped tall stories in Shepheard's Hotel in Cairo.

The cheese was of poor quality, and made one horribly thirsty. For some reason the cigarettes did not. Wingate was strongly against smoking, and at one time proposed to eliminate cigarettes from the ration: he was dissuaded from doing so less by the pleas of the smokers (headed by Fergusson) than by the difficulties of extracting the cigarettes from the cartons in which the rations were already packed. I believe that the presence of cigarettes in the ration saved men's lives; it was noticeable that the smoker felt less hungry than the non-smoker, and non-smokers took to native tobacco to help stave it off. There grew up a standard and honoured joke about the "V" cigarettes, which came down from the heavens with the rest of the rations: "Have one of my cigarettes; I get them specially flown from India."

Incidentally, the orthodox soldiers used to be deeply shocked at our lack of restrictions on smoking. I used to allow any man to smoke at any time. If your men are so under-trained as not to be competent to judge when it is safe or otherwise to smoke, it is time that you went out of business as a commander of guerrilla troops. If a man was guilty of what I called "non-tactical smoking," he was forbidden to smoke for a month. In two years I only had two cases.

With powdered milk we were less familiar than the ordinary British housewife, and complained after we returned to India about its lumpiness when mixed. In our ignorance we had always poured water over it instead of sprinkling it on to water. But we were loud in our praises of the ration as a whole, and of each individual component; all we wanted was more of it; we did not complain about its monotony, and were surprised to hear that such complaints were current. We were openly amazed and contemptuous when we heard that men had complained about having nothing but bully day after day: bully had become in our minds the quintessence of luxury, of a refinement inferior only to bread.

These remarks apply chiefly to the Expedition of 1943. In 1944, as a result of the representations made to and by General Wingate, we fared much better as regards rations; and although we were always hungry, in the sense that we were never satisfied at the end of a meal, we were never short of food. Orde Wingate ordered a large quantity of American "K" ration, the neatest thing of its kind I have ever seen. Each day's ration was contained in three cartons, marked "Breakfast," "Dinner" and "Supper." "Dinner" was poor; it consisted of cheese, biscuits, a lemon drink and some unpalatable sweet; but both the other meals were first class. The total weight of a day's rations was three pounds, and it was arranged that we should have a drop every five days: so that the total weight of food in a man's pack after a supply-drop was fifteen pounds instead of fourteen under the old system of seven days' two-pound rations. This time, thanks to Orde Wingate's persuasive tongue, there were many more supply aircraft, and we never missed a drop except occasionally through enemy action. (The Brigades who stayed in for the monsoon sometimes missed drops on account of weather.)

But although it would be nonsense to say that we were badly off for food in 1944 in comparison to 1943, we were far worse off than any commander would ever allow ordinary troops to be;

and there were two big drawbacks to the "K" ration. First, the very ingenuity of its three meals became far more monotonous than the unvarying monotony of the year before. After three months of a breakfast, dinner and supper that never varied from the breakfast, dinner and supper of the day before, and the breakfast, dinner and supper of the day after, one longed for some break in that horrid, slick efficiency. Secondly, the old medical preoccupation with salt had run completely amok in preparing the "K" ration: almost every item had been liberally doctored with it, and an agonising thirst was the result. There was an excellent soup, for instance, labelled "Bouillon," to drink which was certain torture; its initial relief was followed by a sensation of pickled tonsils. By and large, although we could have done with much more to eat, and although our resistance grew steadily weaker, we fared pretty well on the "K"; and at each supply-drop they used to include something in the nature of a treat, too heavy to carry with us, but suitable for eating on the spot, if time were not too pressing.

In this connection, I have not yet forgiven John Marriott for his share in the Great Onion Scandal. I found him one day smacking his lips over some boiled onions.

"Where the hell did you get them?" I asked.

"Off the last drop," he said.

"We didn't get onions in the last drop, did we?"

"We get 'em every drop."

"Why haven't I been getting 'em?"

"You don't like 'em."

"Damn you, who told you that? I love 'em."

"Oh, well, it must have been my last Brigadier who didn't like 'em," says John, entirely unrepentant. I suppose I got my share after that, but I never fully trusted him again at supply-drops. Normally I hate onions, but on L.R.P. I would eat tripe and tapioca pudding.

Only in one respect, in the way of food, did we fare worse in 1944 than in 1943; and that was during the days of preparation. I am venturing here on a strong criticism of higher authority, not from an innate Bolshevism and not without a soldierly reluctance. But lessons must be learnt and absorbed, and not suppressed from a natural instinct for loyalty. Before the first campaign, we were allowed a generous extra ration during the months of training, in order to build up a "hump" or reserve of fat, on which to take the field. Before the second, although we carried out our training in the same command, we were under a different administration, which contented itself with promulgating two quite irreconcilable rulings. On the one hand they said that we must not do more than so many days a month on light scale rations; on the other, they said that no special ration concessions could be made in our favour.

Now all our cooking had to be individual; the conditions in which we were living precluded cookhouse administration, and our rations had to be carried in our packs, except at the week-ends or the other brief occasions when we were static. The normal rations for a battalion come up in bulk; bully in 14-lb. tins, and other commodities in comparable fashion. It was clearly impossible to tote such items around with us on training, and bully in half-pound tins was not available. The only solution was a compromise—to live light on training, for two or three days at a time, and to have an ample ration for feeding up between times. This required a special allowance in such items as meat, bread, vegetables, milk and so on three or four days in the week, a concession willingly made to us the year before.

The new administration flatly refused to recognise any such need. Wingate was sick, and on the Dangerously Ill list, and could not be invoked. My Brigade was to be the first to go into Burma, two months ahead of the others; it alone had reached the advanced state of training where special arrangements were necessary. Two separate committees of doctors were sent to see the work we were doing, and both advised an increase in rations; both times their report was turned down. I asked for a senior staff officer to come; they sent a junior staff captain, who said that he was already convinced that we were right, but could not persuade his superiors. I asked for the general responsible to come; an answer was received which said that it had been discovered that we were underdrawing our entitlement, and that we ourselves were to blame. I responded by sending all our issue vouchers for the last four months, to prove that we had drawn every crumb which we were allowed under the existing regulations. We were then granted, not the milk and bread and vegetables for which we asked, but two ounces of cocoa and some extra milk per man, as a special concession.

By the time Wingate was out of dock, and had secured a reversal of policy, we were in the train on the way to Ledo and the Patkai hills, and too late to benefit. We could have been twenty to thirty per cent. fitter for our task had our representations been accepted and honoured. I have been on the staff for more than half my service, and I do not subscribe to one-tenth of the ruderies perpetrated by the fighting soldier against the staff; but every now and then one comes across office-bound staff officers without recent experience in the field, who do incalculable harm by ignoring the representations of field commanders. This was one of those instances, and a sad one. The officer responsible had not served in the field for over twenty years. I shall not forgive him.

The lesson must be "hoisted in," as the sailors say, that troops preparing for a long physical ordeal must be fattened for it. This principle can be accepted without being interpreted as an "assault on the accepted ration scale," as these negotiations were described. The accepted ration scale is admirable for the purposes for which it was devised; but you do not feed an athlete entirely on milk, nor a man with a duodenal on red meat. You sometimes hear it suggested that troops should practise living and working on short commons. This is a fallacy, and troops who are likely to have to go short of food must not be stinted during their training period.

The soldier usually grouses about his food, and almost always about the way in which it has been cooked. I remember a man in the siege of Tobruk who found time even there to grouse about the cooking; his grumbling went beyond endurance, and I had to cure him in the end by making him cook for himself. With us, individual cooking was the only possible method and the men became very expert, both in cooking and in making fires. I do not remember them ever being defeated, even by the heaviest rain. They were up to every trick of fire-making, and the sailor, the forester, the keeper, the farmer, the builder, the casual labourer and the ex-Boy Scout all contributed ideas from some long-forgotten past. One old Maori device popped up in my memory from camping days in New Zealand eighteen years

W.G.E.   N before, to which we had resort more than once. You heat stones in the fire until they are as hot as they can get and tumble them into a hole three feet deep; you wrap up chunks of raw meat, the smaller the better, in leaves and put them on the stones; you shovel the earth over the top; and go to sleep. Next morning you dig out your meat, and it is cooked, a hot meal for the morning with the minimum of bother.

I don't think I shall ever grumble about food again. Certainly our men became thoroughly self-sufficient, even the worst of them, whether at cooking, at washing their clothes or anything else. I was immoderately pleased at the tribute of a Commodore of Convoys, who on three separate voyages had brought home Chindits finishing their time. He said that he had never known men so cheerful, so willing, and so well able to look after themselves to their own satisfaction; and he contrasted them favourably with troops drawn from the same kind of homes and environment whom he had taken to South-East Asia each time on his outward voyage, and who, he said, were both helpless and discontented. I suggested that the reason might be partly due to the fact that the Chindits were homeward bound, and the others war-ward; but he insisted that the difference was more profound than that: it was the difference between men who had been used to having everything done for them and men who had learned the fundamentals.

I would say without hesitation that lack of food constitutes the biggest single assault upon morale. It is rarely noticed in the many books that have been written, and the many speeches delivered, upon that subject. Lord Moran, whose lectures on the subject of courage over many years lately culminated in a book, makes no mention of it. Apart from its purely chemical effects upon the body, it has woeful effects upon the mind. One is the dismal condition of having nothing to look forward to. Man is still an animal, and consciously or unconsciously he is always looking forward to his next meal. In this state, one finds oneself saying, "I'm looking forward to something: what is it?" Then comes the cynical answer, "Eating; and there is nothing to eat, and there isn't going to be anything to eat." Then sets in a dreadful gloom; one wrenches the mind away from it, but in a few minutes the question asks itself again, and the same answer chills the spirit. At last the thought is there all the time, and only now and then is a new question asked, "Is there no hope of food?" To this there is one triumphant and tyrannical answer, "None."

The merest promise or hope of food will keep one going a long time. Christopher Burney, writing of his time in Buchenwald in *The Dungeon Democracy*, says: "A man who is really hungry, and who can calculate that to-morrow or the day after or even next week he will be given an extra 200 grammes of bread or an extra litre of soup, lives on that hope and stifles the despair of hopelessness." I shall never forget the new lease of life granted to my servant Peter Dorans and me when, turning out my pack, we found fourteen grains of rice, spilt from some long-forgotten ration, lying black and dirty at the bottom. We cooked them in a tablespoonful of water, and drew new strength and hope from sharing them.

When the hope of food is gone, a new assault develops upon the defences of the mind. This takes the form of a growing dread that soon your weakness may reach the pitch where it will overwhelm you. There is no more heart-rending sight than the man who finally falls, or the man whose struggles to resume his feet are fruitless. You can either remain with him and share his fate, or you must leave him where he lies, assert your leadership, rally your men and push on, one fewer. Your job is to get as many men to safety as you can. There can surely be no greater burden on the narrowing shoulders of leadership than this experience. I will write of it no more; but I think it proper that the race to which these men belonged should know what they suffered without complaining on its behalf. Of all the men whom I have had to leave, wounded, sick or starving, not one reproached me, or made the dreadful duty harder than it already was.

Real thirst leads quickly to madness and death. A man can go two days without water and still keep marching, but at some time on the third day his spirit will break. When at last water is found, the mules smell it, break away from their muleteers and gallop madly towards it; the strength of man's mind varies with the individual, but sooner or later a man will do the same. I have been astonished to find how long a man can carry on marching without food; and no less astonished to find how short a time he can carry on without water.

Water has its dangers, in the impurities which so often lurk in it. Leaping mountain torrents are often, but not always, safe; slow waters, like the Ledan or the Nami, on which many villages are built, are usually dangerous. Centralised purification of water was impossible for us, so every man carried his personal bottle of sterilising tablets. Mike Calvert tells the story of a Gurkha with an uneasy conscience, whom he once saw taking a long pull at his water-bottle. Looking round, he caught Mike's eye on him; a stricken look of guilt came over his face, his hand stole to his pocket, and he swallowed a fistful of tablets, his eyes still meeting Mike's.

Mules are finicky about water, and if it is really bad they will sniff at it and turn away in all but the extremities of thirst. I have often filled our water-bottles from pools which the animals have rejected. Most of our water was consumed in the form of tea, and boiling remains the best way of dealing with it. The sterilising tablets were only used for the bottles. If left to themselves, men drink too much water; medical thought and teaching encourages them to do so, and doubtless medical thought in this, as in the matter of salt, is technically correct. But to drink at every short halt is a mistake, since it is bad for your wind, and gives you what, in the technical speech evolved by us, was known as a "soggy belly." Again, I would never allow men to drink at the beginning of a halt, when one yearned for it most; it is better to wait for five or ten minutes before giving permission. By that time each individual drop will do you more good, and you are less inclined to make irreplaceable inroads on the contents of your bottle. Only once in the twenty-four hours should you force yourself to drink all you want, and more—much more: and that is first thing in the morning on a day when it is going to be hot, but is still cool. I have already mentioned this when describing the march out of bivouac.

Even black or yellow water is tolerable in tea, although occasionally it has a nasty tang of buffalo or elephant. The native tea is not strong enough to drown it, but good old troops' *char* (which I honestly believe that I have come to prefer to the drawing-room variety) will drown most supplementary tastes.

In the bad, foodless days which I have been describing, we never ran out of tea, thank goodness, and we owe many lives to that. Show me the anti-tea or the anti-tobacco crank, and I will joy-fully and contemptuously trounce him.

If you are in the sorry position of having enough water only for a brew of rice, or a brew of tea, but not both, go for the rice. For in it, when cooked, there lingers much water; and you have the rice-water to drink as well.

Food and water, then, are essential to good morale; for a man who is weak from lack of either has literally no stomach for fighting. Apart from them, the courage of a man in good health cannot be compared with the courage of the sick soldier. There was an officer in British Somaliland in 1940 whose pos-thumous V.C. has always seemed to me to be one of the most deserving of the war. (Happily the posthumous part of it turned out to be inappropriate, for he was recovered alive in Asmara when it fell many months later.) Wounded and suffering from malaria, he manned a machine-gun for several days, until he had to be left behind; and a man who is brave with a bad go of malaria is brave indeed.

There is no doubt that in 1943, when a sick man had to go on walking or be left behind, the standard of resistance shown was higher than in 1944, when he had a good chance of being evacu-ated; and this despite the fact that the standard of troops in 1944 was higher than in the previous year. In '43 men went stumbling on when they were far gone in delirium; their instinct kept them going, until they were recovered, while in '44 it sufficed to keep them going only as far as a light plane strip.

Malaria was a serious enemy. The first year, by virtue of the surreptitious and tiptoe nature of the trip, we avoided villages, and thus went far to avoid malaria; the second year we were much in villages and suffered thereby, while those who sojourned near the Indaw Lake had a high percentage of fever. Mosquito nets and cream were impracticable in our type of warfare, and the wonderful boon of D.D.T. had not yet reached us; we were therefore obliged to rely entirely on suppressive tablets of atebrin (1943) and mepacrine (1944).

A comparison of my observations over the two years shows that in the first we were comparatively free of malaria, although

the precautions we took were fewer; which would seem to confirm that the matter of avoidance or non-avoidance of villages
really was the deciding factor. In 1943 we were on the go from
the 25th of January until the 25th of April, a period of 93 days.
Up to the 28th of March, when my column dispersed in the Shweli
Valley, we had taken no malarial precautions of any sort, and yet
we had only six cases, all of which were relapses. Not until the
8th of April did we start taking atebrin, and by then I only had
enough to issue three a week instead of the statutory one a day,
calculating that we should reach the British lines more or less
when we did. Suppressive tablets do not prevent you from
getting malaria; they only keep it under until you can get
proper treatment, and that only until the infection becomes so
powerful that it bursts through. To this point, which some
doctors dispute, I will return later.

From the 10th of April onwards I had only thirty men to
observe, since I was forced to split up into small parties. Of these
thirty, not one got malaria until after we crossed the Chindwin
on the 25th of April. Thereafter, twenty-nine out of the thirty
got it, the exception being John Fraser, who was quite insuffer-
able about his immunity; all these cases developed, as was to be
expected, ten days after we stopped atebrin, and nine days after
we left the notorious Kabaw Valley, where the risks of infection
were high. One case was cerebral, and proved fatal. Other
parties had similar figures, except for those which chose longer
routes, and ran out of atebrin earlier in consequence: they developed malaria on the march.

In 1944 we started on mepacrine six weeks earlier, on the 1st
of March, at a tablet a day, and a crash course, as we called it,
of three a day for five days once in every three weeks. We began
getting primary cases, as opposed to relapses, during the last
week in March. Then one column, through missing supply
drops, was without mepacrine for three days, and speedily reached
a figure of 30 per cent. malaria. After that all columns, even
those which had been taking their mepacrine regularly, began
developing cases; and the only plausible explanation is that the
infection had once again become too strong for the protection.

There was a school of thought among the doctors that if you
religiously took your tablet a day, you could not get malaria.

They claimed that reports from Australia had proved this; they went so far as to say that if you got malaria, it was proof that you had been dodging your mepacrine; and I have had many a row with the doctors over this. Silly stories without foundation were said to be circulating about permanent ill-effects from mepacrine, and it was reported that on some fronts this had led to the troops refusing to take it. It certainly turned you yellow, and I believe that some men did feel slightly the worse for it, although speaking personally I was not affected. However, the contention of the doctors that mepacrine was a certain bulwark against malaria lost a good deal of ground when two of my medical officers themselves contracted the disease in the middle of a crash course. By the time we came out four out of nine doctors had caught it. It was most enjoyable to see them trying to persuade their own superiors (who had been loud in their quotations from Australian statistics) that they had honestly not been dodging their mepacrine.

In one respect we had the wrong attitude to malaria: we looked on it as inevitable; we believed that we were all bound to get it every so often. Good work and propaganda by commanders, doctors, officers and men elsewhere has shown that this is by no means true. Some divisions, like the 17th, early decided that it was nonsense, and demonstrated by results that malarial figures could be cut by thousands if enough trouble was taken—though admittedly they were able to take measures impossible in our way of living. But in one respect we had the right attitude, in that we never treated malaria as a disease meriting evacuation. Unless, of course, it was cerebral, the man would get over it and be fit for work again in a week. Even in 1944, when evacuation was possible, we only applied it in a bad case, or when a man had had it so often that all the marrow (I speak figuratively: I don't want the doctors to mock me) had gone out of his bones. Men whose attacks had run into double figures were not likely to be of much use; they were always relapsing.

Dysentery was fairly scarce, and a man would often claim to have had dysentery when his trouble was the humbler and less romantic diarrhœa. The worst disease of the lot was a form of scrub typhus, which I first heard of from the Americans, and which was to be found chiefly in the Mogaung and Hukawng

Valleys. My own regiment, in Tom Brodie's Brigade, was badly hit by it, and the chances of it proving fatal were high. The American Lieutenant Quackenbush, whom I mentioned in another chapter, was one of two survivors out of a batch of seventeen Americans who got it. There were no cases in my column, and I never heard of any in my Brigade. I gather that the only treatment which could be applied in those early days was an effort to keep down the patient's temperature; once it soared he was lost.

Health in the jungle is not only the business of the doctor or the commander; it is the job of every officer and of every individual. Minor ailments easily developed into major ones, with the danger of being overwhelmed by them not far off; they were like jackals snapping at you to try and get a hold. One such danger was prickly heat. I remember deciding in Delhi, the only hot weather I spent there, that all the advertised palliatives for prickly heat were useless, and that the only one which was any good was the wholly secret and personal remedy of a good scratch. Not so in the jungle; any scratch might start a sore and any sore might spread all over your body. The best preventative of prickly heat is the frequent exposure of the body to the sun; it took a war to get this truth recognised; and whereas of old sunbathing was forbidden, it is now compulsory.

Prickly heat develops where there is tightness of clothing: round the waistband of your trousers, where the weight of your pack rests upon your back, where your rolled-up sleeve chafes the inside of your arm at the elbow. (I always march, and counsel all others to march, with the button of the sleeve undone, and the sleeve itself flapping loose: so, you get some measure of a draught.) I remember two officers having to be evacuated from the results of prickly heat, which had gone septic on them: in one case it was prickly heat pure and simple; in the other it was septic prickly heat joining up with an unhealed bullet wound in the shoulder, received nearly two months before, and infecting it with poison. He was repatriated to the United Kingdom two months later (in his normal turn) swathed from head to foot in cotton wool, and unable to bear the weight of a shirt on him.

All jungle sores are potentially dangerous unless carefully ended. Once on training I lost patience with their prevalence, and announced that the possession of a jungle sore would be regarded as an offence, except where the M.O. acquitted the victim of blame. The solemnity of the announcement was quickly dissipated by the development of two fair stinkers on my own ankles. But there was some sense in the idea, since it brought home to the man that the responsibility was his. Some form of disinfectant should be in every man's personal kit.

Footrot was another serious problem. Splashing through *chaungs* twenty times a day, your feet were never dry; and although we carried three spare pairs of socks one could not always be changing them. Whenever possible we let the air get at our feet: and indeed at the midday halt a general strip would take place: shirts were off for sun-bathing, socks were off for air. Cleanliness was prized; the British soldier is by nature cleanly and seldom has to be urged towards his ablutions.

Where footrot developed, the doctors usually applied gentian violet; but so far as I am concerned, the miracle drug is sulphanilamide, of which a little sprinkled in a wound seems to put the risk of infection beyond doubt.

Another medical rule which was strictly enforced was the order forbidding men to remove ticks from themselves, instead of reporting to an M.O. or medical orderly. Any fool can pull a tick out of himself; but the brute's head usually comes off and stays under the skin. We had so many cases of this happening, risking not only bad sores but an outbreak of typhus as well, that it had to be forbidden, and the medical orderly would do the trick with methylated spirit and tweezers. Leeches in moderation do no harm; *polaungs* are a bore to everybody, but to some more than others. They don't bother me, and neither do leeches; but I have an irresistible attraction for ticks. They appear to regard me as a genuine Dumb Friend.

A personal medical kit, in my view, should have six items: a good disinfectant (we all have our favourite and I have mine); gentian violet; sulphanilamide; adhesive plaster; suppressive tablets; and morphia. The last we carried both in tablet form, and as an ampule for purposes of injection. Other items can be added to taste; some, with proud stomachs, took the wherewithal to curb that pride; some, prone to headaches, took aspirin; some took vitamin tablets by which they set store.

After the first Expedition, few officers and men were fit to go

again; many ended the war still in a low medical category. And
only one, Bobby Thompson, saw Burma through to its latter
end after both Chindit walks. Even Orde Wingate, indomitable
though he was, confessed before his second thrust went in that
he thought no Chindit should operate for more than three
months on end. I believe this to be sound. I believe also that
nobody under twenty-two, or over thirty-eight, should be allowed
to come. Of the over-forties who came in the first year, only one,
a Burmese major called Aung Thin, got out; and of six officers
and men over forty who came in with my Brigade the second year,
only one finished the course, and he was an Animal Transport
Officer with a horse to ride.

In all this talk of health and nutrition, in which I may have
seemed to claim undue knowledge and wisdom, I have not yet
made clear our realisation of the debt which we owe to our doctors.
No commander was ever more lucky than I was in this respect.
The first year I had Bill Aird of Glasgow, the first Chindit doctor
in length of service with the Force, and not the least able nor the
least loved. He stayed with a party of wounded that grim morning when we were broken up. Not all of them got across the
Irrawaddy; not all survived the crossing; but with some—sick
as he was with fever and dysentery—Bill reached the very
Chindwin before he and they were caught by the Japs on the
threshold of safety. He did not live long; he was dead before
they got him to Mandalay; but he will be remembered all the
lifetime of the old hands in No. 5 Column.

And the second year each column was well served, and I
cannot name all the individuals. I can only name Jim Donaldson,
the senior one, a Galloway man with a Glasgow degree, an
English practice, and a world sympathy. He was a born confidant,
and knew many of the secrets of the campaign. And Bill Officer,
the senior doctor of the Force, was outspoken and excellent: we
owe him a lot.

I have mentioned two of the doctors; let me mention one
other rank, of many in my mind. Private Munt of the R.A.M.C.
saw three men with a Bren gun lying wounded seventy yards
out into paddy from the kindly shelter of the jungle, under a
curtain of enemy fire. He brought them in one by one, working
the Bren gun for a few bursts on each trip. Then he went back

and brought in the Bren gun. That was near Thetkegyin, with one of the Recce columns. I put him in for a decoration. A fortnight later, near Mawlu, he was killed while trying to pull off a similar feat. His decoration was never granted, but he too will be remembered. I never saw him; I wish I had.

Lastly, I must mention the famous, the impish, the kindly, the mutinous, the saintly, the wicked, the beloved, the Glasgow-Irish, the always-on-the-verge-of-a-Court-Martial Matron, Miss Agnes McGeary, M.B.E. She cheeked the generals, she scolded the doctors, she mocked the governors, she bullied me, she saved Wingate's life when he was dying of typhoid, she stole for the wounded, she brought many back to health when they would otherwise have died, she raided ordnance stores, she embezzled comfort dumps, she vamped Brigadiers Q, she cheered the dying, she wrote letters to the bereaved; and when she got answers from the bereaved she wrote to them again and again, and still again. She sent me in a clipper for my beard, and a live goose (by Dakota) for my dinner. She was a darling who possessed all our hearts; and in whatever row with authority she is involved to-day, she has all our wishes for a happy issue out of all the afflictions which she so light-heartedly brings on herself for the sake of others. I only hope I am never under her command; indeed, I have but one hope more fervent than that: that she is never under mine.

XI

THE JAP AS AN OPPONENT

IN THOSE six disastrous months between December, 1941, and, May, 1942, when the yellow tide rolled over Malaya and Burma to the frontiers of India, the repute of the Japanese soldier stood danger-ously high—dangerously, because he became endowed in Allied fancy with almost supernatural powers. The Jap himself believed that his ancestors were fighting for him; one set of captured orders included instructions for the soldier even after his demise. If some of the exploits attributed to the Jap in those days by our own soldiery were true, the Jap's belief in his own divinity must have been well founded.

In the later stages of the war, when confidence was regained, the pendulum swung. Indeed, for reasons of propaganda, it swung farther than was reasonable, until we were asked to believe that the Jap was only a moderate fighter after all. I must confess myself to having helped foster that belief. Now that propaganda of that sort is no longer either necessary or healthy, it is as well to sum up the Jap soldier with reasonable objectivity. Victory was not due to any innate superiority of the Allied soldier over the Japanese. The victory in Burma was doubtless won partly by good generalship and partly by good fighting; but it was contributed to largely by the unguarded and immoderate confidence of the Jap, who thought he could safely rely on captured British supplies, and so largely dispense with lines of communi-cation. Thus he destroyed his own army; and thus the same confidence which had brought him strings of victories in the past led him at last to irretrievable disaster.

I am not competent to discuss his generalship, but only his characteristics as an individual fighting man—although I fancy that these characteristics, with their corresponding shortcomings, are mirrored in his generalship. As a fighting man he has two outstanding qualities: his courage and his quickness. He has shortcomings: his gullibility, for instance, and his close adher-ence to the book of the words.

From the earliest days, there were plenty of commanders who refused to be hypnotised by the Jap's apparent mastery of the art of war, and who set themselves resolutely to find the chinks in his armour, even in the depressing circumstances of retreat. On the battalion commander's level, there were such men as Ian Stewart of Achnacone, who commanded the Argylls in Malaya, and Joe Lentaigne, who commanded a battalion of Gurkhas in Burma, and who was afterwards to raise a second Brigade of Chindits, while Wingate's First Expedition was still "in," and finally to succeed Wingate himself as Commander, Special Force. In those days, the Japs had learned how dependent we were on our communications; and, with marked success, they set to work to cut them, or to appear to cut them, on all occasions. It fell to Orde Wingate to deduce, and exploit, their own sensitiveness about a threat to their rear.

To treat first of his virtues, his courage is not seriously in dispute. There are plenty of methods of breaking it down. He is as sensitive as anybody else to heavy concentrations of fire before he is dug in, to the use of flame, to major bombing. But he assaults well in offence, he stands his ground well in defence, and he fights superbly as an individual.

In this last respect he compares favourably with any rival. Few soldiers can be found in other races who are prepared to fight alone and unsupported, to die anonymously and unseen by their comrades, to spit out their last breath without an eyewitness to carry back the news of how they died. Most fighting men have a secret dread of being "missing." They will die almost willingly at the head of their men, or among their comrades, so long as somebody is there who will know what has happened, or what has probably happened. Even the R.A.F. pilot can be sure that his family will know at least on what sortie he was killed. But your jungle fighter who is overrun in his foxhole, or who gets a chance to sell his life profitably but dearly while on a lone patrol, minds most of all the knowledge that he will be missing, and that vain hopes for his return will linger on for maybe years to come.

Yet the Jap will tie himself into a tree so that his riddled body can stay there long after it has lost the physical power to do so of its own volition. He will creep into an enemy bivouac and

open up with his rifle, getting off as many rounds as he can before
he is shot down, and making no attempt to get away. With tiny
patrols he will insinuate himself into a strong position and sell
his life dearly. And he will fight until he has no more breath in
his body.

Many a casualty has been caused by a "dead" Jap. I should
have been one myself, had it not been for the vigilance of my
batman, who saw him start up on an elbow and point his rifle
at my back from three or four yards away. The Jap takes as much
killing as a conger-eel, and is every bit as slippery. (Bill Smyly,
however, was equally slippery once, when he shammed dead
among some dead Gurkhas near Hopin; he had some dead Japs
to show for it, too.) But I will not have the Jap called "cunning."
The "cunning Jap" belongs to the Green Hell School, which
teaches the doctrines of "The Forgotten Army," "Burma, Land
of Snakes," and "How to Live on the Country, in Six Easy
Lessons."

The other virtue in which I willingly award the Jap soldier
ten marks out of a possible ten is in his speed. If the head of your
column should bump into him, you may expect a flank attack
to develop in roughly half the time that you reckon it ought to
take him. He travels light, burdened only by his rifle, his bandolier
and a small haversack; he is usually small, and always lithe and
nimble.

His courage and his speed, then, are his two principal virtues;
and I will accord him four supplementary ones. He digs fast,
well, and as if by instinct; he is underground before the British
soldier has finished spitting on his hands and getting his coat off.

His engineers are good, with the barest minimum of equipment, or more often with none at all. They achieve their results
by a ruthless exploitation of native labour, which they handle with
skilful cruelty.

His camouflage is excellent. I have flown over his positions
at treetop height without seeing a thing. This experience was
most vivid in Arakan, where the British works and camps were
prominent everywhere, and where the Jap-held areas showed no
signs whatever of being occupied. (The enemy's air effort was
negligible, and attempts to hide the British work would have
been a gross waste of time.)

Lastly, he has a grand eye for ground. This manifests itself not only in his choice of defensive positions, but also in minor respects, such as the fashion in which a patrol settles down for the night. Its men explore all neighbouring tracks and short cuts, so that if they have to clear out or fight an action during the night, all ranks are familiar with the topography.

The foregoing catalogue of the fighting qualities of the Japanese may seem grudging; but when you come to consider it, they comprise no mean mental equipment for a soldier. His courage, particularly, is of such a high order that it outweighs many other defects; and even his stupidity is in some sense an advantage to him, or to his superior commanders. Certainly no Jap commander in Burma lost a battle through over-caution, or through lack of drive; whereas his dash and his promptitude in exploring a suddenly developing situation has imposed excessive caution on many a commander opposed to him.

One of my own columns became involved in a skirmish which illustrates several points of moral and tactical importance. The column was engaged on a long outflanking movement through country where water was scarce, and Japs plentiful. They had had a drink one morning—let us say, on Wednesday morning—and it was now Thursday evening. Men and mules were parched with thirst, weary and hot; and the men had been on the alert for possible enemy without respite. A mile ahead lay a stream, marked enticingly and alluringly solid on the map; the intention was to cross it, and to bivouac on the far side. A wide stream could be dangerous to cross, and one always breathed more freely when it was behind one.

Half a mile short of the stream, the column stumbled on a motorable track. It was not shown on the map, so it was presumably new; and recent tyre marks were evident. The column crossed, taking the usual statutory precautions, and reached the stream just as the swift tropical night was falling. A hasty reconnaissance disclosed that the stream had a high bank on the near side, necessitating a downhill scramble of some forty feet. No crossing place was to be seen, and the commanding officer decided to bivouac where he was. He sent out two patrols, one upstream and one down, to look for crossing places to use at dawn; and gave out orders for the night's bivouac.

One platoon, detailed for the north-east corner of the bivouac, moved off in that direction, but before it had gone for forty yards through the teak it found the motor-track, which had apparently taken a jink from the point where they had crossed it a quarter of an hour before. He was just on his way back to tell the column commander, when three Japanese trucks, driving fast, came round the corner without warning, into the heart of the unsuspecting column.

Five minutes earlier, or five later, the column would have been in better shape to receive this sudden gate-crash; but at that precise moment mules were being unloaded, officers were choosing detailed locations for their platoons, and the section normally dropped as "stops" at the moment of entering bivouac were in their proper place at the tail of the column. The leading truck was stopped with a burst of fire; but from it and the other two trucks close behind it emerged some forty Japanese.

The Japs were as surprised as the British, but they bore themselves extremely well. The British mules were all together within a few yards of them, in the act of being unloaded. The Japs opened up on the mules, killed many and stampeded others; for the muleteers, helping to unload heavy burdens such as wireless sets and mortars, knew nothing until the shots broke out, the grenades began bursting, and the mules broke away with their loads half unhooked. The Japs were in the middle of the British and could fight outwards; the British were in danger of killing each other with every round they fired.

Except to their mules the British had few casualties, although among them was the column commander himself: in the act of firing his revolver at a Japanese, the butt of his revolver was struck by a bullet, and his right hand and fingers pulped with splintered wood and metal. The scrap sorted itself out, with the Japs on the outside and the British on the inside; but not until the British had lost much of their most valuable equipment on runaway mules, and had other mules killed. The honours were definitely with the Japs; but it is hard to blame the British.

There is no doubt that in jungle fighting a small party fighting outwards has the bulge on a larger body of troops surrounding them: their chances of survival may be poor, but they are almost certain to inflict casualties out of all proportion to their own.

This applies particularly in the dark, where there is a good chance of making the enemy fight himself, while the dark has the further attraction of offering a good chance of escape to the small party. There was a case in Abyssinia, where a party of Equatorials sped through an Italian stockade making as much noise as they could, and spent the rest of the night listening to the askaris fighting each other. George Astell of the Burma Rifles ran a similar party on the fringe of the Kachin hills west of Broadway, when with about twenty Burma Riflemen he stormed through a sleeping bivouac of Japanese. It was a principle which I taught in training: that small parties in jungle fighting must keep together, so that they know that everyone who is not with them is against them, and positively enemy. Jungle-fighting is not like covert-shooting late in the season; you cannot say, "Cocks only: you can take a high hen if you like"; there must be no holds barred.

Another dogma of the Green Hell School is that the Jap is a born jungle-man. This too is nonsense. Japan is not a jungle country; most Japs are townsmen or paddy-dwellers. It is my experience that the British countryman is no better than the townsman in jungle, after a very short while; and I am quite certain that the Britisher is a better man in jungle, with his superior intelligence, than the Jap. His courage avails him much, but it cannot make up for his failings.

He is gullible, he is quick to react and he is a slave to habit. These characteristics make him easy to ambush, although one must remember that even when ambushed he will fight hard until he is dead. In so far as ours was a harassing role, we had to study the ambush; and the conclusions we reached may be of some mild interest.

An ambush is a trap laid when there is a reasonable fore-knowledge of the enemy's intentions. Such fore-knowledge is usually either derived from Intelligence reports, or from a careful study of the enemy's habits. In our warfare it was usually the latter; and our task was made easier from the fact that his habits were consistent, and his reactions easy to gauge. To draw him into an ambush, one had either to provoke him into moving along a route of our own choosing at a time of our own choosing, or to find a route which he was in the habit of using. The actual site of the ambush had to be suitable to our purpose, and one where he would be moving without caution.

Apart from routes over which he was in the habit of moving, means could usually be found to induce him to move at a certain time or in a given direction. A suitable lure would be a party settling down at ease in a village, or an order to a village to prepare rice to be called for on a given day. News of this was bound to reach the enemy, and he would hasten to the spot by the quickest route. The actual area he would approach with caution; but before that he would travel fast, and that was the part of the journey where an ambush would catch him most unawares.

Where the enemy was likely to travel in motor transport, the setting of the ambush presented some difficulty; for fast-travelling M.T. becomes spread out over hundreds of yards, and the first vehicle into the trap may spring it prematurely, allowing its fellows farther down the convoy to pull up before they reach the danger-point. We met this difficulty by stationing somebody with a wireless set out along the road in the direction from which the convoy was expected. It was this fellow's job to count the convoy, and to warn those in hiding how many vehicles to expect. It is a temptation to try to include too many in the ambush; six vehicles is probably the maximum number which a column ambush can tackle, unless the site is especially suitable, and the troops in the leading vehicles can be prevented from communicating warnings to those following behind.

Ambushes are not an end in themselves; but they constitute a real nuisance to the enemy, tying up troops in unprofitable places, and imposing caution and slowness on all his movements. One has to think out thoroughly beforehand what the enemy will do when the gaff is blown. If you think that the mere fact of the ambush will ensure that the day is yours, you will have a rude shock: he will fight like hell. In Terence Close's ambush on the Banmauk-Indaw road in March 1944, the Japs put up an admirable fight after their initial surprise.

Terence's ambush has a particular interest for me, since I had hoped to carry it out myself the year before. The map showed a point in the road near the 20th milestone which constituted a tempting site for anybody with an ambush-complex. The road appeared to run along the edge of a deep *chaung* on the outside of a curve; the hillside crowded close about the road. We had reason to believe that the Japs were using the road regularly, and I thought that my operations against Indaw would bring more Japs towards the town from the westward. Terence reached the hill above the corner at the hour of dusk, and moved down on to the road in the darkness. The jungle was desperately thick, and the misadventures of both men and mules in the dark were innumerable. Many small gullies, separated by steep ridges, ran down to the main stream and made the descent still more difficult. One mule, with widely spreading sideloads, dropped into such a gully, and fitted it so perfectly that its sideloads rested on the bank while its legs swung helplessly in the air. Its human companions were helpless with suppressed laughter and profanity.

At last some of the platoon commanders decided that the only possibility of getting to their allotted positions lay in going boldly out upon the road and walking along it. As they emerged they suddenly heard the sound of motor-vehicles approaching. Last week, in a London club, one of the officers concerned, telling me these details, confessed that this was his worst moment of the war.

They squeezed themselves against the solid jungle, and froze: there was nothing else to do. Even the mules seemed to grasp the importance of this proceeding, and co-operated to the full. As they stood there, a lorry came past. Had they been in position it would have offered a perfect target; as it was they could only pray, first, that they would not be seen, and secondly, that nobody farther along the road would be tempted to loose off at it. The lorry passed, and they heard another; it too passed, and was followed by another. In all, sixteen lorries drove by, each full of troops, while Terence's men and animals stood like statues. At last there was silence; the ambush position was occupied, and everyone breathed again.

For the next two days only single vehicles passed, and the ambush held its fire. Then, on the evening of the second day, they got a signal from me to break off and concentrate on the Ledan Chaung. Terence asked my permission to wait till dawn, which I gave; and at midnight they caught a convoy of six lorries. One managed to pull up, turn and get away; the troops in the others fought all night. Next morning, all seemed quiet, and Terence, having buried his own five dead, was forming up on top of the hill to march away, well pleased with his night's work. All of a sudden, a small party of Japs who had escaped the slaughter assaulted the hill with their usual monkey-like yells, and enabled him to swell his final score without further loss to himself. The Jap losses amounted to thirty; and the road was not used by the enemy for at least a month.

Another ambush, remarkable for its simplicity, was carried out by a Leicester column on the railway near Pinwe. It seems that a party of Japs came down the permanent way, laughing and chattering and pushing in front of them a trolley. Fire was opened, and the party almost entirely wiped out. Next day, another party came pushing a trolley along the line in almost exactly the same area; but this time they had tied some boughs of greenery to their trolley, and were apparently confident that by so doing they had rendered both themselves and the trolley invisible. Their spirits were forthwith released from their earthly bodies, and were doubtless privileged to continue the fight in accordance with the orders issued to them to meet that contingency—this time, invisible indeed.

The incident of the greenery serves to illustrate the blind faith of the Jap in the power of the textbook. The book said, no doubt, that if you dolled yourself up in greenery, you would not be seen. The textbook served him well in the early days, when the tricks it taught were new. In those days, when he called out English phrases, the British answered; when he fired a few rounds into a post, he drew the fire of the defenders; when he attacked with a few men the rear of a position, the defenders inferred that they were cut off, and withdrew. But people like Ian Stewart and Joe Lentaigne brought back these lessons, and they were learned; and new tricks were not forthcoming. Originality in the field was not part of their mental equipment: witness the frequent attacks on White City—four in three days—from the same direction, at the same hour, with the same preparatory bombardment and apparently the same objectives. Yet his very stupidity drove him again and again to the same hopeless battle —on that occasion in vain; though sometimes, one must admit, his stupidity drove him into a battle so surprising and unexpected that he won it—through sheer stupidity.

But just as the apparent liability of his stupidity sometimes proved an asset, so some of his assets proved on occasions to be liabilities. One example of this paradox was his intense pride of race, his fanatical resentment of anything which he could construe as an insult to his Emperor. To set up a roadblock on a track which he was in the habit of using was to him not merely a military inconvenience: it was also an impertinence, a blasphemy. His fury was so violent that it caused him a brainstorm. He lost what capacity he had for planning his battle; he flew into an imperial, a divine rage. He hurled his platoons, his companies, even his battalions and his regiments against the obstruction without a plan of any kind; and he expended them thus in instalments. Again, White City can provide an example. When first established it was assaulted with two companies: that was reasonable, for he had no means at that stage of knowing its strength. But thereafter he threw against it whatever was available; each new battalion was made to attack as it arrived. Not for several weeks did he learn the lesson that he must build up against it, and by then Mike and I were each strong enough to hustle and harry the build-up with odd columns so that it was never able to put in a really violent assault at anything more than a battalion strength. All these assaults were carried out at night. They were violent enough, and made with great courage and determination; but they only once penetrated the perimeter, and on that occasion the Japs were speedily evicted.

In short, teasing the Jap was easy, and it was also the quickest method for giving confidence to fresh troops; the Japs would fall in swathes, and prove conclusively that their immortality was exaggerated.

Orde Wingate had three sound slogans for fighting the Japanese which stood the test of time.

"Don't be Predictable."

"When in Doubt, Don't Shoot."

"The Answer to Noise is Silence."

Predictability was a Jap sin, and it was sheer gain to us. Ourselves, we went to great lengths to observe this basic Wingate law. Only once was it badly broken, and from that breach sprang all our troubles in 1943. Our whole Force, less certain columns outside the ring, allowed itself to linger in the great loop formed by the Shweli and Irrawaddy Rivers, long enough for the Japs to become aware of it. They knew that we must break out, and lined the rivers to prevent our doing so. We had excuses in plenty, but the Law knows no excuses, and that particular law is fundamental. We never offended again.

"When in Doubt, Don't Shoot."

I believe that in New Guinea the Australians followed a different teaching, and continued to believe in it. I have heard, for instance, that, once bivouacked for the night, they forbade all movement outside the perimeter, and brought down a heavy fire without question if such movement were heard. I prefer the Wingate teaching; the other leads to trigger-happiness and jumpiness and mutual slaughter. We never forbade movement outside the perimeter; although anybody going out had to be properly cleared before doing so. Certainly, if this slogan had not been learned and taught *ad nauseam* we should have had a lot of unnecessary firing. As it was, men repeated it in moments of stress, and it induced self-control and self-confidence of a high order.

The same applies to the last slogan, "The Answer to Noise is Silence." The Jap relies on noise. He shrieks when he goes into action; he fires shots at random when he thinks he is on to something suspicious. If he is answered by noise, he knows the most of what he wants to know: that somebody is there; whereabouts he is and his approximate strength. All this knowledge he has won for the price of a few rounds. If, on the other hand, he gets no answering cry or shot, he is either falsely reassured or thoroughly discomfited; if the latter, he has lost the moral initiative, and the seeds of nervousness are sown in him. And again, he who answers with silence knows that he has given nothing away, and feels himself to be a Strong, as well as a Silent, Man.

For the worst thing that can befall the commander of a small force in a jungle encounter is the loss of control. When indiscriminate shooting starts, you have begun to lose control; from there it is only a small step to losing moral and physical control of your force. When that disintegrates you are sunk; and soon you will be fighting other elements of your own men. For a long time I had a haunting fear that one of my officers and four men, whom I had to leave behind wounded in 1943, had been hit by the fire of another platoon. Of the five of them, two died on the spot, one was murdered by Burmese, and the fourth died of gangrene, malaria and dysentery on the way to Rangoon. Only the officer survived two and a quarter years in Jap hands; and I was never more relieved in my life than I was to learn from his own mouth the precise circumstances in which he and his men had been wounded; and to know that he had seen the Japs who had hit himself and his men actually discharge the very bullets from a few yards away.

The introduction of the American hand wireless of the type known as " Walkie-Talkie" in 1944 made this business of control much easier; but one still had to keep one's mind on the problem throughout every action, however small. This applied particularly to what we called the Encounter Drill—an immediate action to be applied when meeting the enemy head-on. The idea was for the leading elements to pin him immediately, while elements farther back in the Column automatically carried out a hook analogous to the scorpion's sting. The Jap suffered from the same problems, and had less wit in overcoming them, so that he often inflicted casualties on himself—again resembling the scorpion, who in certain circumstances stings himself to death.

I have already given the Jap credit for good digging. When he had time to make elaborate defences, they were always good; although we never encountered in the interior of Burma anything so elaborate as that remarkable fortress which he built himself at Razabil in Arakan, and which gave such trouble to the 7th Indian Division in 1944. (I believe Mogaung, which Mike Calvert captured after bitter fighting in August of that year, was tough, but I have never met anybody who saw both and was able to compare them.) The Jap's performance in this respect was the more remarkable in that he was short of all the tools and appliances of which our engineers, even in that theatre, had in comparison such a profusion. He improvised well, and his *panjis* of bamboo stakes, sharpened and hardened by fire, were horrible things. To the present generation of Englishmen they appeared new; an earlier generation met them, or something very like them, at a place called Bannockburn rather nearer home.

It was always hard to induce the British soldier to dig, until he had experience of what happened when he didn't. It took Stukas to teach him in Europe and North Africa and Greece and Crete; in Burma he learned it at the hands of Japanese infantry —no mean tribute to that infantry.

One form of defence which I tried in vain to get Wingate to ban was booby-traps. I have no notion how many Japs were killed on our booby-traps; I know that I lost over twenty killed and wounded on traps set by other Chindit brigades. In 1943 several columns used them by setting them in their wake upon tracks where they suspected that the Japs might be following up. No great damage was done: on that occasion we knew when we were clear of each other. But in 1944 there were many columns operating in the same general area; and although they were bound to report what tracks they had trapped, so that other columns could be warned, there was such a glut of traffic on all wireless sets that either the reports or the warnings failed to get through. Captain Chet Khin, my old Karen ally, who was commanding one of the Queen's Reconnaissance platoons, had six casualties in one day from booby-traps laid by a certain column in another brigade. Such losses induce in one a feeling of helplessness and bitter anger.

Booby-traps in such circumstances should only be allowed, in my view, as part of the definite defences of such places as Aberdeen (where I did use them) or White City (where Mike used them most effectively); or on demolitions after they have been blown, to harass attempts at repair. Otherwise they are a menace, and I have never regretted casualties more than the unlucky men thus lost or maimed through thoughtlessness. In Long Range Penetration, lack of ordinary foresight or imagination is the unforgivable sin. One cannot think of everything, but the probable results of light-hearted booby-trapping would be obvious even to a Japanese.

One last gibe at the Jap must be allowed me. He is a rotten shot. He handles his mortars well, getting them up into the forefront of the battle with a skill that we never equalled; but at good old-fashioned musketry he would never get his proficiency pay in the British Army. We found on the other hand that the Burma National Army, whom we bumped up against several times, were much better shots. If I remember rightly, they were armed with British rifles, which may help to account for the marked difference.

In 1940, soon after we were kicked out of Norway, I heard a broadcast by a Scottish serjeant which has always stuck in my mind as the epitome of bad taste. I have never heard any reflections on the behaviour of British troops in Norway, in what must have been a most unpleasant campaign against miserable odds; but it was unbecoming for a man who had taken part in it, and who was now in the safety of the United Kingdom, to mock the German fighting man, and to declare in ranting tones how much better we had proved ourselves, man for man. In decrying the Jap soldier, now that the war is over and he no longer has it in his power to put the wind up me as he has so often in the past, I hope I have not been guilty of the same breach of taste. With all his shortcomings he was certainly a courageous fighter, from whom we learned some bitter lessons, and from whom we have still some to learn in the way of absolute devotion to one's cause, and almost absolute disregard for one's own life. Despite what the newspapers said, he rarely gave himself up while he could stand.

Nevertheless, we must not forget that he is a barbarian; and when we are urged, as we shall certainly soon be urged, to exhibit towards him a spirit of Christian forbearance, we must stretch our memories and make them long. Personally, I shall remember that out of eighty of my men who reached his jail in Rangoon, fifty-two died; I shall remember that sixty more are believed to have fallen into his hands who never reached Rangoon at all; I shall remember what the twenty-eight survivors have told me about their own sufferings, and about how and why some of the others died. And if I am asked to remember that some of them are Christian, I shall recall how it was one of them, who proclaimed himself a Christian with his opening words, who personally devised and superintended the tortures to which one of my officers was subjected. The devil should pray that he be spared his due.

XII

THE LIGHT PLANE FORCE

LATE IN NOVEMBER of 1943 we were in training in the Central Provinces of India. Our date of readiness was only a couple of months ahead. Individual training was over, and we were beginning to train as complete columns. My Brigade lay on the border of two small independent States, ruled by Maharajahs; the eight columns which it comprised were camped by the side of an artificial lake formed by the Gangaw Dam, and by the rocky Ken River running out of it. On either side of the lake and river lay a dry and thorny jungle, in which we trained; and downstream from us two more British Chindit brigades were also bivouacked. The remainder of the Force was some forty or fifty miles to the westward.

From time to time, General Wingate would summon us to conference at Jhansi or Nowgong or Gwalior, to comment on the progress of the training. At one such meeting he introduced a small, broad-shouldered American colonel with a square jaw and a quick smile, newly arrived from the States. Phil Cochran had come to command No. 1 Air Commando, which itself included the Light Plane Force. We did not know until long afterwards that he was the hero of an American comic strip corresponding roughly to Buck Ryan; but so (thinly disguised as "Flip Corkin") he actually was. I have never followed the adventures of Flip Corkin, but if they approach the variety and excitement of Phil's they must be good stuff.

Wingate sat down in his chair, and helped himself to a cup of tea brought by his villainous-looking but faithful servant Bachhi Ram, who had shared his fortunes that spring in Burma. Phil took the stage. For half an hour there poured from his eager mouth a fantastic stream of advertisement. One really blushed to hear him. His boys were marvellous; there was nothing they couldn't do. They would fly us into Burma, and they would fly us out. "I've hurd about yew boys an' all your waalkin'; I feel real bad about all that waalkin'; maybe yew think I'm kiddin'; well, we can always dream, cann't we?"

He had us laughing, he had us entertained, but he failed utterly to convince us. Wingate looked at us from the stage, to see how we were taking it, and his fierce eyes had a twinkle in them at our obvious disbelief. It was usually his rôle to startle us, and to make us wonder whether or not he really believed what he was telling us. To-day Phil Cochran was stealing his thunder.

At the end of the meeting I tackled Phil direct. He had spoken about his light planes, which took off (so he said) in seven hundred and fifty feet—the Americans always speak of feet where we speak of yards. Some of them had already arrived at Karachi, where they were to be assembled. I told him outright that I found his claims hard to believe, but that I would like to give them a fair try; and could I have the first experiment? My brigade was to be the first to take the field, and thus had the least time in which to train with his crews; and I should welcome the chance to see whether or not the aircraft had the performance which he claimed for them, and whether or not they could really operate on the rough landing strips which were all we could hope to build them.

Phil struck the bargain immediately, and gave me a firm promise that I should have the first try-out; and the chance came about a fortnight later. I had set an elaborate scheme in which the Ken River represented the Chindwin; four columns represented British parties returning from a trans-Chindwin raid; the other four represented Japanese trying to intercept them. "The British" were starting from a point in Panna State some twenty-five miles beyond the river; the "Japs" could move or lie up at will anywhere they wished between the "British" and home. My Brigade headquarters were remaining static by the lake; they alone could be reached by road, since the country beyond the river and lake had no motorable tracks at all.

The scheme was due to last three days. We had hoped the aircraft would arrive before it started, and had briefed the columns in their use; the type, length and surface of the strips which they were to prepare, and the maximum height of trees permissible at either end. There was no question, of course, of building strips in the jungle proper; it was a matter of smoothing out existing patches of pasture. Some delay prevented the aircraft from reaching us before the columns left for the exercise; but we had a strip and petrol all ready for them to land on near my headquarters, and had arranged to notify the columns by wireless when they should arrive.

The troops had been out a day, and the "British" were free to start their homeward move, when Captain Smith and Serjeant Chambers arrived with their two "L.5's." Smithy was to be my squadron leader on the actual campaign, but this was the first time I had met him. He was big and burly, sallow-faced, rather reserved to start with, cap on the back of his head, an engaging smile. Chambers was dark, very quiet, the best pilot in the whole outfit; I got to know him well, and have flown many hours with him since in Arakan, Burma, and India. They had barely arrived when a genuine S O S came in from one of the columns. A man had been kicked in the groin by a mule, was unconscious and totally unfit to be moved. They were building a strip, which would be ready at half-past three in the afternoon. Had the light planes arrived, and would they come and get him? It sounded like the perfect test of whether or not Phil Cochran's claims were genuine or empty boastings, of whether or not light planes could really land at short notice to evacuate casualties.

It was then about half-past one, and there was plenty of time in hand before the strip could be ready. Smithy and Chambers settled down to luncheon with the rest of us. An hour later we drove out to the strip, and for the first time I found myself looking at an L.5—that ugly but serviceable contraption to which thousands of our men were to owe their lives in the next few months. Its own mother could not have called it beautiful; it looked like Tenniel's picture of the "Bread and Butter Bird" in *Through the Looking Glass*; the "flying mess-tin," as our men speedily christened it, was its aptest title. The clumsy, narrow wings were secured to the fuselage by round tubes which looked like the frame of a bicycle; and altogether it looked as if aircraft design had gone back to the days of my Uncle Alan Boyle, who once held the long-distance record of six hundred yards, and was the first man to fly over the Brooklands sewage farm.

Smithy took the pilot's seat, and I twisted myself into the passenger's place behind him. We took off, and soon the jungle

and the rapids of the river were spinning away below us. Higher
we rose, until we saw the whole stretch of the Panna and Bijawar
jungles for many miles around. I had told my column that for
the purpose of the exercise all aircraft were to be treated as hostile
by both sides, except by such columns as had actually summoned
them on a mission; and the careful search for signs of troops
all around the countryside disclosed only one party—two or
three tell-tale columns of smoke rising from beside a stream,
itself betrayed by the darker green of the scrub along its length.

Although it was even now only three o'clock, half an hour
before the estimated time when the strip was to be ready for us,
we bore away for the place where comrades of the injured man
had wirelessed that they were building it. Flying at fifteen
hundred feet, we soon saw some fifty figures working like ants
on a patch of pasture not far from the river. We circled them
once, coming lower as we did so; and then Smithy throttled
back, and shouted to me in the sudden silence, "Do you wanna
land?" The strip looked desperately small, but I nodded bravely;
and we came lower yet and had a shot at it. The first time we
were scarcely low enough, and did another circle; the second
time we touched down on the extreme edge of the strip. I saw
that we were at the downward end of a hill, and that the far end
of the strip was well over the crest. However, we bumped to a
halt; and were immediately surrounded by fifty soldiers with
picks and shovels, stripped to the waist, sweating from their
labours, and all agog to see the new toy.

Frank Larman, a squadron leader in the R.A.F., who was
afterwards killed near Mohnyin, had been supervising the work
with a sapper officer; and he said he had tried to wave us off, as they
weren't ready for us. "Wal," said Smithy, "if you finish all the
strips as good as this, I reckon we'll be O.K." He regretted having
said that many times afterwards; because thus encouraged, we
proceeded to try them much too high, and I fear that our optimism
cost a number of aircraft before we were done.

The injured man, groaning and grey with pain—for his con-
sciousness had returned—was hoisted into my seat in the aircraft, which was to take him away and come back for me. She
took off amid the cheers of the crowd: we had arranged for an
ambulance to wait at the strip, and the news spread round the

Brigade like wildfire, at the end of the exercise, how the poor
fellow had been safely in hospital twenty minutes after leaving
the ground.

For those of us who earlier in the year had so often had the
misery of abandoning our wounded, this first demonstration of
the powers of the light aircraft lifted a great weight from our
hearts. Nor did this good omen play us false. The pilots were as
stout as the aircraft; and to the end of my days when I think of
America, or when I hear Americans mentioned, my mind will
flicker across the boys of the Light Plane Force before it finally
focuses on the relevant context.

We got to know them only gradually, as they joined us one
by one. They came in twos and threes, as they completed the
process of assembly at Karachi. The officers came and stayed
two or three days and went—Andy Rebori, a red-haired architect
from Chicago; Sam Edwards, small and young; Hap Arnold;
Smithy himself; Walt Barger the Communications (*anglicé*
Signals) Officer, who as an amateur before the war had communicated over the air with Tommy Moon, my own Signals Officer.
They were a light-hearted lot; and Andy and Sam fairly made
our Christmas for us. They arrived for duty on the 23rd of
December, and were easily prevailed upon to stay and celebrate.
The Prime Minister of Bijawar State had invited me to bring a
party out shooting with him on Christmas Eve, and Andy and
Sam came along with the rest. We saw nothing of moment
except a large bear, which Duggie Dalgleish shot twice in the
chest: it only said "Woof," in much the same tone as an uncle
surprised by a hearty nephew in frolic, and shambled off un-
heeding.

We had the benefit of the light planes on all our remaining
exercises; and on one occasion at least we shook them. I wanted
to go and see my rear headquarters some fifty miles away, and
to take my brigade major with me. Robbie, my senior sapper,
built a strip (admittedly under protest) 200 yards long, instead
of the 280 which had been agreed upon as a minimum; and in
due course two L.5's arrived. After a couple of visible sniffs at
it, they landed. The pilots introduced themselves: they were two
serjeants we had not met before, rejoicing in the names of
Schnatzmeyer and Amspoker, the first an old hand, the second a

lad still under tuition. "Snatch" looked chewingly at the strip, and said: "Wal, we *gaht* here, but I dunno 'bout gettin' aout of here!" Under his directions we knocked down a few trees, filled in a few holes, and added perhaps eight yards to what we had. Then, not much reassured by Snatch saying: "Boy, I'm gonna keep my eyes shut!" I clambered into his aircraft, and put John Marriott into Amspoker's. We revved up with troops sitting on our tails, and then roared flat out along the little space we had; twisted and jinked among the trees at the end, and so were free of the air above the forest.

It was the same firm of Snatch and Amspoker that flew John and me up to our concentration area at Ledo, while the Brigade steamed across India in its fleet of trains. An L.5 is not designed for long journeys, and we grew heartily tired of our cramped positions in the back seat. We went to Delhi first, where I had business, and spent two last nights of comfort in the luxury of the Viceroy's house. Thence it took us three long days of flying at a modest hundred miles an hour to reach Ledo, in the far eastern corner of Assam. Each day we set off in the bright chill of an Indian winter's dawn (it was January); landed two or three times for petrol and food; and reached our stopping place for the night in the last few minutes before it dropped heavily on us like a theatre curtain. Ledo itself, on the third day, we made only just in time; for the ground was already dark, the sun had already dropped, and the vast stretch of black forests yielded its glimpse of Lakhapani strip in the last minutes that we could have discerned it. In his jubilation, Snatch essayed a stylish upward turn before swinging in to his landing; and in that instant the engine stuttered and cut out. He called loudly on the Deity, applied stick and rudder just before she stalled, and in triumph shouted, "I got her whipped!" We glided smoothly down upon the dusty runway, hardly distinguishable by now from the pine-like woods on either hand; and the engine started again as we rolled along it.

Here, during the next few days, I saw other L.5's under General Stilwell's command, bringing in wounded Chinese from the fighting a hundred miles to the south. The Chinese made quiet and stoical wounded, on the whole; they looked small and still and shrunken. One at least was dead when I saw him taken out

of the plane; and I wondered how much he had known of what
he was fighting for, and whether he was any wiser now. I had
had much the same feeling in the Syrian campaign, when I saw
Senegalese fighting Senegalese, some for Vichy, some for de
Gaulle, according to the side which their officers had backed.
But for some chance, this might have been a Chinese from some
other area under some other control, or maybe even from an area
of China—if such there were—where none knew of the war. But
these thoughts are unhealthy before a campaign, and I put them
from me as the dead Chinese was carried away.

Although we used them in many other rôles, it was for the
evacuation of wounded that the light planes were originally
given us, and this remained their chief task throughout the
campaign. No provision had been made for this need on the
British fronts (I use the word "front" as opposed to the Chindit
battle-areas behind the enemy lines), as it had always been hoped
that normal means of evacuation would be possible. But as the
season wore on, and the Japs cut off forward troops in more and
more places, some of our planes were detached from us to work
in such areas as Tamu and Arakan. The composite squadron thus
formed was commanded by Chambers. In the early stages of the
campaign, we stuck to the system of independent squadrons, each
attached to a parent brigade; but later, when several brigades
were working in the same general area, and when casualties to
aircraft had reduced their reserves, the squadrons were amalga-
mated and worked as one. By that time several of the pioneer
squadron leaders had been recalled to the States, and the combined
squadron was commanded first by Bill Lehacka and then by Dick
Boebel. I make no apology for naming these names to the reader:
they mean a lot to us.

The L.5 carried two passengers, or three if the strip were long
enough. A far better aircraft, of which we had only a few
scattered through the squadrons, was the L.1. This wonderful
little machine carried four passengers with ease, including one
stretcher case; but the model was unfortunately obsolete, and as
they became casualties they could not be replaced. The rôle of
casualty evacuation had not been foreseen when they were first
built, and the twin purposes for which the L planes were designed
were artillery spotting and liaison work; for these the 5 was

better than the 1, and the latter had been suffered to go out of production. They were therefore very precious, and whereas the loss of a 5 was regarded as all in the day's work, each loss of a 1 cast a gloom on us. Stomach wounds need stretchers, and only a 1 could take a stretcher. We husbanded them as much as we could, and in the end L.1s were only sent out when they were asked for specifically, and sometimes not even then.

Unlike the 5, the L.1 had to be cranked with a handle from the ground. This foible was a source of embarrassment one day to myself and Serjeant Fiske. Fiske was a real character who often flew me around; he had been a bar-tender in Chicago in an establishment which had included Al Capone and others of his profession among its clientèle. He was a man entirely without nerves, and an excellent pilot. On this particular day, I had arranged to fly south from my fortress at Aberdeen to meet Tom Brodie, who commanded 14 Brigade. Tom and I had been ordered to carry out a converging attack upon the same objective, he from the south and I from the north; and the delicacy of the timing made it essential that we should meet.

It was better for Tom to choose the place and time of meeting than for me. I was comfortable and stationary at Aberdeen; Tom was in an area hotching with Japanese, and it would hardly be fair to ask him to leave his Brigade in the situation in which it found itself. I therefore signalled him asking him to make a strip at his convenience where I could visit him. He named a time and place; it was some fifty miles away, and he wanted me there at three o'clock. Fiske and I left at 2.30; I recollect that some mail had just arrived, and I read it as we flew south, lying on my belly on the planking designed to take a stretcher. At the junction of the Taung and the Meza I took over navigation; I knew the district and Fiske didn't.

To make a light plane strip, you select a paddyfield with good approaches, and remove as many bunds as may be necessary to give you the required length. There is thus no difficulty in recognising the strip from the air, since the dark green lines represented by the bunds are replaced by brown lines running where turf has been removed. We duly saw the strip, but could see nobody upon it, a disconcerting moment which has come my way more than once. We descended gingerly, and saw plenty of friendly uniforms among the trees on the edge of the field; and thus reassured Fiske landed, taxied to the end of the strip and switched off. Our ears were then assailed with the unwelcome sound of small arms fire; and Tom Brodie, emerging from the bushes with one of . his colonels, told us apologetically that some Japs had arrived to interrupt our proposed conference.

Visions of a leisurely gossip over a cup of tea deserted me at once. Our conference was hurried, and no irrelevant topic entered into our talk. In less than five minutes, feeling somewhat conspicuous upon the open paddy, Fiske and I walked back to the "ship." I climbed in and resumed my position on my belly. At that moment, Fiske gave a loud cry, and with a picturesque oath, declared that he had forgotten the cranking handle.

"Can't we swing the thing?" I asked.

"Wal, it's a thing that's never bin done," said Fiske.

I remarked that on the whole it seemed to me that now was the time to try. I was just getting out to go to the airscrew while Fiske tried tricks with the controls, when out of the bushes came one of Tom Brodie's R.A.F. officers, who very civilly applied himself to the job instead. He sweated at it fruitlessly for some time, and I had fully resigned myself to abandoning the aircraft, and continuing the campaign with Tom Brodie's Brigade instead of my own, when at last she fired, Fiske revved her up, the Flight Lieutenant lit out for bush, we taxied down the strip and were speedily airborne. Thereafter, whenever I was going out in an L.1, I was always fussy about seeing the cranking handle before we took off.

I have memories of another L.1 trip with Bill Lehacka. This time we were going over to see Mike Calvert at the White City. I cannot recollect exactly when it was, but we at Aberdeen had heard a lot of noise all night, with a great deal of mortar fire and shelling. It looked as if trouble had boiled up there again, as it did from time to time; and a light plane going over early in the morning had been fired on and unable to land. (We discovered afterwards that the pilot had tried to land on the Dakota strip instead of the light plane strip; and as the Dakota strip bordered a copse which at that time was held by the enemy, the fact that he had been fired on was not surprising.) I had some troops in the vicinity, and thought that they might be of help to Mike in relieving pressure on his defences; I was also keen to discuss with him the general situation.

Our journey over was uneventful; and although we felt a trifle nervous going in, we got down without mishap. The Japs had been trying to get in all night, but at dawn, with Mike's guns and mortars playing on their concentration areas, they had pulled out again. The prolonged bombardment had produced only two wounded Gurkhas, whom Mike asked me to take back to Aberdeen with me after our conference. I also said I would take back Peter Fleming, who had come in from India to have a look round, had accepted an invitation from Mike to spend the night with him, and who (I may be doing him an injustice, but I think not) was overdue from G.H.Q. in Delhi. Now Peter Fleming was a big boy at school when I was a little one; I used to be frightened of him; but on this happy occasion, having put one (stretcher-case) Gurkha on the stretcher platform, and inserted another underneath it, I climbed up behind the pilot with my legs round his neck, and put Peter in the Black Hole in the bottom of the aircraft, where he couldn't see a thing, not even daylight. Thus, with our departure punctuated by an occasional mortar burst, we took off for Aberdeen; with Fleming, sometime Captain of the Oppidans, underneath, and with Fergusson definitely on top.

Another trip from the White City to Aberdeen was less fortunate, but furnished the occasion for one of the epics of courage characteristic of the pilots of the L.P.F. Serjeant Solomon F. Eudy, of Texas, was older than most of the "boys"; he was slow spoken, as befitted his farming background. One day he went over to the White City to collect some wounded Gurkhas; the Japs were fairly close in at that time, and had inflicted some casualties on the garrison the night before. Three miles west of the City his engine conked; he brought his aircraft down skilfully among the dry teak trees, and then for the first time examined his charges in detail. None could speak English; only one could walk. Two of the three had been wounded in the legs, the third in the head. I would have been the last man to blame Eudy if he had decided that his duty was otherwise; his job was to fly, and his aircraft had crashed; but he resolved to get his men in to safety. Aberdeen was fifteen miles to the westward; the White

City five to the east; he rightly decided that he could never get the men to Aberdeen, and resolved to work east to the fringe of the forest, and to await his chance to cross the paddy back into the White City.

It took him two days. He and the other man who could walk carried the two who could not, three or four hundred yards at a time. Twice he left them all, to take their water-bottles to water, through jungle which he thought (and rightly) to be full of Japs. He brought his Gurkhas at last to the edge of the jungle, and, as all seemed quiet, he started to drag them across the open paddy.

Half-way over, one of the occasional Jap air-raids burst on the White City. Eudy froze, and he and his three companions, hungry and thirsty, lay motionless on a stretch of green as flat and featureless as a billiard table while the Zeros whooped and swooped around them. Then they resumed their painful crawl across the open. Mike had summoned more light planes from Aberdeen to come and collect his wounded from the raid, and one of these, passing over, saw Eudy and his men as they were crossing the paddy; the pilot reported them to White City and a patrol went out and collected them. I recommended Eudy for a British Military Medal; he had, after all, been succouring citizens of the Empire; but I was fearful lest on some technicality, because of his being an American, he might be denied it by some unimaginative creature at Headquarters. I am glad to say that he was duly awarded it; and I hope that some day he may receive the medal itself at His Majesty's hands.

Of the many errands of mercy which sent the light planes skimming out just over the tops of the trees from their various bases, the vast majority were completed without incident. The pilots were briefed, took off, loaded up, returned, received a new brief and repeated the process without interruption. Many of them, at busy periods, when fighting was the fashion, carried out seven or eight such missions a day. When things were easy, they dozed in the shade of a tree, played games of dice or cards or curled up in their neat jungle hammocks. But they had always to be prepared for the worst. If a risk was taken, the price for it had usually to be paid. When two of them (senior enough to know better) were sent to land Jim Harman and his men on a sandbank in the Chindwin, and went (it was a hot day) in a pair of shorts and nothing else, they were asking for trouble; and they got it. A week in the jungle without food, without a knife, without a weapon, stripped to the waist at night when the mosquitoes and leeches are thirsty, will teach you a lesson beyond all need for what the schoolbooks call recapitulation. They were picked up, those two, and carried out many more missions during the campaign; and they always carried thereafter, boots, shirts, a blanket, a carbine, a couple of grenades, compass, map, water and a week's provisions.

Another time I got Smithy to land Jim Harman (who was always thirsting for adventure) with a couple of men on a completely unreconnoitred natural landing strip near the Indawgyi Lake. I wanted Jim to carry out a diversion on a Jap-frequented road, so as to impress the enemy with our ubiquitousness. On the way home, Smithy saw some Japs. This was too much for his high spirits; and he spent a happy ten minutes pelting them with grenades and spraying them with a tommy-gun, from a few feet above their heads. Even when not tempting Providence, adventures of a roughish kind were not far round the corner for the light plane pilots.

Murphy crashed one day when out to pick up some wounded men from my old battalion in Tom Brodie's Brigade. Whenever his comrades came to pick him up again, the Japs just beat them to it, and he was what Phil Cochran would call "waalkin'" for over a fortnight. Two others, one of them a doctor, flying side by side in a C.64, got one bullet from near the railway line which neatly went through the inner leg of each. Another, flying out to our guerrilla detachment at Sima Pa, just over the border into China, landed on the strip, rather like Fiske and me *chez* Tom Brodie, to find the Japs in possession, and had to abandon their plane altogether; they were rescued some weeks later, venturing nervously back on to the strip near the wreckage of their own aircraft. Yet another, flying a medical officer out to a particularly nervous strip close to a strong Jap force, to pick up two wounded men, made a bad landing and broke his undercarriage. The doctor made a splint for it after two hours' work with a couple of bamboos, and they flew out again, bringing the casualties with them.

Sometimes their troubles came upon them through carelessness. I will not reveal the name of the pilot who flew me down to visit one of the columns of the Queen's Regiment under Terence Close, which was lying at a village a few miles west of Indaw. Terence had sent me a signal saying that he was ready to hold it "to the last tomato"; and flying down there I found him and his officers (including my old friend Chet Khin) sitting around sun-bathing and eating their way through a heap of tomatoes eighteen inches high, brought to them by obsequious villagers. I heard their gossip, and then went back to the plane. Without taking care to reckon up the length of the strip and the amount of boost which we required for take-off, the pilot pulled back his stick and opened her out. As we got near the end I became nervous; I could feel no sign of her lifting, and guessed we had little in hand. At last I felt the pilot desperately pulling back the stick and her nose rising; and then I felt her tail-wheel strike the ground very hard indeed. She shuddered, recovered, and soared into the air; and we spent the next few minutes flying along at such an angle as would permit of looking at our shadow on the ground and trying to make up our minds as to how much of a tail we had left. We couldn't see for certain; the pilot, throttling down, said he thought we had better go back to Aberdeen, where we would make sure of getting her repaired, than to the strip by my then Brigade headquarters, which was a battle headquarters, without facilities, and somewhat near the enemy. We did so, and it was as well that we did; for as we touched down at Aberdeen, we also collapsed on to the ground amid a cloud of dust; and I was sorry for the pilot's sake to find that Phil had flown in from India that morning, and was present and available to tick him off for having hazarded my allegedly valuable life.

It was Clint Gaty—Colonel Clinton B. Gaty—who first started the fashion of using L.5's for target indication. Flight Lieutenant Gillies had been with John Findlay of the Queen's when Findlay's patrol had wandered at will round a Japanese ammunition dump. Gillies knew precisely where it was, and with Clint flew over it in a light plane to confirm that he could recognise the spot from the air. We flew him out to India to lay on a bomber raid with Phil Cochran's Mitchells; and the following morning he and Clint marked the target area with smoke grenades while the bombers came in and destroyed them with incendiaries. It was a thoroughly successful raid, the first of many such; when the light plane flew at treetop height to make sure of the target, and the bombers merely dropped their eggs where they saw the smoke fall. Systematically by this means the whole important dump area of Indaw was set afire dump by dump, and destroyed without the loss of a man over a dozen successful raids.

Occasionally, even in that well-paddied area around Indaw, it was impossible to find a paddy large enough to build a strip three hundred yards long. For such places as these we used a helicopter. Great strides have been made in this type of aircraft even in the short time which has elapsed; but the helicopter of 1944 had a range of only eighty miles; and the problem of getting it into Aberdeen was tricky. The difficulties were ingeniously overcome without my knowledge. Petrol was flown in to some of the strips which we had constructed during our southward march, being carefully timed to arrive two or three minutes before the helicopter; the helicopter arrived, filled up and took off; and so speedily was each operation accomplished that the air-strip was occupied and deserted again all within five minutes. The first bounce was at Haungpa, the second at Minsein; and the Japs, who had been watching the strips ever since their original construction, arrived in each case too late to prevent take-off.

By the time we left the Indaw area, there were at least fifteen strips in the neighbourhood. The process of building them was simple: the nine- or twelve-inch paddy bunds could be removed by a platoon in a couple of hours. As we grew more experienced, we realised that the native type mattock employed by the local inhabitants was a far more effective tool for this purpose than the picks and shovels which we carried ourselves; and thereafter the strips were always built by locals under the direction of our own men. At Auktaw, where the Leicesters built a strip for the evacuation of their wounded while they were fighting at Inwa, the Japs came and blocked it with heavy logs. When next we needed to fly off wounded from that spot, we found it altogether quicker and easier to build a new strip alongside the old one, than to clear the old one of its logs. From then on, the Japs realised that the blocking of strips was not worth while, and they never bothered to do it again.

Chambers, Snatch, Amspoker, Clephis, Samp, Fiske, Christian, Murphy, Burrell, Tom the Chinese, Potlucky the Pole, and all the others: I know your faces and remember most of your names. When we Chindits are old, garrulous and thundering bores, we will remember what you did for us, and tell our children. In the future our countries may lose their present understanding, and squabble ; but we shall not forget the L.P.F., nor what its light-hearted pilots did for us in their ramshackle planes.

XIII

SIGNALS AND ANIMALS

"SIGNALS," they told me at Camberley, "are the handmaid of the General Staff; but there are limits to the liberties which may be taken with a handmaid."

There were few limits to the liberties which we took with our signals; and there were few calls which we made upon them to which they did not respond. Their difficulties in jungle are great; and most of the time we were asking them to cover immense distances in conditions for which they were not designed. I cannot be technical; indeed, wireless telegraphy, radio telephony and spoof telepathy have often seemed to me to have much in common. Even John Marriott, a competent ex-Signals officer in his own regiment, declared his belief that half the time the Signals were making up their own messages; but this was mere badinage, and on both trips the Signals did a splendid job.

In 1943 our main set for talking back to India was the F.S.6, while we also had three "21" sets, for domestic chatter to any detachments which we might send out from the Column. We had also a huge R.A.F. set called a 1086, which took up three mule-loads, and which, when assembled, looked like a street-organ. In 1944 we had "22" sets for all purposes, other than R.A.F., for which we still retained the street-organ.

The marriage of the two subjects of signals and animals within a single chapter is no *mésalliance*, for they were closely linked. All the worst, heaviest and most awkward mule-loads were signal loads; the sets themselves were bad enough, the batteries were worse, and the charging-engines, for charging the batteries, were the worst of all. I forget now what the brute weighed, but the two biggest mules in each column were earmarked for the charging-engines, and unless one rang the changes, and made them carry turn and turn about, a sore back was certain. The signallers became expert muleteers as well, and the best muleteers were always allotted to the signals mules, as having the most important loads.

I have described elsewhere how the signallers' and cipherers' work began when ours finished. Such poor privileges as were in our gift went to these men and to the muleteers. If some luxury came our way which would not go round the column, it went to these fellows in turn. I remember enviously watching them guzzling tinned peaches which came to us one drop: a tin between every two men, instead of between every six or eight, as would have been the case had we issued them all round the column. This was poor recompense for all the extra work they had to do; yet they never groused or grumbled, and took the greatest pride in their work.

The lack of a decent man-pack set, with speech over thirty miles, was a great nuisance. The Reconnaissance Platoon, when properly handled, should be working twenty or more miles ahead of the main column; all John Fraser's best work in 1943, when he occupied that position in my No. 5 Column, was accomplished at that range. But in order to speak back to me he had to have wireless ; and in order to have a wireless he had to have a mule; and in order to have one mule he had to have two: for mules hate going singly, and give endless trouble when made to do so. The only man-pack set available in India had too short a range for this purpose. In 1944 we were given a new set known as a "B2," which weighed some thirty pounds, and which was said to have these qualities; but we only got it at the last moment before leaving railhead, the crystals had not been properly tested, and only two sets out of nine in the Brigade ever gave satisfaction. Moreover, it was a brute to carry; even local coolies pressed into service mutinied and bolted after a few miles, and I for one did not blame them.

We thought the "22" set excellent. It was said to be temperamental, but we did not find it so; it was said to be delicate, but we thought it remarkably robust. I have seen it several times hurtle down a hillside on its mule's back, without either mule or set being one penny the worse. Some of the more athletic mules invented a sport called, "Putting the Wireless Set"; the record put, in my experience, was some twenty-two feet; and the wireless worked even after that.

The trouble with wireless in that country was the jungle-filled valleys, which does odd things to radio; the inevitable thunder somewhere between us and our base in India, usually in the hills west of the Chindwin; and the unvarying fade-out half an hour to an hour after dark. The Americans in Aberdeen had a powerful set which bored through most thunderstorms, but even it was swamped at times. Most of our wireless traffic was cleared at the midday halt of three hours, which was statutory throughout my Brigade; and one could usually count on an hour after getting into bivouac before the atmospherics overwhelmed us. If there was still much traffic outstanding, the tireless signallers would rise early, and put in an hour's work before dawn, when conditions again were usually all right.

Each battalion had five " 22" sets, three with the senior column and two with the junior. Operational messages were all passed through Brigade Headquarters, but columns had to be able to speak to Air Base direct to pass their Q.Q. messages concerning supply drops. In 1943 all messages had to go through Brigade, with the result that there was one continuous jam of traffic from the moment we crossed the Chindwin on the way in, until the final disaster near the mouth of the Shweli River, when every set in the Brigade but three went off the air for good. Throughout the campaign only the most vital messages could be passed. In 1944 we were determined to avoid this mistake, and a new system of command was devised, based partly on proposals framed by John Fraser and myself.

Each Brigade had a Rear Brigade Headquarters, to act as a Poste Restante. If for any reason, such as enemy action, a column had to be on the move between twelve noon and three, and could not receive its messages from Brigade Headquarters, Brigade would pass its messages to Rear Brigade, and the column would collect them from Rear Brigade when an opportunity offered. Rear Brigade intercepted all signals, from columns to Brigade, from Brigade to columns, or from either to Air Base; so that at any given moment Katie Cave, my second-in-command sitting at Rear Brigade, knew exactly what all of us inside Burma had communicated with each other. In addition, two or three times a day, Rear Brigade would broadcast a Situation Report, compiled from the information received through listening in, which all columns could receive.

Rear Brigade also acted as the channel between me and Orde

Wingate's Headquarters. Any orders which Wingate wanted passed to me, he gave to Katie; anything I wanted passed to Wingate, I signalled to Katie.

The system worked pretty well. The chief trouble was the gap between Rear Brigade and Air Base, which were separated from each other by a hundred and fifty miles of air travel, and a thousand of surface travel. Anybody wishing to go by road and rail between the two had to travel by road to the railway at Manipur Road Station, and thence half-way round Assam to reach air base at Sylhet from Force and Rear Brigade Head-quarters at Imphal; since the direct route from Imphal to Sylhet via Bishenpur was only traversed by a rough track, barely pass-able even for a Jeep. When in March 1944 the Japs passed to the offensive, and cut the road between Imphal and Manipur Road Station near Kohima, Imphal could only be reached by air; and during that month, when the Japs were on the verge of breaking into the Imphal Plain, and were within a few miles of Rear Headquarters, Wingate ordered the whole shooting-match to fly out to Sylhet. This happened at the awkward moment described in Chapter V when I was spread-eagled on the Kyagaung Range above Indaw, hungry for news from every quarter, and unable to get it; since my Rear Brigade Headquarters was, liter-ally and in every sense of that undignified word, in flight.

From then on, Katie and John Stobbs were alongside each other; and certainly, if a third Expedition had materialised, as it very nearly did, Rear Brigade, Force Headquarters and Air Base would surely have been together. There was, it is true, a move on foot, chiefly for reasons of economy, to amalgamate Rear Brigades into one vast Force Headquarters; but all the Brigade Commanders were fighting strong rearguard actions against that unwelcome proposal.

Each Brigade Signal Section, while remaining one unit, was split between Rear Brigade in Manipur or India, and Main Brigade in the field with the columns, the senior Signals officer being in the field. I was lucky in having an extra Signals officer with me in the shape of Jack Hallett: he had been sent to me in error as an infantry officer, and I naturally played the idiot boy and put him as longstop to Tommy Moon. The Signals people at Force Headquarters had their revenge on me by stealing the extra cipher operators whom I had trained for Rear Brigade: I had proclaimed abroad my belief that the approved cipher establishment was too weak, and had trained a lot of sick and sorry, hammer-toed and wall-eyed, weak-kneed and malarial, as additional cipher staff for Katie. The insufficiency of cipherers is a lesson which we learn in every campaign and forget with every victory.

Another such lesson is the misuse of signal priorities. In this matter Wingate himself was the chief offender; he never sent a signal with any priority lower than Most Immediate. He had an awkward habit of despatching circular signals to all columns, either of exhortation or (more often) of reproof. There was an occasion in 1944, when Mike Calvert had completed his fly-in, when Wingate decided to send out a flamboyant and eloquent "Order of the Day," which completely and utterly jammed all my wireless sets throughout the whole Brigade for forty-eight hours. A similar curse fell on the commanding officer of a battalion of my own Regiment in North Africa, when the Germans were launching an attack, and he was trying to get through to the gunners to bring down their S.O.S. shoot. He was told by the signallers that there was an incoming call from Division with priority over his. Fuming, he waited for it; only to hear the voice of his Divisional Commander saying, "Now, all good luck to you. You realise you must hold on to the last man and the last round?"

To which he replied:

"To hell with the last round! I'm trying to get the first round to go off, if you'll only get to hell out of this and off the line!"

Signals, once framed, required careful watching, since they were quick to go out of date: and a signal of burning urgency at one moment, which had missed its chance of despatch, might have to be killed before it cluttered up the air at the expense of another message of later and greater import. The sheaf of signals, enciphered and ready for despatch, had to be constantly reviewed, and some of them selected for massacre. Unlike ordinary warfare, where a wireless station can either transmit on the move or only moves intermittently, in our warfare a wireless station only halted intermittently: the aerials would be up within five minutes, and the signallers on the air within seven; and from then on messages would be flowing out and in until the mules were being saddled up to move on again. Cipherers, to save time, would encipher and decipher even on the move, stumbling over roots upon the track, and calling out the figures to another man marching behind them with the book.

The more weary signallers and cipherers become, the more liable you are to get corrupt groups and meaningless messages. The highest praise I can bestow on these men of mine is to proclaim the rarity of corruptions in their work; and that I can do with a clear conscience and deep gratitude.

Of mules I should like to celebrate the virtues in a great epic poem. I love them from the tip of their Bolshie ears to the outer rim of their highly suspect hind hooves. The patient eyes and courageous hearts of the great family of mules move me with a real affection.

When mules first came into my ken near the Betwa River in India, in 1942, I knew nothing of them; and the pundits surrounded them with such an aura of mystery that I began to wonder if I should ever learn even the elements of their management. There was a tendency to regard them as the property and responsibility of the Animal Transport Officer, and to regard him as the Monarch of the Muleteers. Until that attitude was abandoned, we never did any good with our animals. The main essentials of animal management are common sense. The initial fitting of the beast's saddle is the job of an expert; once that is done, every platoon commander can learn the rest. Thereafter, the proper loading and handling of his own mules is his responsibility, and, as they say in Scotland, no other body's.

My predecessor in command of 5 Column made the initial mistake of sending for training as muleteers the worst men in his column. It was too late for me, in that year, to reverse his decision, but much was done by making the muleteers realise how important they were. The following year, the various battalions in my Brigade played fair, and argued, reasonably, that other things being equal, transport drivers, with their traditions of maintenance, should make the best mule-drivers; and it was so. We were lucky to have a number of ex-Yeomanry troopers with commissions suitable for immediate employment as A.T.O.s; and for Brigade A.T.O. we had Bill Dixon, who had gone to Sandhurst the hard way, having enlisted as a trooper in the 4/7th Dragoon Guards after leaving school. One column had an English horse-dealer, another a Border farmer; and in short there was not a dud A.T.O. in the whole outfit. After the campaign was over, and our mules had flown back to India, we got a pat on the back for their condition at every level, finishing with the Director of Remounts and the Army Group Commander— a chaplet of compliments which I pass on with a graceful bow to those responsible.

The bigger mules, for heavy loads such as the signal equipment and the mortar bombs, were mostly South African or Argentinian; the smaller, which were so tiny that we called them mice and minnows, were Indian. By that stage in the war there was a critical shortage, and the cry for mules was ascending to heaven from Maungdaw to Fort Hertz. The smaller ones, which at first were despised, proved to have hearts of gold; one tiny one, which carried, along with some H.Q. stuff, some of my own possessions—the one privilege I allowed myself—was known as the Brigadier's mule, and was affectionately christened "Brodie," out of compliment to the Commander of 14 Brigade. (I don't think he knows this—yet.) Provided they were properly looked after and properly loaded, those beasts would go for ever.

Properly looked after and properly loaded—both were matters for common sense. To see that the back was clean before the saddle was put on; to see that nothing in the way of twigs or mud was adhering to the underside of the saddle when it was put on; to see that the loads were decently done up in the loading-ropes; to see that they were scrupulously balanced so that neither side was heavier than the other; to see that the saddle was precisely in the right place; to see that the girth was fully tight, so that only two fingers could be worked between it and the animal's belly; to make sure that the buckle of the girth did not come where the load bore upon it; to see that the breechings and breast-ropes were right; to see that the girth was still tight twenty minutes after starting, when the animal might have "blown;" to see that the saddle was not whipped off the mule immediately after halting, when he was still hot and sweaty; to see that he could drink in comfort, and was allowed to go on drinking "the other half," after his first series of gulps, followed by the inevitable look round; to see that his back was massaged and his hooves cleaned out; to watch eagerly for the first appearance of a gall, so that it could not develop: these were the chief matters of concern. One lapse on the part of the muleteer, one stage with a burr under the saddle or a high-riding buckle, and the mule might be out of action for a month, and would join that tell-tale procession of mules without a load, which betrayed inefficiency or carelessness somewhere.

We had a few, a very few, spare animals; and as a campaign wore on these decreased. Every column had a list of the order in which stores and equipment should be jettisoned. If a disaster should happen in one's mule-train, one must know at once, and without having to think it out, what was to be chucked away and what was to be taken on. In Brigade Headquarters, Brodie's load was top of the priority list, and it was jettisoned on the Kyagaung Range, when we had to have *pakals* (tin tanks) of water dropped to tide us over a waterless week. Some of the animals, such as those carrying the Vickers machine-guns, had special saddle-fittings, and this complicated the problem a trifle; but for most loads we relied upon the universal carrier, a shoddy-looking affair whose usefulness belied its appearance.

The men became passionately fond of their mules: not only the muleteers, but the whole platoon who owned them. I have seen men weeping at a mule's death who have not wept at a comrade's. I have seen men jeer at another platoon whose mules were having to be helped to their feet, when their own had successfully negotiated whatever obstacle had proved too hard. David Rose in my Regiment tells of how he saw a Jock grab hold of a mule's hairy ear, bring it down to his mouth like a telephone receiver, and say into it, "Hallo, there!" The mules did more than their share in keeping us in a good temper; and their fabled obstinacy, translated into terms of sticking to their job through thick and thin without urging, is a rare and fine quality. Their determination not to be left behind was pathetic; and I shall always remember as one of the saddest sights I have seen the spectacle of a mule refusing to leave its half-section, who was succumbing to a bullet-wound. They were two animals which always refused to be separated and had to be worked together;

they had come to us together, and the men who brought them told us that they had never been apart. By the banks of the Irrawaddy, one of them lay down and died; the other stood and nuzzled it long after the breath had gone out of its body; at last it consented to come with us, but it was never any good again. It pined away to nothing, and at last we had to eat it.

There are certain loads which mules hate, such as anything with a really loud rattle or chunks of raw meat. The wildest mule I ever saw was one which was asked to carry a load of dixies on training. (Dixies are great metal cooking-pots, perhaps eighteen inches long and twelve deep.) They got him loaded all right, but having taken one step he heard behind him a noise like a thousand kettles. He took some quick paces to get away from them, and the nasty noises pursued him. There followed a performance between him and the cook-serjeant, who was still vainly hanging on to his head, which looked for all the world like two strange associates on a see-saw. The cook-serjeant went up and the mule went down; the mule went up and the cook-serjeant went down; then the mule "put" the cook-serjeant (who was a better object for the purpose than any mere weight) and galloped away into Central India with the dixies on his back clanging like the bells of Notre Dame at every bound; nor was he seen for a week. What became of the dixies, like the bandicoot in *The Charity that Began at Home*, no one ever knew.

I have heard it said, and seen it written by an officer with experience in "V" Force in Arakan, that mules in the jungle offer such problems of feeding that they are a hindrance on deep patrolling. I do not subscribe to this view. Provided you can get either unhusked paddy or bamboo (or, better still, both), they will do well. The quantity of bamboo-leaves which a mule will devour is fantastic, and amounts to at least twenty pounds a day. To keep him at the top of his form, however, he will do better on proper feeding, and we worked for the purposes of supply-drops on three pounds a day.

Horses and ponies, on the other hand, did not thrive on bamboo or paddy, and both years they wasted fast. They could not keep going like the old mule, and were out of condition within a few days of leaving roadhead. Their numbers diminished at a shocking rate, and they were susceptible to all sorts of woes which passed by the mules. I do not remember losing a single mule from fatigue or exposure; only from battle-causes, accident, drowning, or on one occasion when we had an outbreak of anthrax, probably caught from a pool where elephants had been drinking. We were always afraid of surra, but by avoiding old standings and lighting smoke fires we seemed to get away with it. With horses and ponies we had endless foot troubles, however carefully we shod them; the mules were unshod as soon as we left the road, and did well in that condition.

Horses and ponies were primarily for carrying casualties, and also gallopers. The A.T.O. and his serjeant were usually mounted, and they were the only individuals who had horses as of right: others requiring them asked the A.T.O., and were allotted one for their immediate need out of a pool. We used them also to carry the packs and equipment of men who were sick, but not sick enough to ride; it was the brutal truth that many men got better more quickly if they were kept moving; and the mere reprieve from carrying one's pack was almost enough in itself to effect a cure. I am not at all sure that I should have got out of Burma myself in 1943 had I got on a horse after being wounded in the muscle of the hip: although marching was painful, it prevented any stiffening setting in, and after a few days I was able to walk as well as anybody.

Horses were useful for intercommunication, but not as much as we had hoped; for a jungle track is rarely wide enough for a horse to pass a moving column. At a halt, even the short halt between each hour of marching, the rule was for the track to be completely cleared so that one could walk or ride from the head to the tail of the column without trampling down the resting men. It was the normal practice at each of these halts for an officer from the head of the column to ride half-way down, where he met another coming up from the tail; they would have a word with each other, and then return to their starting point. At supply-drops, too, there was usually a horse handy for whatever officer was running the drop; the dropping zone was often half a mile from the bivouac, and it was highly desirable to have mounted orderlies on duty between the two.

Some extremely gallant actions were performed by mounted men on different occasions. In February, 1943, a young officer of

the Burma Rifles by the name of Toye rode forty miles through
hostile country from Tonmakeng to Myene to bring Wingate
news of Japanese movements; and the following month a
corporal in my own Column (and, I am proud to say, from my
own county) undertook a hazardous ride on my call for a volunteer. I had had several men wounded whom I had to leave, and
I wanted to get hold of some Burma Riflemen to travel back to
the spot where I had left them to induce the local villagers to
take them into their care. It was getting dark, and I knew that
five miles along a certain track there should be a section of
Burrifs. I asked for a volunteer to get on a horse, ride out along
the track, which none of us knew, and try to locate this section.
We were just about to blow a bridge on the railway; we had
already been in action that day in the neighbourhood; another
column was making trouble a few miles to the south; and all
the Japs in the neighbourhood were on the *qui vive*. It was a job
I should have hated myself; but Corporal McGhie volunteered
to go, mounted a horse, and rode off into the darkness. He
found the Burrif section, and returned with Lance-Naik Ba U
and two men, who went back to the scene of our fight only to
find the Japs in possession. I remember thinking, as McGhie
rode off, that I was witnessing a brave act, undertaken in cold
blood and loneliness. Later in the campaign both McGhie and
Ba U became missing; but Ba U escaped in 1944, McGhie was
found in Rangoon in 1945, and I submitted the names of both
for the Military Medal. I know McGhie got his, and I hope Ba U
was also lucky.

Elephants I never acquired, although at various times other
columns had the use of them for short periods. I believe there
were about eight thousand working elephants in Burma at the
time of the Japanese invasion, and most of these were owned by
the big firms. Some were turned loose and roamed the country;
a few were taken into hiding by their *oozys* or drivers; most were
worked for the Japs. Mike Calvert managed to pick up a few both
years, and in 1944 had what was almost a regular elephant train
working for him in the Kachin hills east of the railway. He had
had bad luck with one or two supply-drops, in that wire and
defence stores intended for White City were dropped by mistake
on one of his floater columns in the hills, while foodstuffs in-

tended for the columns fell in White City. He used his elephants
to move the stores down to where he needed them. My Leicesters,
once, when extremely hungry, had a supply-drop in the Auktaw
Reserve Forest, which consisted entirely of barbed wire and
booby-traps intended for Mike, and not much good as articles
of diet.

Elephants are more vulnerable than mules to the criticism
made by the "V" Force officer in Arakan—that their feeding
problem outweighs their usefulness. They eat like gargantuans
(whatever those may be), and belong, moreover, to a strict trade
union which severely limits their working hours. They can
carry reasonably great weights, and are remarkably agile in
what they can tackle; they make splendid pioneers, crashing
down thick jungle in a few minutes which would take a gang
of slashers several hours. But my knowledge of elephants is entirely hearsay, and I had better not talk about them any more
for fear of uttering some solecism.

Pack bullocks are by no means to be despised. Their great
virtue lies in their independence of grooming: they take no
looking after, and a "bullocketeer" (a horrible word which I am
ashamed to admit having coined) had nothing to do but prod
the animal along with a stick. They offer no forage problem,
since they graze contentedly on whatever offers. They are slow
movers, slower than mules; but the average speed of a column
is so liable to constant checks and minor halts that they do not
really impose much delay on one's movement as a whole. They
have two principal limitations: first, the extreme difficulty of
fitting a saddle to them; and secondly, they cannot carry more
than about thirty pounds a side, as opposed to seventy a side on a
small mule and ninety on a large. But—and this is a big but—
they constitute a welcome reserve of meat on the hoof, and a
little beef a few hundred miles into Burma is thoroughly welcome. In 1943 I took three pack bullocks to carry extra forage
for the mules, and we ate them all before we reached the
Irrawaddy. I felt a bit of a cad eating them after all they had done
for us; but that did not deter me from giving the order. Like
the Walrus, I held my pocket-handkerchief before my streaming
eyes; and like the Carpenter, I kept asking for another slice.

The "bullocketeers" felt little pity for their charges, however;

they were hurt by the complete coldness shown to them by the bullocks whom they had prodded so far. The mules were quick to distinguish between their own muleteers and the other two-footed animals around them; the bullocks remained supremely indifferent, and so died unlamented.

People laughed at our bullocks, as we marched them up the Manipur Road; they seemed to think that they added the last comedy touch to a comedy farce. They were wrong. If some of the formations on that front, who proclaimed so loudly that they were bogged down by lack of mules, had tried out bullocks, they would have found them excellent substitutes. Although they would have had limitations in forward areas, they could profitably have been used to replace mules in the back areas, thus making the mules available for the front line.

One more animal completed our menagerie—our dog. Two months before the 1943 Expedition started, during a conference at Brigade Headquarters, Orde Wingate told every column commander to produce two men for training with Army dogs at Dehra Dun. I remember the occasion well, because it produced from an officer of one of the Gurkha columns, who must have spoken without thinking, the odd remark that he didn't suppose it was any good sending Gurkhas, as the dogs presumably only understood English. I chipped in gravely to say that I didn't suppose the dogs had a very extensive vocabulary, and that in the course of two months it should be possible to train up the Gurkhas to the same linguistic standard as the dogs: which went down terribly badly with the Gurkha officers.

In due course the men went. I sent Anders and Cummings; and they came back at Christmas time with Judy, a Staffordshire bull-terrier bitch. She carried round her neck a leather satchel of the same pattern (to my amateur eye) as cavalry officers wear on their cross-belts. She was trained to run between two men. Say, for instance, that I was sending out John Kerr's platoon (as I did at Tonmakeng) on detachment, and wanted Judy to run between us: Anders would go with John, taking Judy with him, while Cummings would remain with me. Once in position, Anders would send Judy away: she would run to Cummings where she had last seen him, at my Headquarters. Then, if Cummings sent her away, she would run back to Anders. We used her several times, working from outposts back to Column Headquarters, and she was extremely good.

Nobody except Anders and Cummings, her two masters, was allowed to speak to her, feed her, pat her or take any notice of her. In the end, both her masters were killed or missing, and thereafter she shed her professional status and became a mascot. She got out to India in due course with one of my dispersal groups, was embezzled by an officer, and was last heard of serving with him somewhere on the North-West Frontier. She is entitled to the 1939-45 Medal and the Burma Star, and I trust that she has been duly invested with both.

On the Scottish National War Memorial in Edinburgh Castle, not only the men and the women, but the animals are remembered, from the horses and mules of the gunners and the R.A.S.C. to the mice used by the tunnellers to test the air. That is right and proper. So do we remember the animals that shared our wanderings with us, and most of all the mules. They could not have shown more spirit or devotion, more pride in their endurance, if they had known and rejoiced in the cause in which they were working. Some are dead, some are still serving, some, no doubt, retired. May the living have good masters in their lives, and may their loads sit lightly and balanced on their willing backs; and may the dead enjoy good grazing and frequent supply-drops in the Elysian pastures.

XIV

A. AND Q.

ONE OF the joys of Long Range Penetration was that you were largely shorn of your administrative tail. In modern war the proportion of men actually engaged in fighting the battle has become smaller and smaller, and the number of men required to support the fighting greater and greater. It would be wrong to suggest that we were not a major administrative headache to those behind us; but the privilege of having the headache was largely delegated to the unfortunates at Air Base, who became for this purpose the whipping-boys both of Wingate's own Headquarters and of ourselves in the field.

The credit for building up the supply dropping system must go to Peter Lord, a retired officer of the Border Regiment who was appointed Staff Captain to Wingate's original Brigade at the end of 1942, and who eventually became King of the huge Air Base system which nurtured us in 1944. Few know it; but Peter Lord is to Air Supply what the Wright brothers were to the aeroplane. The first year the whole Expedition was supplied by Burbury's 31 Squadron, R.A.F., with three Dakotas and two Hudsons. The Hudsons were a failure; they could not fly down to the speed of the Dakotas, who waddled like a Thames Barge just over our heads; they flew so fast that half of the parachutes which they dropped turned inside out, like a funny-man's umbrella, as soon as they opened and their loads came down woomp and smashed. 31 Squadron did us proud; their spirit was exemplified by the unknown aircraftman who always dropped the morning paper on us at the end of the last run of the drop, and was wildly cheered by the men on the ground.

In 1943 the first two supply-drops were on a grand scale, catering for Brigade Headquarters and five columns. With so few aircraft, they took three days to accomplish, and it seemed incredible that the Japs should not get wind of them and fight for the drop. They didn't; but I was glad that after that we had drops to individual columns. My own column was unlucky; we were the leading column for much of the time, and it was thought that a drop on us a few days ahead of the main body would give away Wingate's intentions to the enemy. The result was that I only got two drops, both beyond the Irrawaddy, and my total receipt of rations over more than seventy days amounted to only twenty days' worth of food.

We had Royal Air Force officers with us, and they were always first class. In 1943 they were invited to volunteer for a special mission, of which the nature was unspecified; they all thought they were going to fly some new type of aircraft; and their language when they heard that, instead, they were going to march more than a thousand miles was not of the choicest. Their duty that first year was primarily to organise supply-drops, and secondly to get experience: we used to torment ours, Denny Sharp, by describing him as "Officer in Charge of Droppings," which he didn't like. It turned out that the task of running a supply-drop was easy for those with a little experience, and did not in itself require an Air Force officer at all. The finding of suitable Dropping Zones had to be fully understood by all Column Commanders and Reconnaissance Platoon Commanders.

To start with, we thought that a supply-drop must take place on open paddy; but as we gained in experience we found that other sites would do equally well. A dry *chaung*-bed, or thin jungle where the parachutes, even if they were caught up in trees, could be easily retrieved, were often used. Far the most important thing was to ensure that there was no obstacle to the circling of the aircraft at three hundred feet. If the drop took place from a greater height than that, half the parachutes would drift away from the dropping zone and might never be found. The aircraft would drop four or five parachutes on each run, and they would circle to port: so that while an obstacle to starboard might be acceptable, an obstacle to port was not. Nor was it desirable to have an obstacle even outside what one considered the range of the aircraft's circuit (which we reckoned at three miles); it put the pilots off, and resulted in a bad drop.

The task of a Reconnaissance Platoon Commander detailed to find a supply:dropping zone was therefore not easy, especially in ill-mapped country. We were often cursed by the dropping pilots for choosing a mediocre site when they could see a good one only a couple of miles away; they forgot that they could see everything from up in the air, while we had to struggle painfully through solid jungle to find a place, and could never get a view at all.

In 1943, daylight dropping was the rule, and, the Jap air effort being negligible, interceptions rarely took place. I am often asked why the Japs did not see these drops in progress and come to interrupt them. In point of fact, they sometimes did; I never had one interrupted myself, but Brigade Headquarters were unlucky twice. An opposed supply drop is impossible; the parachutes come down all right, but they cannot be collected, nor their contents distributed. All the same, it is not easy to judge from jungle precisely where a drop is taking place. Once, when I was ordered by Wingate to meet him at a drop on a certain *chaung*, I could see the aircraft circling all round me, but it took me two hours to find where they were actually dropping their supplies.

The second year the Jap air effort was more in evidence. It was thought wise to have daylight drops only as far as the Chindwin, and thereafter night-drops only. Experience showed that night-drops were more successful; the pilots had to take especial pains to drop precisely over the line of fires which indicated the dropping zone; and the results were more accurate, even though they dropped from a greater height by night than by day. One disadvantage of night drops was that it kept tired men up all night when they should have been rolled in their blankets and asleep, whereas a day drop meant some relief from marching; a stern column commander, on the other hand, eager to cover his mileage, used to chafe at the waste of good marching time resulting from a daylight drop. We used to look forward to a daylight drop as affording a rest; even though people as tired as we were start off more wearily after a meagre half-day's rest than after a normal midday halt. Limbs and muscles grow correspondingly stiffer; and we were to learn, before the end of the campaign, that after several months of marching, even a three days' rest does you as much harm as good.

The essence of a good supply drop lies in foresight, a speedy pick-up and a speedy distribution. Your site should be four hundred yards long at the least to allow a good pilot with a good crew of shovers-out to drop four or five parachutes on each run. You lay your fires in the shape of an L: the bay on the right-hand side of the letter being sanctuary, and the parachutes and free drops falling on the left of the letter parallel to the long arm. You select your firemen, to build and tend the fires; your pickers-up, complete with mules and muleteers, to bring in the loads (which have attachments to enable them to be hooked on to the mules' harness); your dumpmen, to run the dumps to which the stores are brought according to their nature—Food, Boots, Clothing, Equipment, Ammunition, Explosives, Petrol; your recorders, who count the number of loads dropped in each run. These recorders sit at several vantage-points, noting what is dropped; beside them sit markers, who draw a chart and mark in each load which has fallen outside the proper dropping zone, showing on their chart the direction in which it has fallen and the estimated distance. In addition, there are various officers to co-ordinate the work of each party. The secret is to have every available man properly employed; not forgetting the protection of the area, patrols watching for interception, and an alarm post to which everybody repairs in the event of trouble. If it were not for this last, any battle which might develop would turn into an all-against-all.

I have long since lost count of how many supply drops I have had; but I have never not been gladdened by the sound of the planes arriving. We would greet them with a recognition signal flashed on an Aldis lamp, and then they would circle once or twice before beginning to drop. If all was going well, we left them alone; if not, we could speak to them on the radio. With daylight drops it was normal for the aircraft to fly around after each other in a circus, each dropping as it flew past; with a night-drop this was apt to be dangerous, and it was thought safer for each aircraft to complete its seven or eight circuits and fly home, being relieved by another. When all was done the collection and distribution would begin. It was our pride to complete this as quickly as possible; and we soon learned that mail must not be issued until everything else was done: otherwise everybody knocked off surreptitiously to read the latest from home. It was always a slow business, and a column was seldom ready to move off inside four hours after the drop was finished.

One's feelings at a supply drop were mixed. One was intensely relieved to know that one had rations for another five days; at the same time one was rueful in contemplating the enormously increased weight of one's pack. Mail was the greatest joy; and the misery when there was none was beyond comfort. Sometimes it was definitely missing; on a bad drop, such as we had more than once on the Patkais, one knew for certain that it had gone drifting away down into the depths of the valley below; once it was dropped on the Japs instead of on us; once, we think, it was stolen by natives, who, when they got used to the process around Indaw, were always hanging about in the deep field in hopes of high catches.

Boots and clothing were dropped free; so was fodder for the animals. These were dangerous loads, and we had a number of casualties; one fatal one which I remember was on an unfortunate armourer, not on duty, sleeping half a mile from the dropping zone. Boots and clothing were never damaged through being dropped free, but sometimes a parachute would fail to open, with the worst results to its load. All food, however, was valuable, and even damaged tins had to be brought in to a special dump, from which each platoon received a proportion of the broken stuff as part of its rations: it "counted." Anybody found munching, or filling his pockets, from a broken container was liable to the severest punishment, even if he hadn't eaten for a couple of days.

Almost everything that came down in a drop was useful, with the sole exception of some of the cushion-like material used for breaking the fall of the more delicate items, such as wireless sets or batteries, petrol for the charging engines, or charging engines themselves. The acid in the batteries, incidentally, was jellified in some mysterious way, so that it could not spill. Parachute cloth made excellent handkerchiefs and sweat-rags; a sweat-rag, tied round the neck, was almost an essential garment, for we sweated till the pores of our skin were sore. Furthermore, parachute cloth was the best possible currency among the locals, who had been unable to buy new clothing since the war, and were dressed mostly in rags. A headman who helped us was more grateful for a gift of parachute cloth than for a tip of fifty rupees. Indeed, we learned that parachutes were changing hands for thirty rupees apiece, and that Tonmakeng, where we had our second Grand Drop in 1943, became a rich village from its windfall in this material. The cords that attached the canopy to the load were particularly useful, and were issued in fair proportion to the platoons in exactly the same fashion as the stores and rations. It was light, silken stuff of an incredible strength, and the men would wind it round and round their hats like a *puggaree*. It had a hundred uses, varying from mule-lashings to bedding-lines, picket-ropes to boat-painters. For hundreds of miles they were my trousers' only source of upkeep.

We kept down to a minimum the amount of wireless traffic incidental to a supply drop. Each column carried a little booklet in a waterproof cover, in which were micro-photographs of many pages of typescript. Here under various headings was listed every conceivable requirement. The Medical section included obscure drugs with yards of Latin names; the heading "Padres' Requirements" included portable pyxes and Communion Wine; mortar-bombs and split-pins, spare barrels for Vickers guns, armourer's tools, wireless coils, boot-repairers' awls— everything was included. Opposite each item was a code number, which was all that had to be quoted on a signal. Air Base did the rest.

There was also a "Standard Drop" which never varied. If your current column strength was four hundred and twenty men, you said so in your signal, and you got a Standard Drop for that number of men, plus special items which you quoted out of the little booklet. All this information was embodied in a signal called a "QQ" which told Air Base when and where you wanted your next drop. Air Base then told you whether or not you could have it; this depended on what the Army airily calls "other commitments." Eventually, with luck, you got a signal from Air Base called a "Q.K.," which told you that the drop was on. We in the field had no conception of the worry and the flurry that went on at Air Base; we only knew that thanks to Katie Cave (who watched our interests from Rear H.Q.) and John Stobbs at Air Base, we got what we wanted.

Even in 1944, however, we were always short of aircraft.

Wingate, exploiting to the full the license given him by Mr. Churchill and President Roosevelt, had requested and obtained the transfer of a large number of Dakotas from the Middle East to support our thrust; 117 Squadron, the champion of all supply-dropping squadrons, came to us from Italy as a result of these negotiations. But various circumstances conspired to poach these precious aircraft from us: the surrounding of British and Indian forces in Arakan and Manipur, the need to switch divisions to hard-pressed points within S.E.A.C., the insistence of General Chiang Kai Shek for increased tonnage over the Hump were among the factors which drew on our reserves of transport support: with the result that we could never get anything like all we needed. We were never stinted in food, but we were hard hit over things like clothing and boots.

Nor were these always of good quality. A man's personal belongings, apart from warlike equipment, was reduced to the very minimum, but even so it took a good deal of maintenance. On his head he wore an Australian type Bush hat, far the best jungle hat I know, with the possible exception of the rather expensive floppy creation made of spun-glass which some officers managed to buy. The Bush hat made an excellent pillow; it became floppy and shapeless so that it did not catch the light or show up in any way, and made it unnecessary to use the camouflage netting and scrim so beloved of the orthodox; a stout chin-strap kept it on your head even when struggling through the thickest jungle. Someone in authority tried to induce me to subscribe to the official view that the khaki beret would be just as good: this was so palpably untrue that I could not possibly perjure myself by meeting him even a quarter of the way. Had I thought that a round hat without a chin-strap was any good for jungle wear, I should have worn my own Balmoral instead of getting myself up like a Digger. Steel helmets we never wore, nor did we ever pine for them.

On our bodies we wore the ordinary issue bush-shirt. The ideal would have been the Angora material made in bush-shirt pattern, but these did not exist, and it was no good wanting them. It was galling to visit, as I did between campaigns, the Long Range Desert Group in Syria, where they were training for the war in Europe, and to find that they were allowed to send liaison officers home to order whatever fancy stuff they wanted. I did not grudge them their good luck; but I was a horrid shade of green with envy. India and South-East Asia had rightly been put lower in the scale of priorities than North Africa and Europe, and this deprivation of the right to devise and obtain special kit was part of the burden. We got the best of what was going in our own theatre.

Trousers were of ordinary khaki drill, and all right for the purpose. The quality of boots and socks, however, was a legitimate source of complaint. The Indian boot is an instrument of torture for the European foot. My complaints about it on training were so loud and so penetrating that a high official (European) in the appropriate supply department was sent to see my Brigade. He arrived without warning in my absence, visited two of my units, and sent in a report that the boots had not been fitted or altered with sufficient care. I wish I had been privileged to be present during his visit; I should have asked him how he proposed to fit boots dropped by parachute; I should also have given him half an hour to fit a pair of his own boots to his own satisfaction, and then marched him fifteen miles in them. He also inferred in his report that anybody but a fool would have realised that every new pair of boots needed to be broken in gradually. How one does that on Long Range Penetration I do not begin to know. I shall never cease to regret that I was not there when he came, or that he never came again after I had seen his report.

The boot trouble was overcome by some bright boy cornering a supply of South African boots, which were first-class. Even then I got one supply drop of Indian boots; but the tenor of my radio messages was such as to make the whole stratosphere break out in blisters, and it never happened again.

The standard of sock was low—so low, that when you got a new pair of socks wet, there was a shrill whistling sound, and each sock shrivelled up into a little hard, wet lump in the toe of your boot. Many men learned to march without socks at all; for those who continued to use them, we got them dropped three or four sizes too large, and shrank them into something approaching the right size though not, alas, the right shape. My own practice was to wear two pairs of socks in an outsize pair of boots; but even so the socks were so small after one wetting that the top of them was well below the top of the boot, and the heel half-way along the sole. The sole of the foot was pretty hard by then, and provided one changed the socks around fairly often, so that the lump was not always in the same place, no harm was done; on the other hand, I developed sores round the top of the boot, where it chafed against the bare leg. I don't say that long marches can ever be a pleasure, but they can be saved from annoyances like these.

For a long time we could get no boot-repair outfits for the use of the cobblers who were attached to every column; and there was also a shortage of boot nails. Good boots therefore disintegrated for lack of nails, and whole new boots had to be dropped to replace them.

A man carried spare socks, rubber shoes, spare shirt and trousers. Shorts were not acceptable, as they could not be worn at nights owing to mosquitoes. The Balaclava helmet was a godsend, especially at night, when it acted as a partial mosquito net. The uses of a groundsheet and blanket are obvious; the life-jacket, which was designed to help cross rivers, turned out to be an excellent container for such things as rice or paddy, and was used for those purposes more than for making the men amphibious. Mess-tins proved short-lived: the bottoms fell out of them after only moderate use. Water-bottle, canvas *chagal*, ration-bags, toggle-ropes (for which the far better parachute cord was quickly substituted), jack-knife and *dah* were the chief remaining items. Of these the *dah* was the best friend.

The *dah* was the perfect knife for its many purposes. To the native of Burma it is his own tool—his knife, fork, spoon, spanner, walking stick, shot-gun, axe, trowel, spade and personal weapon of defence. This is not to say that he has not excellent mattocks and other specialised implements; but he carries his *dah* with him wherever he goes, and does wonders with it. The British soldier swiftly became adept in its use, although never to the standard of the native. Walking in my accustomed place at the head of the column, my *dah* was always in my hand, and in fact was almost a physical extension to my arm.

You can safely test the jungle-worthiness of a soldier by the condition in which he keeps his *dah*. If, after a month in the jungle, a soldier is to be found with a blunt *dah*, he is no good.

One sometimes happens on a reasonably good soldier whose rifle has rust on it: one is cross with him, but one realises that it may be a mere lapse. No soldier, on the other hand, could have a blunt *dah* and be unaware of it: for the *dah* is in use all day and every day, and a few minutes of every day must be devoted to sharpening it.

The *dahs* issued by Ordnance in India proved to be of poor material; it was impossible to keep an edge on them. We complained of this, and were visited as a result by some Ordnance official, who asked us to elaborate our grouse. I explained how one bout of five minutes' cutting serrated the edge like a saw. He was horrified, all right, but not for the reason we meant.

"Do you mean to say you've been trying to cut *trees* with them?" he asked, scandalised.

"Well," I said, "what else is a *dah* for?"

"I'm not quite sure," he said, "but not for *that*."

He was a perfect example of the type of officer I call "pit ponies" who spend their lives in offices and blink when they get out in the open air. Heaven forgive me, I have been one myself often enough. In the end, we managed to get rid of our Ordnance *dahs*, and to replace them either with *kukris* (which, with their curved blade require some skill in handling) or with the American type, through the kindness of a senior member of General Stilwell's staff. This was a whippy, broad-bladed affair—a little too whippy, in fact, but of such excellent steel as to outweigh this trifling disadvantage. The British issue machete was too short for the purpose; one had to stoop to whatever one was cutting, and even then stood a good chance of skinning one's fingers.

I have said, more than once, how much of our training consisted of trying to learn afresh arts of primitive living which must have been instinctive in our forefathers, but of which our civilised and pampered generation had no need. We felt all the time that we were rubbing along somehow on a meagre equipment, and we thought we were terrific chaps to be able to do it. The men of the Burma Rifles showed up the hollowness of this claim. From them I learned another lesson in sociology.

It was a subtle rebuke to us and to our civilisation, to see how much more value the Karens of the Burma Rifles derived from the same equipment that we thought meagre. The simple gifts of the Royal Army Ordnance Corps—the groundsheets, the parachute cord, the *dah*, the this and the that—which to us were the ordinary clumsy articles of issue, were real treasures to the Burma Riflemen. They saw at a glance the myriad uses to which they could be put, which were veiled from our spoiled Western eyes. With groundsheet, *dah* and parachute cord, the Burrifs could lash up a tough canoe in fifteen minutes' cheerful work. If they had no cord, they could make string from the outside of the bamboo, or from the bark of dozens of different trees, in a few minutes longer. If they had not groundsheets, they would make a raft in only a very few minutes more. They knew at once which woods, which bark, were suitable for these purposes; whereas the British soldier, to start with, would make an elaborate and ill-shapen boat, put it into the water, and then, with eyes like saucers, watch it sink.

"Blimey!" he would say. "I thought wood floated!"

And the Burrifs would laugh like hell, but never nastily.

Whatever ignorance there may be in this country about those splendid little men, Karen or Kachin, there are twenty thousand British soldiers who will always remember them with real affection, and glowing admiration.

To be perfectly fair, the Burrif soldier had his limitations. He did not excel at attacking in a set-piece battle; he saw no future in dying in a foxhole before an enemy assault. But in the tip and run action, in the teasing of Jap forces, in bold and resolute scouting, in the sudden and dramatic brush, in deep and fruitful patrolling, in map-reading, in compass-work, in the good old "eye-for-country" stuff, he had no equal among British or Gurkha: about Indians I cannot speak, never having seen them fight in jungle country.

If one came to a *chaung* with steep banks, and sought a way across it, sending patrols up and down to find a mule descent and ascent, the Burrifs would bring back an answer in half the time it took a British soldier, slipping through the undergrowth like minnows among water-lilies. And even when they could not speak or read English, they read maps with the penetration and intuition of astrologers. The Jock or the Tommy tended to concentrate upon the written place-name, which, in Burma, was a snare and delusion; the Burrif looked at the drainage system, the watersheds, the valleys.

I must not digress too far; I want only to illustrate how these men, who had only lately come into contact with civilisation, had a much truer sense of even the humblest advantages which civilisation confers; and that we, the more civilised, once separated from the protection of civilisation, were unable to exploit its most basic benefits to our advantage in anything like the degree of the humble and enthusiastic and faithful Karens and Kachins. Not the least of what we owed them was the power, derived largely from them, to make do with what we had, and to be ingenious in finding substitutes for what we had not.

The job of the Administrative Officer in each Column was no sinecure; for him, the constant self-congratulation of the Column Commander that he was shorn of administrative worry must have been irritating beyond bearing. All the Column Commander had to do was to calculate and keep in mind the day and hour when rations would run out, and to be sure that he would be in a place and tactical situation suitable for a new supply drop. It was the Administrative Officer who had to ascertain, and approve or veto, the needs of each platoon and individual, and calculate how far the normal allotment of three aircraft per column would meet the needs of the column at that particular drop. It was he who had to persuade a platoon commander that, even though his men's toes were sticking through their boots, the said boots must be made to last another ten days. It was he who had to persuade the Column Adjutant that unless he was given a bigger share of the wireless time during the next two days the Q.Q. would not be cleared before the drop was due. It was he who had to supervise the distribution of the drop when it arrived, and deal with the inevitable complaints, claims and counter-claims. It was he who had to keep the nominal rolls in order, report casualties, record promotions and discharge all the "A" duties of the Column. In 1943, when we were short of wireless sets and wireless time, no casualties could be reported until after the campaign; and the *yakdans* or leather panniers containing our few documents fell into enemy hands when the mule carrying them fell over a cliff on to the gratified Japs below.

In that year my Adjutant, Duncan Menzies, had kept a full

transcription of every signal in a large notebook, writing out the messages in English words and Greek characters, as a security measure, and then destroying the originals. This book was on him when he was captured by the Japs at Zibugin, on the fringe of the Kodaung Hill Tracts; but we never discovered what, if anything, the Japs were able to make of it.

Except for the Administrative Officer, and his Colour-Serjeant, the burden of the Administration fell on Air Base, where Peter Lord presided over the combined D.A.Q.M.G.s of all the Brigades who were supported in turn by the Quartermasters of the Battalions. From time to time it was suggested that this organisation was extravagant, and that a centralised staff would be more economical and efficient. All we Brigade Commanders fought this proposal tooth and nail. No centralised staff, however good, could ever feel the direct personal interest and responsibility towards the column in the field which illumined every routine duty discharged by John Stobbs and his colleagues. Every man felt that he had friends at Air Base; and this was a direct and considerable contribution to morale. Every supply drop, for instance, brought me a book: *The Pilgrim's Progress*, *Kenilworth*, *The Vicar of Wakefield*, and a dozen other books all reached me during the 1944 walking tour. (I found solid stuff suited my campaigning appetite.) And it was not only to me, as Brigade Commander, that such services were performed; every platoon had its agent at Air Base, selected from some man with hammer toes or fallen arches who could not pass the especially rigorous medical examination which we applied to all the men. No impersonal system could possibly have induced the same feeling of being cared for; it was one of those imponderable factors which make for enhanced morale, and which are recognised all too seldom.

We went, also, to great lengths to avoid the cross-posting of men to other units—a system which can cause more discontent in a formation or regiment than is officially admitted. War is hateful at the best of times: one of the few things that makes it tolerable is the privilege of fighting it with one's friends beside one, another imponderable which is too often ignored, especially by those without recent experience of the field. Speaking as a Brigade Commander, I would rather take the field short of fifty men in each unit, than have those hundred places filled with strangers; one can carry the principle too far, but thus far I would willingly go. I do not approve of the volunteer principle, by which units temporarily employed on dull duties lose the cream of their men to units in the limelight, and by which the volunteer becomes glamourised; I do not approve of danger pay except in certain very special cases. Once a man is in the King's uniform he is a soldier, and goes where he is sent. Contrary to a widespread belief, the Chindits were not volunteers: they were ordinary units detailed for duty as Chindits, with unsuitable material pruned away. There were a certain number of volunteer officers, and some of them were excellent; but ninety-nine per cent. of the officers and men of Special Force were detailed to become Chindits in the ordinary way of duty, and they did their duty well.

It is by no means sure that because a fellow volunteers for a dangerous job he will be good at it; it is not even sure that his heart will be in it. The motive that impels him may be one of a dozen. One can have nothing but sympathy for a lad, young, keen and fit, who feels that he is missing the war, and volunteers for anything that comes his way. Brought up on tales of gallant deeds, he wants to assure himself that he too can stand discomfort and fear, and be capable of endurance through hardship and privation. But nobody can tell, until he has had experience of these things, what they will really be like: he may be sure that they are quite unlike whatever he has pictured. I interviewed many officers who volunteered for Chindit duty between the two Expeditions. A high proportion were young and keen, but wholly without experience. Of those I took, some turned out well; a few, whose imagination had built them a false picture of what endurance means, failed badly. The most useful type is that which has had some experience, didn't like it much, but wants to go again with his eyes open, knowing something of what war is like, yet confident that he can stand another helping. The man who really enjoys hardship is a rarity and a freak.

This is more relevant that it might seem. The posting of officers and men is too often regarded as a mere administrative problem, and the moving of "bodies" in the same light as the moving of commodities and stores. A horrible habit is current in certain circles of talking about "bodies"—so many "bodies" to this unit, so many "bodies" aboard that ship. No staff or regimental officer under my command ever uses that expression twice. If you start talking about officers and men as "bodies" you are in danger of thinking of them as such; and then it is time that you were outed from whatever job confers that privilege upon you, and are yourself made into a "body" within the meaning of the Act.

There was one more administrative function which fell upon the devoted officers and men at Air Base. In 1943 the chief worry of us all was our inability to write home. We were naturally forbidden to tell our families what we were about to do; we could not even warn them that for the next three or four months they would not hear from us. The thought of their anxiety at the sudden cessation of letters was intolerable. I hit on a solution which I put to Orde Wingate, and which he accepted: that an Air Mail Letter Card should be dispatched each month to our next of kin on our behalf, telling them that we were fit and well, but, owing to operational reasons, unable to write as usual. It ended with a request that they should continue to write to us.

These Letter Cards were printed, and although they doubtless caused some perturbation at home, they prevented our relations from worrying unduly. Only in one home did they have an un-expected effect; the Staff Captain, Peter Lord, whose signature appeared on the cards, had an angry letter from the mother of a subaltern in one of the columns demanding to know what Peter meant by saying that her son "could not write as usual:" he hadn't written home for over two years.

Otherwise the cards were a success, and the second year they were used again, although this time we were able to send out mail from time to time, by the medium of light aircraft taking wounded back to Aberdeen or Broadway, and thence to India by Dakota. It says much for the credit of the postal authorities in India, and at Special Force Headquarters in particular, that on the second walk I got my mail from home more quickly and regularly than at any other time during my spell abroad of over four years.

XV

BEYOND THE CHINDWIN

BEFORE THE late war, the expression " Behind the enemy's lines"
conjured up the most delicious vision of adventure, beside which
all other adventure was anæmic. But since 1940 it has been
almost a routine affair, and every theatre has had its behind-the-
lines element. Apart from various organisations so secret that
they must not be mentioned in writing (even though they may
apparently be discussed freely in London restaurants) we have
seen the exploits of the Special Air Service Brigades, the Long
Range Desert Group, the partisans of Greece and Albania, the
British representatives with the Maquis, "V" Force in Burma,
the Patriot Forces in Abyssinia and several others. These were
deliberate; but there were also many instances of British officers,
cut off in retreat or remaining behind of their own volition, who
organised parties for sabotage or intelligence, and experienced
in two or three years enough adventures for two or three excep-
tional lives. Some of their names are known fairly widely, some
not at all. It would take a lot to beat the stories of Freddie
Spencer-Chapman in Malaya and Ivan Lyon in Singapore, and
Seagrim in the Karen hills and David Stirling in Libya; yet
there may be even better tales to tell, and others which will never
be known.

For instance, in March, 1943, my Column and I were toiling
up a dry *chaung*, called the Myauk Chaung, some ten miles east
of the Irrawaddy opposite Tigyaing, when we saw, painted on a
boulder in the middle of the river bed:

$$\boxed{\begin{array}{c} \text{To} \\ \text{R E} \end{array}}$$

A mile farther up the stream we found a single arrow painted on
another boulder, pointing up a tributary. We followed it but

found nothing. Water was scarce thereabouts, and there were no villages for eight or ten miles, except upon the Irrawaddy itself. We never solved the mystery, although we invented several possible solutions. The reader's guess is as good as mine; but my own, for what it is worth, is that a party of Royal Engineers, coming out of Burma in the great evacuation of 1942, got so far on their way to India, and became exhausted for lack of food or because of ill health and weakness; perhaps a few volunteers pushed on to try and get help, while the rest of the party went into hiding in the hills, leaving these clues to the direction in which any rescue party should seek them. This is a long shot, and I have never been able to learn of any such party. Perhaps the volunteers fell into enemy hands.

The experience of being behind the enemy lines, once rare, is now common; and other people's views on it are certainly as valid as any of mine. It would be idle to deny that the sensation of campaigning in that topsy-turvy way includes an element of especial excitement; but it is also exhilarating, so long as things are going well, in the knowledge that you, and not the enemy, are setting the pace. It is only when you are tired or hungry or dispersed that you begin to wonder if you really are setting the pace, or whether the initiative has not passed to the enemy. When that feeling once gets a grip of you, you are in danger.

Throughout 1944 we were in great strength, and we retained the initiative up till the end. In the first half of the 1943 performance we were also, in piquet parlance, the Major Hand. But I am glad, in retrospect, that my education has included the experience of being hunted, of being on the run; for without doubt that experience, which was ours with a vengeance in March and April of 1943, is well worth having. It has come the way of many men, including illustrious historical figures—King David, King Robert Bruce, Prince Charles Edward; and it encouraged one at bad moments to remember that these, at least, had had a happy issue out of their afflictions, which were quite as unpleasant as ours.

Mike Calvert once enunciated several golden rules for successful Chindit fighting. One was, to place your men where they had got to fight, whether they wanted to fight or not. It is easy in Chindit warfare to dodge a battle; all you have to do is to

take to the jungle and remain in it. Commenting on the 1943
Expedition from Radio Saigon, the Japs said, quite fairly, that
any fool could march round the jungles of Upper Burma and
get away with it. One sometimes had to take oneself severely
to task before sticking out one's neck: it was easy to find an excuse
for not doing so.

Mike's second rule, still more profound, was, "Have a sense
of history." You must see your fighting in perspective, and at
the same time as you remember the past, you must remember
that you and your men are making history yourselves. I like to
trace the similarities between our own campaigns and those of
Robert Bruce. He, indeed, was fighting in his own country, and
we in a strange one; but he, like we, was engaged in liberating a
country from an oppressive enemy who, nevertheless, could rely
on help from the nervous and the Quisling-minded. His little
force, in the hills of Galloway and Carrick in 1304, was three
hundred strong, only a little less than one of our columns. He,
too, practised column dispersal when in trouble, each party
making for an agreed rendezvous where they could concentrate
to renew their raids upon the enemy's supply dumps and communications. He, too, built up "secure bivouacs" and "strong-
holds." As a boy, I had read the great epic by Barbour, the Arch-
deacon of Aberdeen, the Fourth and Fifth Books of which tell
this part of the story; and I had visited many a time the site of
his secure bivouac at the head of Glen Trool, his ambush on the
south side of the Loch, his rendezvous at Craigencallie.

Often in Burma I recalled passages from the poem which
might have applied equally to ourselves:

> "In Glentruewall a quhile he lay
> And went weyle oft to hunt and play
> For to purchase thaim venesoun
> For than deer war in sesoun."

There were little anecdotes, too, which touched us particularly
close. One was the tale of how the King was attacked by hostile
villagers when, as was his wont, he had left his perimeter one
morning early to satisfy the calls of nature, accompanied by only
one man. We had the very same rule, that any men leaving the

perimeter for that or any other purpose, must go in pairs, and be armed. It was lucky that King Robert had the same rule, and was thus able to dispatch his assailants.

Again, when John of Lorn, a Highland Lord allied to the English, was pursuing him with a superior force, and was close on his heels near the Ayrshire and Galloway border, Bruce ordered his column to disperse into small parties and to re-assemble near Clatteringshaws. We of Wingate's first Burma march were taught exactly the same doctrine, and passed it on, in turn, to our men. It sounds all right; but there was one point about it which none of us foresaw: that the morale of these small parties was subject to dismay and depression. The sensation of suddenly finding oneself in a small party rather than in a big was analogous to finding oneself in a small boat instead of a large liner. Bruce might not have thought of it in those terms, but he would have recognised the mental experience; and one felt a close kinship with him accordingly.

After the campaign, when I was sent to the Middle East for a month on a lecture tour, I revisited my favourite place of pilgrim-age in Jerusalem—the stone let into the pavement of the Scots Church in memory of the "Pious Wish of King Robert Bruce, that his Heart might rest in Jerusalem." I reckoned that he would have understood the background of my lecture better than I could convey it to my audiences.

I split up into small parties on three occasions in 1943: once to confuse the enemy's pursuit after carrying out various demoli-tions on the Mandalay-Myitkyina railway; once in the course of a skirmish, when I was trying to burst through a strongly held village in a hurry; and finally to confuse pursuit and to facilitate foraging on the way home. Even the first time, when the initiative was still distinctly ours, each "dispersal group" suffered a drop in morale, and the worries of each dispersal group commander immediately increased. Not only was his personal responsibility, for navigation, leadership and purpose, automatic-ally enhanced; but each such leader, severally and jointly, had to think hard about the eventual reunion at the rendezvous. And this constitutes no ordinary headache.

Detachments are often necessary and often effective; but they are always a worry, and no experienced commander in our form of warfare sent off detachments light-heartedly or without deep thought. Especial foresight is necessary. There are probably not enough wireless sets to go round, and the rendezvous cannot therefore be altered once it has been chosen and announced. There is a classic example of a Column Commander, who had been surprised and ambushed, trying to alter his rendezvous in the middle of the ragged battle which resulted: some of his groups went to the old one, some to the new, and the column disintegrated completely.

The choice of a Rendezvous is not always easy. There were certain rules about them: they must always be forward and never back; they must be easy to find, even by people without maps; they must be natural and not man-made objects, since man-made objects are liable to change, move, disappear or be duplicated. Thus a road was not permissible, since a road shown on the map might have fallen into disuse, might follow a new alignment, or new roads might be built in the same approximate area and direction; more likely still, there would be other tracks in the neighbourhood, and a heated argument would take place as to whether this broad track was or was not a road within the meaning of the map.

Wingate also insisted that a Rendezvous must be a line and not a point: you might miss a point, whereas you would only overshoot a line through ill luck or sheer lack of care. In practice, these restrictions more or less limited one's choice to the line of a stream running across one's axis of approach; and the stream itself must of course be remote from habitation and from frequented tracks. The Rendezvous was changed daily or more often still: at any given moment of the day or night, every officer knew what Rendezvous was current.

Waiting at a Rendezvous for the others to show up was always a beastly business. There was often some unlooked-for circumstance which made for doubt, either as to whether this was certainly the right place, or whether all the detachment or dispersal group commanders would be sure it was the right place. Or perhaps one had under-estimated the time which it would take people to get there, and arrived oneself only ten minutes before—or perhaps ten minutes after—the Rendezvous was due to close. One might be able to tell whether people had already been and gone, or one might not. It was never the practice, in areas where the Japs or unfriendly locals were thick on the ground, to take one's whole party to the Rendezvous; one left them in hiding near by, and sent a patrol, or went oneself, to the Rendezvous, with all caution. It might easily have happened that the enemy had caught a prisoner and extracted from him by torture the exact place and time where he was to meet the main body. We know now that this precaution was well worth taking. All the officers who returned from captivity after Rangoon was recaptured had been tortured when first taken to make them divulge where they had expected to meet me again. They had all replied that I was a cantankerous devil who never told them a thing.

In point of fact, with this very possibility in view, I told the Rendezvous only to officers, although they were allowed to pass it on to N.C.O.s when necessary. I used to tell officers my general plan for the next week, so as to give them a reasonable chance of finding me again if they missed me at a Rendezvous; usually I gave a Second Rendezvous. It was with much misgiving that I divulged to them plans as much as a week ahead; one wanted to put everybody in the know, but with the risks of torture one simply dared not do it. In no circumstances were officers allowed to pass Second Rendezvous on to N.C.O.s or men. Officers pleaded with me for permission to do so, so as to lessen the chances of men being lost for good; but this was one of the many cases in which one had to harden one's heart. In the long run it was in the man's own interests to know nothing if he was caught; to give him vital information when he might be put to the test of torture was not fair.

I lost three men altogether on the first expedition—lost in the literal sense, on the line of march. The first was a private soldier who was found to be missing after a midday halt: he was never heard of again. The second was a man who walked out of the perimeter to fetch water from a waterhole a hundred yards away, and failed to return: he was probably lost; a careless man, who takes no heed of exactly where he has gone, can easily get lost a hundred yards from bivouac. The third I lost only one day later: he too nipped out of the column when it had only moved a hundred yards out of bivouac, to pick up some article of equipment which he had forgotten: he never caught us up again. Both these last two were lost in an area remote from villages, where I was quite certain that we were miles away from any Japs; yet both fell into Jap hands, the first after wandering for a day, the second within five minutes. The first died in Rangoon jail, like most of the others; the second survived and is back in this country—it is from him that we know what happened. His story illustrates how barren we were of information when there were no villages in which to seek it. It was a shock to me to learn from him, two and a half years after the incident, how close on my tail the Japanese were without my knowing it.

To be the hunter, as we usually were, is exhilarating beyond words. To be the hunted, as we were for six or eight weeks, is hell. It would be tolerable if one had plenty of food and was fit and had a certain amount of information; but when hungry, sick or wounded, and completely ignorant of what is going on, and of where your enemy is—that is what Clint Gaty used to call "non-habit-forming." You must recognise the symptoms before they develop, and appreciate the moral situation before it is upon you, so that the men under your command may meet it when it comes with a resolute spirit; for, as the Book of Proverbs puts it, "a man that is without spirit is as a city that is broken down and without walls."

One of the earliest symptoms is a tendency to credit the Jap with omniscience. You begin to feel that he knows almost everything, and is certain to guess the rest. It seems to you that the route by which you have decided to travel must be the obvious choice, that the defile through which it will take you the day after to-morrow is bound to be held, that the valley you must cross the next day is patrolled day and night, and that the native who saw you as you crossed that strip of open paddy will have rushed to Katha to report you. It is extraordinary how often some trivial incident occurs which seems to confirm this worst fear.

There were many signs and portents in those sorry days when we were on the run which betokened evil. These were the columns of smoke which sometimes certainly were, but which more often probably were not, signal fires lit by native agents. There were footprints of the unmistakable Japanese rubber shoe, which one would suddenly find afresh on the track, and which one knew only too well belonged to no potentially friendly Man Friday. There were the mountainous elephant droppings. There was the tendency to light out for bush on the part of villagers, a sure sign of the closeness of Japs. We heard sentries talking. We found cigarette packets dropped. We saw the lights of lorries. Once we stared at Japanese across four hundred yards of river, while they stared back at us. We met guides returning from leading Jap troops into villages where we were going. Once John Fraser walked into a village to buy rice, and saw a Jap sentry leaning against a wall a few yards from him with a rifle beside him. Most exciting of all was the sound of motor-lorries on roads quite near us, and the sound of railway trains on the hostile railway which was the main artery of Jap communication. I can never walk along a railway track now without remembering the night when my companions and I skulked at the foot of the embankment near Mohnyin, while a long train pulled past us five yards above our heads in the darkness.

I repeat, all these were in the evil days, when the sum of my orders and the whole of my object was to get my battered remnant out to India without loss, and when it was touch and go whether even that modest aim was within our physical, let alone our moral, powers. When Mike Calvert crossed the same railway in much the same condition the same week a hundred miles to the south, the temptation was too great for him altogether (for he is a most irrepressible officer): he stopped, and blew it up again. As far as I was concerned, there was no temptation; all I asked was to be allowed to cross it in peace. In fairness to myself, I might perhaps be allowed to add: first, that we were in worse physical case than Mike's lot; secondly, that we were in the hand of Kachin guides who would have been made the scapegoats for any prank; thirdly, we were actually being pursued; and fourthly, we had no explosives left. The last excuse resembles that of the French *maire* who offered Napoleon many excuses for not affording him a salute with guns: "lastly," he said, "we have no guns."

> "Man cannot tell, but Allah knows
> How much the other side was hurt."

Lord Wavell quotes these words of Kipling as illustrating his favourite military maxim; and they were very appropriate to us. Wingate always advised us, when we felt that spectre of Japanese omniscience creeping up on us, to think not of "The Japanese," but of one specific Japanese of the same rank as ourselves. He counselled us to picture the headache that we were giving to Major Watanabe, our opposite number, who was getting hell from his superiors for being outwitted by our antics. This was wise indeed. Poor Watanabe! I grew quite sorry for him. The sweat was streaming down behind his spectacles in the miserable hut to which he had been driven by the allied bombing as he sought to sift the good intelligence from the bad. Then he would hurry on his equipment, march twenty miles to intercept us, and find us once more vanished, into the boundless and silent forest. Later, when he and I were both Brigadiers, he was faring no better; and he had not had a pleasant leave travelling in the Middle East and seeing hosts of old friends in the course of a thoroughly boastful lecture tour, living on the fat of Egypt and Palestine, drinking Clos Maryut and Wolf Kummel. He had spent his monsoon wondering how so many of us had slipped through his fingers, and considering how the deuce he could do any better when we came again, as we were sure to do. All the same, if I ever meet Watanabe—but there is no longer any need to pretend that he is real.

For the Japs were not really omniscient. They must have picked up a good deal, but their powers of deduction are limited, and their sense of responsibility for passing on what they had learned to their neighbours was negligible. It was perfectly evident that one could commit a crime in one individual's area, and pass on into the next without one's dossier following one. Their only really co-ordinated move against us in 1943 was when they surrounded us in the Shweli-Irrawaddy bag; and that must have been directed from their Army Headquarters in Maymyo or Mandalay, which were beginning to be threatened by our direction, and which were located at the heart of a communications system well adapted to the necessary deployment. On that occasion their information was foolproof, for they must have had news of all our crossings of the Irrawaddy. One column crossed at Tagaung on the 4th of March; mine at Tigyaing on the 10th, in broad daylight, the Japs arriving in time to fire on the last boat; Mike Calvert somewhere between the two on the 12th, and becoming engaged in rear when his crossing was half done; two more columns and Brigade Headquarters, a thousand men in all, at Inywa about the 20th. They were watching the Shweli, and knew that we had not crossed it; they knew also that only a few had broken out of the narrow entrance to the bag at the south. They needed no clairvoyance to tell them that we were still there; and to do them justice they reacted with exemplary speed, and made their dispositions well. Wingate made one effort to break out at a single point; it failed; and thereafter began our trek back to India in small parties, breaking through the Jap cordon more or less simultaneously at different points. Although only about half of us got back to India, many more got out of the actual bag, only to be picked up when they collapsed, or to be intercepted on some other easily patrolled line between the Irrawaddy and the Chindwin. Several parties, including one under my own medical officer, Bill Aird, were actually caught on the Chindwin, a fate narrowly escaped by Wingate himself. Gim Anderson, the Brigade Major, spent an unhappy twenty-four hours hiding in elephant grass on the east bank, while the Japs tried to burn it down.

It is often and quite truly said that the surest way to obtain high morale is for the troops to be certain, before ever the battle begins, that they are going to win. That cannot be disputed. Early in the war, however, no such certainty was possible —neither in Europe before Dunkirk, nor in North Africa in 1940 and 1941 when there were fewer troops and less equipment than were at the disposal of the Eighth Army later on. Happy are they who have not seen, and yet have believed. I was not in France, but there was nothing wrong with the morale of those who fought in North Africa in the early days of the Western Desert and Tobruk and Keren, and whose Africa Stars bear neither the figure 1 nor the figure 8. And in Burma in 1943 and 1944, we were still in the early stages of the Japanese War, since it had been wisely ruled that the German War enjoyed the top priority. We had to build morale in other ways; we could not be sure of winning. It is a measure of Wingate's greatness as a leader that he promised his men hardship and death as the probable price of their success, and they followed him with loyalty and pride. Every man knew, for instance, that to be wounded, to the degree of being unable to walk, meant to be abandoned. How many leaders dare tell their men that, especially when the enemy has the reputation for cruelty of the Japs? Wingate dared to do so, and still his men were proud to follow him.

It was a serious handicap that no publicity could be given to the Chindit expeditions while they were still in progress. My views on publicity are Victorian, and it is with great distaste that I read interviews in the Press with any but the most senior officers. But in North Africa and Syria, it was of great importance to the morale of the soldier that he should be able to hear on the B.B.C. in the evening some account of the week's fighting, if not the fighting of that very day. That fillip was denied us; we could not be sure of winning, and we could not afford to have our doings announced on the wireless while we were still engaged in their performance. We had to rely on other methods of maintaining morale.

Nevertheless, in passing, I would say that there were two respects in which this task could have been made more easy. The first is a common cry, of which the Kings of Intelligence must be heartily sick, but the temptation to cry it again is too strong to be resisted. It is hard to believe that the gain to Intelligence through the systematic suppression of the names of units outweighs the moral gain which would result from their publication. Again, I am old-fashioned enough to find it distasteful to hear the names of individuals trumpeted to the world in the newspapers or on the wireless news, for deeds which should properly be accredited to their Regiments.

The second point could have been remedied, and remains sore. When Special Force first took the field in 1944, it was described for Security reasons as the 3rd Indian Division, a very proper precaution. The mention of "Special Force" would immediately have caused Japanese ears to prick. But after Wingate's death, a decree came out from a source which cannot now be traced, saying that in future "3rd Indian Division" would be our proper title. A less appropriate name could hardly have been devised. We had seventeen British battalions, three Gurkha, three Nigerian and one of the Burma Rifles; we had British gunners and

American airmen; there was no Indian unit in the whole force, and only three (and they Gurkhas) belonging to the Indian Army. This was an exceedingly sore point with the men, and rankled hard; I confess to having shared it in full. Good wine needs no bush; the deeds of Indian units in the war speak for themselves without having to assume the laurels of non-Indian units. Many people, both in India and at home, were deceived into thinking that we included Indian units . Even Mr. Amery, then Secretary of State for India, illustrated the deeds of Indian troops by a reference to the "3rd Indian Division."

There were other minor annoyances, but on the whole we were well looked after. General Scoones, who commanded IV. Corps during both expeditions, was a staunch friend to us, both in the matter of helping us tactically and in mothering us generally. In 1943 he fed us generously from his scanty stores of food when we were inward bound; and as each of our bedraggled parties returned to his Corps area on the way out we were royally received. Every time I opened my mouth, either more food or a fat cigar was rammed into it by General Scoones or Brigadier Roberts, his B.G.S., and a former commander of 16 Brigade.

In 1944 morale received strong reinforcement in the way of padres. The previous year we had had none, and I was personally opposed to taking in anybody whom I did not regard as essential. An abuse of language which has become common is the use of the word "essential" when "highly desirable" is really meant; and I felt that we should rigorously cut out everything under the headings of "would be nice to have" or "might be very useful." Boot-repairers and doctors were essential; padres, to my mind, were only desirable.

I ate my words before the end of the campaign of 1944. Going in at the top of the batting list, as we did, our establishment of padres was not up to strength; we were supposed to have, and the other brigades did have, one padre for each column. I only had three in Burma; my senior padre was left at Air Base, where he did wonders for us in the way of sending in comforts and looking after the wounded. Padres were well worth having. Behind the line campaigning is sufficiently jumpy by nature as to make every man-jack engaged in it anxious to travel and to fight under the best possible auspices. Everybody felt the better for

the short service we held for the Brigade before entraining for
Ledo and the war. It lasted less than a quarter of an hour; the
lesson was the famous passage from Joshua, Chapter 1, verses 1-9;
and the only hymn, accompanied by the band of a concert party
which was in the neighbourhood, was "Guide me, O thou great
Redeemer," to the fine Welsh tune *Cwm Rhondda*.

The padres held services where and when they could, usually
on the occasion of supply drops, when there was a check in the
marching; all services were undenominational; one cannot be
bothered with denominations in the jungle, and indeed it is a
pity to be bothered with them anywhere else. I and my servant,
both Presbyterians, attended an Anglican communion service
somewhere between the Chindwin and the Uyu, when we and
the Queen's were awaiting a supply drop. A splendid Roman
Catholic padre with the Gunners held services for all. In my
own regiment, in 14 Brigade, the padres held five minutes'
prayers every night, going to a different platoon in turn, so that
those from other platoons knew where to go if they wished to
take part; and I gather that these were always well attended. I
wish we had thought of it.

Again, at the end of the campaign we had a short Thanks-
giving Service; and this time also I made it my business to find
out what the men felt about it. We had a printed Order of Service,
and copies were offered which could be sent home to their families:
almost every letter going out from the Brigade enclosed a copy.
Three days later, we read in *The Times* a speech by a diocesan
Bishop at home, to the effect that the modern soldier took no
interest in matters of religion; which provoked my senior padre
to such fury that he wrote a rude letter to his Lordship, with my
complete approval, telling him that he was talking through the
episcopal hat, bootlaces and all.

I believe that the fighting man is deeply interested in religion,
which has suddenly become a matter of urgency. That interest may
wane in the light of peace, because the fighting man, having
beaten his sword into a ploughshare, turns away from the glass
and straightway forgets what manner of man he was. It is our
mood at the moment of deliverance that needs crystallising. I
hinted at this in a previous book, and it drew down on me, to
my great discomfort, a barrage of proselytising, amounting

almost to intimidation, from adherents of the Oxford Group; so I hasten to add, for my own protection, and that of the ex-soldier, that the answer, in my view, does not lie in that direction. I am no Oxford Grouper, and I do not propose to embarrass myself by drawing aside unduly the curtains of my mind. But in those weeks of fugitive marching which was our lot in 1943, much thought that was vague became real. Why did this chap collapse, and the other chap keep going? Why was that fellow shot dead, and the other still able to stagger along with a couple of wounds? The moral character of A, the prayers put up on behalf of B, had no relevance. Yet one had the feeling that it was foreordained which should survive and which should not, although how the choice was made was not for us to guess.

For the last month, we were all quite sure that, if only we got out, nothing on earth would ever have the power to worry us again; the greatest discomfort, the worst fear, the most cruel anxiety would be powerless against us once the present tyranny should be overpast. And then, one evening, we came to the British lines, crossing the Chindwin in a small boat in relays, and finding ourselves all at once among friendly folk. We did not feel truly delivered until the following morning, when we stood at the crest of the watershed dividing the Chindwin Valley from that of the Kabaw, and knew that the nightmare was behind us. There we halted, and gave rein to our thoughts at last. We thought of those still struggling out behind us, of those whom we had left without hope, of those who had fallen into the enemy's hands, of those who were soon to learn of their bereavement and of those who had months and years of doubt and anxiety before them. We did not forget to remind ourselves that we were not out for ever; that we had had, in some degree, a hiding which we must go and avenge as soon as we were rested and recovered: we knew that even then; although of the thirty men around me only four were sufficiently mended physically to come in again on the second walk eight months later.

But that sensation of deliverance, on Easter morning, 1943, in contrast with the sufferings of the weeks before, was so intense as to remain as a talisman for ever against depression or faint-heartedness. We have only to be down on our luck or out of sorts to remember that day and be whole again. We can never

again be so low; and although we can never experience quite
that same feeling of jubilation and resolution for the future, we
can remember it and draw encouragement from it; and just as
we can never again be so elated, we can never again be so cast
down. And there must be many others who have been through
similar situations, with a similar talisman from an almost
identical mood.

Finally, those weeks engendered in us a totally new sense of
values. We had all been in the same boat: inflexible discipline
and a strong sense of comradeship had brought us out of our
troubles. I had had to affect a callousness alien to one's natural
instincts; but everybody knew its purpose, and nobody minded.
There was no recrimination and no bitterness. And I find intolerable the bitterness that exists to-day in national life and
international relations. Just as officers, N.C.O.s and men all
realised then that our fates were linked, and that each had his
part to play in whatever position he was filling, so such a realisation ought to be general throughout our nation. There is no
room for bitterness between class or party, nor, least of all, has
any class or party the right to question the sincerity of its
opposites. The Conservative or Socialist leader may very properly
point out what he considers to be wrong in his opponent's
political creed; he may expose what he considers to be its fallacies;
but he is black in guilt when he lightly ascribes to those who
disagree with him motives less worthy than his own.

Those of us who have been especially lucky to come through
the war have no right to refuse any call to public duty, and when
one is asked (for instance) to stand for Parliament it is one's duty
to do so. But the rancour with which the election of 1945 was
fought, by both sides, is the worst augury for the future of our
country which has shown itself since the war. The gloomiest
feature of all was the suddenness of the plunge into these depths
of bitterness; and not even the atomic bomb has made us surface
yet. It is hard to believe that the British nation, whose public
men snarl at each other with such malignity now, is the same
race as stood united in 1940.

*If the foot shall say, Because I am not the hand, I am not of the
body; is it therefore not of the body? If the ear shall say, Because I am
not the eye, I am not of the body; is it therefore not of the body? If*

the whole were hearing, where were the smelling? The eye cannot say unto the hand, I have no need of thee, nor the head to the feet, I have no need of you. There should be no schism in the body; the members should have the same care one for another. Whether one member suffer, all the members suffer with it; or one member be honoured, all the members rejoice with it.

We learned a great deal in Burma, about an infinity of subjects; but I believe that this was the biggest lesson of all. We have had our forty days in the wilderness, and we know.

RETURN TO BURMA

(*An Elegy for the Chindits*)

O comrades whom we left unsepulchred,
  O comrades whom we laid in shallow graves,
O lightly sleeping comrades, have you heard
  The sound that beats insistent as the waves?
Up the dark alleys of the jungle-tracks
Where once you stumbled with your monstrous packs,
  It flows, the tide that liberates the slaves.

I heard you speaking in the quiet nights
  When all the birds are hushed, the crickets still,
When the pale fire-flies with their shuddering lights
  Cruise in the archipelagos of the hill,
When up the mighty corridors of teak
Along the secret woodway from the creek
  Pads the great cat returning to his kill.

When the black shadows reach across the path,
  When from the village dies the evening smoke,
When from the mere steams the sun's aftermath,
  When in the marsh the frogs begin to croak,
The hour when we were wont to bivouac,
To choose our sleeping-place and leave the track,
  Kindle the fire and put the rice to soak.

Then you have spoken, for you have desired
  To know our varying fortunes, how we fared,
Trudging in weariness but still inspired
  To press again the venture that we shared.
Then in the night I was aware of you,
So lightly laid as still to share the dew
  Falling on us your friends for whom you cared.

Forest to forest, range to distant range,
 Across the vales your voices speak and say:
"Here where I lie, to-day was nothing strange—
 Heard you, my comrade, anything to-day?"
And one makes answer: "Here where we two lie
Four hundred of our countrymen went by—
 We saw them laughing as they went their way."

And one beside a track more distant yet,
 One from a group of graves, some old, some new,
Says soberly: "To-day our comrades met
 The enemy by our thicket here, and slew
Twoscore and ten; and some of ours who fell
Lie with us now, and have brave tales to tell."
 And voices call: "Comrades, we welcome you."

But you who fell beside us, pioneers
 Shorn of the future—you who chose to be
The hopeless van of the victorious years,
 The heralds of the day you could not see:
You we have steered on as a seaman's mark,
Your graves shine forth exulting in the dark
 The leading lights of ultimate victory.

O comrades all, the known and the unknown,
 Sleep still at last: your vigil is despatched,
The black defences of the night are down,
 The outmost wicket of the day unlatched.
This day beyond your graves our armies reach,
The hosts are come for whom you made the breach,
 And now at length the enemy is matched.

        December, 1944.

APPENDIX A

ORDER OF BATTLE, 16TH INFANTRY BRIGADE

Brigade Headquarters

Commander:	Brigadier B. E. Fergusson, D.S.O., The Black Watch.
Brigade Major:	Major J. H. Marriott, M.C., Leicesters.
Senior Officer, Burma Rifles:	Major J. C. Fraser, M.C., Burma Rifles.
Intelligence Officer:	Capt. W. Kinnersley, Leicesters.
Signal Officer:	Major T. Moon, Royal Signals.
Staff Officer, Royal Engineers:	Major J. W. Robinson, R.E.
Medical Officer:	Major J. Donaldson, R.A.M.C.
Animal Transport Officer:	Major W. G. M. Dixon, Sherwood Foresters.

Rear Brigade

Second-in-Command:	Colonel F. O. Cave, O.B.E., M.C., Rifle Brigade.
D.A.Q.M.G.	Major J. Stobbs, Queen's.

Units

1st Battalion The Queen's Regiment.

No. 21 Column:	Lt.-Col. J. F. Metcalf (evacuated wounded).
	Major E. B. Clowes.
No. 22 Column.	Major T. V. Close.

2nd Battalion The Leicestershire Regiment.

No. 17 Column:	Lt.-Col. C. J. Wilkinson (evacated wounded).
	Major D. Dalgliesh, M.C.
No. 71 Column:	Major H. N. Daniell.

51/69 Field Regiment, Royal Artillery.

No. 51 Column: Major A. C. S. Dickie, Burma Rifles.

No. 69 Column: Lt.-Col. R. C. Sutcliffe.

45th Reconnaissance Regiment, Royal Armoured Corps.

No. 45 Column: Lt.-Col. C. R. T. Cumberlege (evacuated sick)

Major G. Astell, Burma Rifles.

No. 54 Column: Major R. A. G. Varcoe (evacuated sick).

Major E. Hennings (killed in action).

(The apparently haphazard numbering of the Columns was due to security reasons.)

APPENDIX B

*Extract from article entitled " Report on the Health of 401 Chindits"
by Lt.-Col. J. N. Morris, R.A.M.C., dated 15 June, 1945, in
The Journal of the Royal Army Medical Corps, and reproduced
by kind permission of the R.A.M.C.*

These men came from all parts of Britain, belonged to different
formations and presented manifold disorders, but they tended to
conform to a clinical pattern and the group spirit was strong
among them. What we learned to call "the Chindit syndrome"
soon emerged—the frequent association of long hair and long
dirty nails; superior intelligence, morale and manners; fatigue
and hunger, pallor and loss of weight, skin sepsis, diarrhœa and
malaria.

Of the 401, 19 were officers and 382 other ranks. The striking
positive features are the frequency of multiple disorders (I think
it may safely be said that each patient had two or three conditions
requiring hospital treatment), and the immediate evidence of
malnutrition to an unexpected degree. On the negative side the
very low incidence of psycho-neurosis was unexpected after two
and half years' experience of a British General Hospital in India.

The three cases (of psycho-neurosis) among the 401 Chindits
were mild; only two, as far as I could see, were related to the
campaign, and these cleared up quickly. The infrequency of
neurosis is in keeping with the high morale of these men as
observed even in hospital.

INDEX